A CENTURY OF CYCLING

A CENTURY OF CYCLING

The classic races and legendary champions

WILLIAM FOTHERINGHAM

A CENTURY OF CYCLING
by William Fotheringham

This edition first published in 2003 by MBI, an imprint of
MBI Publishing Company, Galtier Plaza, Suite 200, 380 Jackson Street,
St. Paul, MN 55101-3885 USA

First published in Great Britain in 2003 by Mitchell Beazley,
an imprint of Octopus Publishing Group Limited,
2–4 Heron Quays, London E14 4JP.
© Octopus Publishing Group Limited 2003

Text © William Fotheringham 2003

The information in this book is true and complete to the best of our
knowledge. All recommendations are made without any guarantee on
the part of the author or Publisher, who also disclaim any liability
incurred in connection with the use of this data or specific details.

We recognize that some words, model names and designations, for
example, mentioned herein are the property of the trademark holder.
We use them for identification purposes only. This is not an official
publication.

MBI titles are also available at discounts in bulk quantity for industrial
or sales-promotional use. For details write to Special Sales Manager
at Motorbooks International Wholesalers & Distributors, Galtier Plaza,
Suite 200, 380 Jackson Street, St. Paul, MN 55101-3885 USA.

ISBN 0-7603-1553-1

Set in Franklin Gothic and Gill Sans
Printed and bound in China

CONTENTS

FOREWORD

As a cyclist I became aware of the stature of the great races in various ways: from the things the fans and press would say, the way my team mates would talk to the Belgians when the northern Classics came round, and to the French when it was Tour de France time. For the professional cyclist, the value of the races is in their very importance. To win a Classic or a major Tour gets publicity for your sponsor, that's what you are paid to do. Winning these races is your job, and in turn this was your biggest reward. The pleasure in winning is not always fully visible at the finish; because it leaves such a deep impression, it takes time to sink in.

When I was racing, there was no time to dwell on the importance of the greatest races; I was too busy racing, thinking about what lay ahead, doing my job as I had to. For example, in the Tour of Flanders, I would see people hanging down the hedgerows on the cobbled hills, packed up there, but my focus was what was in front of me rather than what was to either side. I was thinking of what I was doing, what was going on in the race, where the next hill was, and whether I was in the right position in the bunch. I would never get beyond that. In the Tour de France, it would be the same in the mountains.

Even in the build-up to the biggest races, you have conflicting feelings about them. I would not be jumping out of my skin in the run-up to Paris-Roubaix, for example. It's the best Classic to win, but it's the most horrible to ride, because so much can happen; there are so many crashes with the other riders, and the motorbikes and cars travelling with the race. I would not look forward to it. But if I was ruled out beforehand, as happened several times, because of a silly crash that left me with a broken bone somewhere, I would be intensely disappointed, because of the wasted months spent working towards it.

If Roubaix is the greatest Classic, the race that made the biggest impression on me during my career was the Tour de France. It has such a following in Europe, and is the only race that's truly known all over the world. Doing well in the Tour is an aim which is much easier to explain to people – everyone knows where France is – even if, sometimes, when I would ask people to guess how long it is, they would say "five or six days?"

In Ireland, as a young cyclist 30 years ago it was hard to find out about the great races and riders. My children, Nigel and Stacey, who are nine, know that Erik Zabel goes for the green jersey in the Tour de France, Lance Armstrong for the overall classification. They have a vast depth of knowledge compared to what I had as a cyclist of 14, because it's all there on the internet and in the newspapers.

But that mystery just made it more exciting to ride alongside Eddy Merckx as a young pro. To see him at the start or ride next to him was a marvellous feeling. Bernard Hinault had massive presence as well: he was a rider who would take control. Riders would attack when he had said the peloton should take it steady, and he'd roar at them "you'll never win another race!" Miguel Indurain would never have done that: Joe Bloggs could go up the road and he'd never make a sound. But even I used to admire Miguel, because he was such a gentle guy and a great bike rider.

As a participant you see the greatest bike races from a very particular angle. Most of the time when I was racing in the Classics, the major Tours and the world championships, I was too bound up in what I was doing to think of their place in cycling history, and to appreciate the status they have for cycling fans and the press. That's changed a little now that I've retired, now that I'm spending more time talking to my fellow commentators at Eurosport and to the fans, and that I have more time for reflection. That's why I can feel the importance of a book such as this, which will give you that knowledge I found so hard to come by as a young teenage bike rider.

Sean Kelly
October 2002

RIGHT In the autumn of his career, Sean Kelly wins the 1991 "race of the falling leaves", the Giro di Lombardia. Just behind on Viale dell'Industria, Monza, is the Frenchman Martial Gayant.

INTRODUCTION

Deep in the Pyrenees, on the outskirts of the small town of Sainte Marie de Campan, in the deep valley between the Tourmalet and Aspin passes, an old stone barn stands end on to the main road. The building looks anonymous, and would be were it not for a metal plaque on its side. This was once the "Eugène Christophe forge", the lettering proclaims.

This building saw one of the cruellest episodes in the history of the Tour de France. In the 1913 race, Eugene Christophe struggled down the Tourmalet with his forks broken and laboured for hours to repair them in the forge, his chance of winning the race quite gone.

Christophe's story is foremost among the race's myriad legends, and rightly so. The episode is a perfect microcosm of the Tour and of road cycling: long and arduous physical effort, the intervention of the malign hand of fate, the struggle against overwhelming odds.

It sums up professional cycling's essence in another, important way: this has always been a sport of the open road, in the same way that motor racing was in its infancy. What lies ahead cannot be predicted – foul weather, accident, mechanical or physical breakdown.

Therein lay the original romance of racing around France, for example, or from the French capital to the Belgian border. Much of of this allure is still there, whereas motorsport has gradually been forced onto one anonymous circuit after another.

Participants are now better protected than in the pioneering days, but they cannot always foresee the hidden pothole at the strategic moment, the sudden change from headwind to crosswind, the hail shower that turns a stretch of cobbles into a skating rink, or the unexpectedly steep hill.

In that sense, today's sport is a place where Christophe and his fellow pioners would still feel perfectly at home. They would also recognise the great amphitheatres of the sport – Galibier and Tourmalet in the Tour de France, the Stelvio in the Giro d'Italia, the Old Kwaremont and Muur at Geraardsbergen in Flanders have changed only superficially since they were first climbed: road surfaces may improve – in

Flanders they get worse – but the gradient and the effort remains the same.

No other sport uses an entire country as a backdrop for its showcase events. On a three-week Tour such as France, Spain, or Italy, the scenery is ever-changing as entire regions with their own culture and physiognomy are crossed in a single day. And the single-day Classics have the strongest sense of place, rooted in the culture of a particular region.

Finally, a sport of the road is uniquely accessible for the fans. To feel the essence of the greatest bike races, they have only to get on their bikes and sample for themselves the Koppenberg, the forest of Wallers-Arenberg, or the wall of the Alto di Angliru.

Such is the richness of 100 years of cycling history that the difficulty for the writer is not what to include, but what, reluctantly, to leave out for the sake of clarity. I have narrowed the definition of "great races" to the three major Tours and the single-day Classics, but to do so is frustrating: there are events such as Paris-Nice and the Dauphiné Libéré which are worth an entire book of their own.

Such a sport breeds a certain kind of hero, and by and large the "giants of the road" of cycling have been individuals of iron will, each driven by his own particular obsession.

Lance Armstrong's meticulous attention to every detail, weighing every gram of food, is mirrored by Eddy Merckx's night-time visits to his garage to check his bike. Henri Pelissier's rantings against the demands of race organisers in the 1920s were echoed 60 years later in Bernard Hinault's blistering attacks on the sadists who had the temerity to make him race over cobblestones.

Each great cycle race is a peripatetic soap opera, with a constantly moving backdrop, and a cast continually evolving as circumstances change. One morning's villain is the following afternoon's hero. The greatest of stars can be laid low by a puncture or sudden illness.

The men, however, are not the foundation stones in this story. In the century since Henri Desgrange founded the Tour de France generations of cyclists have come and gone, but the allure of the open road remains the same.

LEFT A few words about the great men of cycling pushing themselves to the limit in search of glory words about the great men

TOUR DE FRANCE

In 100 years Le Tour has survived world wars, scandals, skulduggery, drugs, death, and strikes. "La Grande Boucle" (the Great Belt) encircling France is now the peak of the cycling calendar. Unmatched in the sheer physical demands it makes on competitors, it scales the Alps and the Pyrenees, and the prestige it brings to the winner is cycling's greatest prize – the coveted yellow jersey. Who are the men and what are the milestones that transformed this 3,500-km (2,200-mile) marathon from a newspaper marketing stunt into the world's greatest annual sports event, and a national institution that obsesses France every July?

LEFT To the victors the spoils on the Champs-Elysées: Laurent Jalabert, Lance Armstrong, Robbie McEwen, and Ivan Basso were King of the Mountains, overall winner, points winner, and best young rider in the 2002 Tour.

TOUR DE FRANCE

THE MOST GRUELLING SPORTS EVENT IN THE WORLD, A FABULOUS EXCUSE FOR A PICNIC, AND A UNIQUE INSIGHT INTO FRENCH CULTURE – THE TOUR DE FRANCE IS ALL THESE THINGS AND MORE.

"It is the festival of a summer of men, and the fête of all our countryside, with a passion which is particularly French; so much the worse for those who cannot share in its emotions, follies, and hopes." With those words, the writer Aragon welcomed the Tour de France when it returned to French roads after World War II in 1947.

Only the two great wars have stopped the Tour, the focal point of French summers for the last century. It has grown from an outlandish, mammoth publicity stunt into the world's largest and most demanding annual sports event. In that time it has remained surprisingly true to its original formula, visiting all of France, on public roads, and free to the public.

Viewing the Tour, be it in vineyard, cornfield, or mountain pass, is a French family tradition. The parents who cling to their children as the *peloton* (the main group of cyclists) speeds through were once toddlers themselves watching Eddy Merckx and Bernard Thevenet from their parents' arms. The grandfather in his chair halfway up the Galibier pass could well have seen Fausto Coppi and Gino Bartali do battle on that same piece of tarmac half a century ago.

The millions of fans now come from all over the world, often to ride their bikes up the great Pyrenean and Alpine passes, to paint their heroes' names on the road before cheering them as they wobble painfully through. What still sets the Tour apart from other great sports events is the way it goes out to its fans. It is, in the words of the late Geoffrey Nicholson, the only form of international conflict that takes place on the doorstep, apart from war itself.

Every town, village, and hamlet in the country hopes that one day it may wake up to the sight of the gendarmes lining the roadside. Then it will be time to set up the barbecue, get out the chairs and tables, or often the tractor and trailer for an elevated view, put up the bunting, write the name of a local cyclist on a piece of cardboard, and let the greatest free show on the planet begin.

"That moment of silence, of unimagined expectancy," wrote Keith Bingham in *Cycling Weekly* in 1990. "Then the mass of bronzed and muscled men on their glittering machines swooped in with a great whoosh of air, the vacuum tugging at spectators' hair, sucking up paper hats and dust in the wake of mayhem on the move. And then the crowd sighed and gasps of wonder were drowned out by the thunder of 50 service vehicles howling through."

THE ROOTS OF THE TOUR

While the Tour is now regarded as a vital piece of French national heritage, on a par with its film or car industry, its roots lie in a national scandal – the Dreyfus Affair. This followed the jailing of a Jewish army officer, Alfred Dreyfus, wrongly accused of passing military secrets to the Germans. The controversy divided the nation.

At the country's leading cycling paper, *Le Vélo*, the editor, Pierre Giffard, was pro-Dreyfus. The financial backer, Count de Dion, supported Dreyfus' accuser, the Chief of Staff Count Esterhazy. When Giffard wrote an editorial in the pro-Dreyfus paper, *Le Petit Journal*, calling for Esterhazy to be guillotined, de Dion cut off funds and set up a rival daily, *l'Auto-Vélo*, printed on yellow paper – *Le Vélo* used green. The editor was Henri Desgrange, a former professional racer who had been forced to give up his job as a lawyer because female clients objected to his riding a bike with bare calves.

In dire need of a gimmick to boost his paper's sales, struggling at around a quarter of *Le Vélo*'s 80,000, Desgrange adopted his assistant Géo Lefèvre's idea for a round-France cycle race over six marathon stages: Paris–Lyon–Marseille–Toulouse–Bordeaux–Nantes–Paris, with a total of 13 rest days. There would be no pacemakers, at a time when it was

RIGHT The heroic days: Fausto Coppi leads his great rival Gino Bartali over a pass in the 1949 race, the event where Coppi became the first man to win both the Tour de France and the Giro d'Italia in the same year.

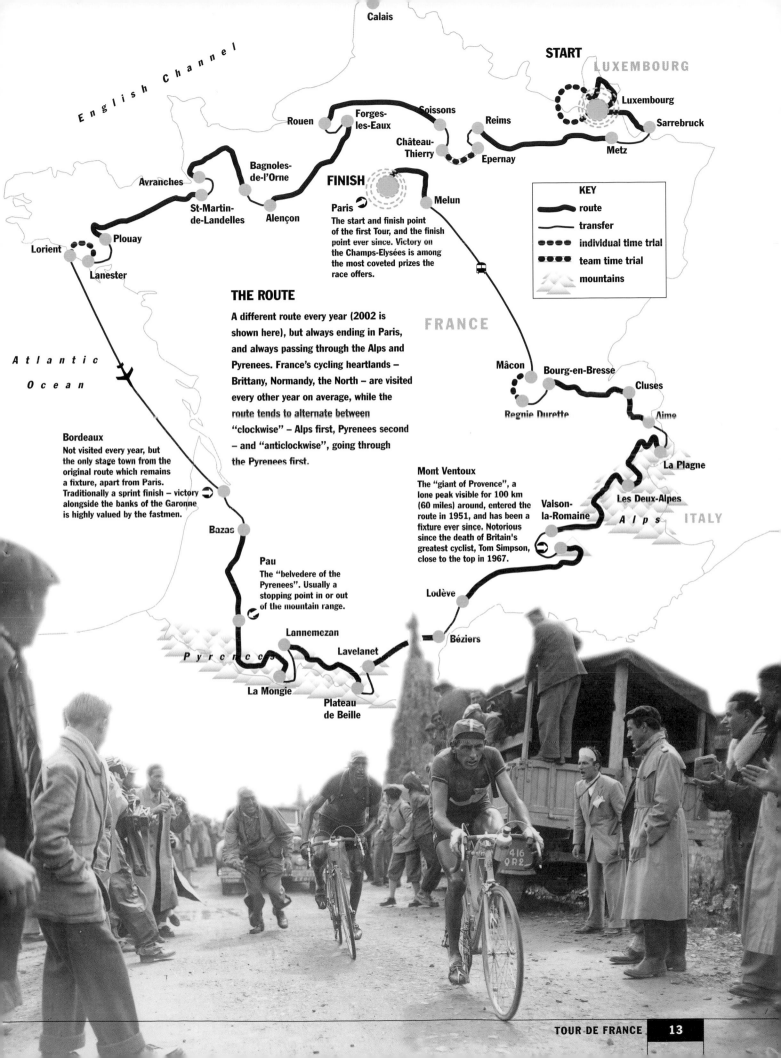

Calais

START

LUXEMBOURG

Luxembourg

Sarrebruck

Metz

Reims

Soissons

Epernay

Forges-
les-Eaux

Château-
Thierry

Rouen

Bagnoles-
de-l'Orne

Avranches

St-Martin-
de-Landelles

Alençon

Melun

FINISH

English Channel

Lorient

Plouay

Lanester

Paris

The start and finish point
of the first Tour, and the finish
point ever since. Victory on
the Champs-Elysées is among
the most coveted prizes the
race offers.

THE ROUTE

A different route every year (2002 is
shown here), but always ending in Paris,
and always passing through the Alps and
Pyrenees. France's cycling heartlands –
Brittany, Normandy, the North – are visited
every other year on average, while the
route tends to alternate between
"clockwise" – Alps first, Pyrenees second
– and "anticlockwise", going through
the Pyrenees first.

FRANCE

*Atlantic
Ocean*

Mâcon

Bourg-en-Bresse

Cluses

Regnie Durette

Aime

La Plagne

Bordeaux

Not visited every year, but
the only stage town from the
original route which remains
a fixture, apart from Paris.
Traditionally a sprint finish – victory
alongside the banks of the Garonne
is highly valued by the fastmen.

Bazas

Mont Ventoux

The "giant of Provence", a
lone peak visible for 100 km
(60 miles) around, entered the
route in 1951, and has been a
fixture ever since. Notorious
since the death of Britain's
greatest cyclist, Tom Simpson,
close to the top in 1967.

Les Deux-Alpes

Valson-
la-Romaine

Alps

ITALY

Pau

The "belvedere of the
Pyrenees". Usually a
stopping point in or out
of the mountain range.

Lannemezan

Lavelanet

Lodève

Béziers

Pyrenees

La Mongie

Plateau
de Beille

KEY
route
transfer
individual time trial
team time trial
mountains

customary for tandems or triples to assist the competitors in major races.

The aim was to outdo Le Vélo's two promotions, the Bordeaux–Paris and Paris–Brest–Paris races, so Desgrange and his writers, Lefèvre and Alfonse Steinès, hyped his new event to the skies. An editorial two days before described the race as "a gigantic concept which will have the whole of France on its feet, not for a few hours, but for 19 days [. . .]. Men like you will be fighting ten times in a row on courses as hard as Bordeaux–Paris. Remember the admiration and stupefaction you felt when Maurice Garin or Hippolyte Aucouturier arrived in Paris covered in dust and mud after riding for hours and hours, climbing uphill, cascading downhill, watching the moon replace the sun in the sky and the sun come up in the east, all that while we continued our everyday lives, remember all that and you will see the grandeur of the task that these same men will undertake."

Some 60 cyclists paid their five-franc entry fee and lined up on 1 July 1903 outside the Reveil-Matin café in Montgeron, a suburb of Paris. They were given nicknames – "the Furniture-makers' Champion", "the Prince of the Miners" – and it was the handlebar-moustachioed Garin, known as "the White Bulldog" or "the Little Chimneysweep", who led from the off and returned to Paris on 19 July, escorted into the Parc des Princes by 2,000 cyclists waving their hats in the air.

Desgrange's event was a triumph. A vast civic procession was organized in Garin's home town of Lens, in the north. *Le Petit Journal* newspaper wrote, "the success and fame of *l'Auto*'s Tour de France have been as great as its importance." Sales went from 30,000 to 65,000 overnight. The big rival, *Le Vélo*, would eventually close.

Never forget that this was all about newspaper sales. Garin's last act before going home was to hand Desgrange a handwritten account of his race for publication in *l'Auto*. It included these words, which still ring true: "You have revolutionized the sport of cycling, and the Tour de France will be a key date in the history of road racing."

THE ROUTE DEVELOPS

In 100 years, the Tour's basic format has changed surprisingly little, compared, for example, with the difference between Formula One and early motor races. Desgrange tweaked the format slightly over the 20 years after the race's foundation – the first Tour was decided on cumulative time, as is today's race, but for a short while he flirted with deciding it on points. There were switches from trade teams to national squads, and back again.

The race distance increased drastically, from the 2,400 km (1,500 miles) of the first Tour to around 5,400 km (3,400 miles) by the 1920s, but the stages were shortened to minimize the time the riders spent racing in the dark, when they were vulnerable to hostile fans. This in turn meant increasing the number of stages, and correspondingly reducing the number of rest days; by the 1930s, the format was similar to that of today, albeit with longer stages, and four or five rest days rather than today's two.

Constantly in search of headlines, Desgrange sent the riders into the annexed territory of Alsace-Lorraine

ANTONIN MAGNE

was "no glory without virtue", and who won his first Tour in a style that would be familiar to Lance Armstrong. For four weeks before the race he lived in the Pyrenees, climbing the cols of the Pau–Luchon stage every other day, working out which gears to use. During his reconnaissances, he noticed that the descent of the Aubisque was highly dangerous, being covered in huge stones, and he planned his attack there to win the yellow jersey.

Later in life he was a massively influential team manager over a quarter of a century, notably for Louison Bobet, Raymond Poulidor, and Britain's Barry Hoban.

NATIONALITY	French
DATES	15 February 1904–8 September 1983
NICKNAMES	Tonin le Sage (the Wise One); le Taciturne
PROFESSIONAL	1926–39
MAJOR WINS	
1931	Tour de France.
1934	Tour de France; GP Nations.
1935	GP Nations.
1936	World Road Championship; GP Nations.

in 1905, first getting permission from the German governor, Count Zeppelin, and extended the route to include the whole of France. The Pyrenees were crossed in 1910; the Galibier in the Alps – where the statue of "the Father of the Tour" now stands – a year later; and in 1919 he produced his masterstroke, the yellow jersey, to counter complaints that the public could not see who was who when the race passed.

The early Tours were a matter of every man for himself, with the riders strung out one by one across the countryside, but as road surfaces and bike manufacture improved in the 1920s, team tactics became more important, as the riders tended to stay together in one group. To break the grip of the great cycle firms, Desgrange banned trade teams in 1930, and divided the field into national squads, with their costs paid by *l'Auto*.

An extra source of income was needed, so he dreamed up the "publicity caravan", a cavalcade of floats advertising anything from cheese to car tyres. The caravan remains a key part of the Tour, as eagerly awaited – and taking far longer to pass – than the

NATIONALITY	French
DATES	22 January 1889–1 March 1935
NICKNAME	la Ficelle de Fer (the Iron Wire)
PROFESSIONAL	1911–28
MAJOR WINS	
1911	Giro di Lombardia.
1912	Milan–San Remo.
1913	Giro di Lombardia.
1919	Paris–Roubaix; French national title.
1920	Paris–Brussels; Giro di Lombardia.
1921	Paris–Roubaix.
1922	Paris–Tours.
1923	Tour de France.
OTHER RESULTS	1914: Tour de France, second.
	Tour de France: seven stage wins; eight days in yellow jersey.

HENRI PELISSIER

Rebellion against figures in authority was the hallmark of France's best all-round cyclist between the wars. It began the moment Henri Pelissier walked out of the family home in Passy, outraged that his father wanted him to work in the family dairy rather than try his hand at cycling.

CYCLING'S FIRST FAMILY

Pelissier's story is also that of two other men, his brothers Francis and Charles: cycling's first family. While Henri first made his name in Italy before World War I broke out, with wins in the Tour of Lombardy and Milan–San Remo, Francis turned professional after the Armistice. This was a time when the great French cycling marques were banded together under the banner of "La Sportive", a closed shop with the aim of preventing professional racers pushing wages up.

The Pelissiers wanted nothing to do with it, and were taken on by a small manufacturer, JB Louvet, in 1921, on condition that they win the Paris–Roubaix Classic – the pair of them against the 120 "La Sportive" riders directed by Alphonse "the marshal" Baugé. The pair duly finished first and second – their only regret being that Francis punctured, meaning they could not cross the line together.

Not that things always went the brothers' way: in the first Tour of the post-war era, 1919, Henri took the

yellow jersey early on, but the entire field attacked him on the stage from Brest to Les Sables d'Olonne. After chasing for some 290 km (180 miles), he was on the point of regaining the field when the race organizer, Henri Desgrange, came alongside and ordered them to stop working together, as it was against the rules.

Pelissier abandoned, and he walked out again the next year, after winning two stages, when Desgrange penalized him two minutes for throwing away a tyre belonging to the race organizers, as all the riders' equipment did.

PELISSIER VS DESGRANGE

The popular champion and the all-powerful race organizer and editor of the newspaper *l'Auto* had a fraught relationship. "Never forget," said Desgrange before one Paris–Roubaix, "*l'Auto* made you what you are." "Never," screamed Pelissier. "I'm the one who made *l'Auto*. Look at your sales on Sunday morning when I win ..."

Desgrange was a secret admirer of Pelissier, noting in one editorial that he had all it took to be a champion, "including a nasty streak", and his 1923 victory in the Tour, including a lone escape over the Col d'Izoard, coming after 12 years of Belgian domination, caused him to wax lyrical. "This win has the classicism of a work by Racine, the value of a perfect statue, a faultless canvas or a piece of music destined to stay in everyone's minds."

The incident that made Pelissier truly celebrated ended the truce. In 1924, during a stage of the Tour that

started in Le Havre in the middle of the night, Pelissier put on two jerseys, one issued by the Tour organizers and one of his own. He threw away the latter when the sun came up, and was reported to Desgrange. There was a public altercation, and Pelissier abandoned the next day, in the little town of Coutances in Normandy, with Francis and a close friend, Maurice Ville.

They were found drinking hot chocolate in Coutances Café de la Gare by the journalist Albert Londres, whose interview with the trio, originally entitled "Les Martyrs de la Route", is now universally known as "Les Forçats de la Route" – the Convicts of the Road – the term that became synonymous with the outrageous demands made on the men of the Tour.

Pelissier complained, "Anything they wouldn't make a mule do, we have to do", adding, "The road to the cross had 14 stations: we have 15." Then he and his brother opened their pillbox: "... cocaine for the eyes, chloroform for the gums ... and do you want to see the pills? We ride on dynamite."

Pelissier's turbulent life had a fittingly turbulent, if tragic end. His wife Leonie committed suicide in 1933, and two years later his girlfriend Camille shot him during a violent argument, with five bullets from the same pistol that had ended Leonie's life. As for his brothers, Francis made a career for himself as a team manager, specializing in winning Bordeaux–Paris, while Charles won a record eight stages in the 1930 Tour and went on to become one of France's most popular cyclists of the 1930s.

LEFT Philippe Thys carries the victor's bouquet after stage seven of the 1920 Tour de France, the race in which he became the first man to win the Tour three times.

cyclists' ability to go beyond normal levels of endurance and suffering: "industry mixed with heroism", as Aragon put it in 1947.

The Tour was taken into the mountains as early as 1905, when Desgrange sent the riders up the Ballon d'Alsace, in north-east France. First to the top was René Pottier, who climbed the 12 km (7½ miles) in around 40 minutes, side by side with the 1904 winner Henri Cornet, "panting, pouring with sweat, their chests emitting a 'han' sound like that of a bellows in a baker's oven", wrote Desgrange. Pottier strained a knee muscle with the effort of the climb, and later withdrew, but returned to win the following year. He did not live long to enjoy his success: he hanged himself in January 1907 in his sponsor's warehouse following an unhappy love affair.

The Ballon and the other mountains of 1905, Col Bayard and the Cote de Laffrey in the Alps, were mere molehills compared to the innovation of 1910: the crossing of the Pyrenees during a marathon 320-km (200-mile) leg from Luchon to Bayonne. Steinès suggested the idea to Desgrange, who dismissed him as "crazy", but still sent him to reconnoitre the Aubisque, Tourmalet, Aspin, and Peyresourde passes.

"There are no roads," said Desgrange. "No one risks their necks on the Aubisque apart from goatherds and woodcutters, and their tree trunks carve ruts big enough to sink a donkey." Steinès negotiated payments for the local engineers to make up the roads, and set out over the Tourmalet by car – until the snow became too deep and he was forced to continue on foot in his city shoes.

"You see the poles pointing out of the snow," said his guide as he left him. "They are 12 feet tall, and mark the road." Soon the poles disappeared under the snowdrifts, and Steinès eventually struggled into the town of Barèges, on the other side, just as the search parties were being prepared. "Perfectly practicable," he telegraphed Desgranges.

"The Father of the Tour" was not present on 21 July when the riders left Bayonne at 3.30 a.m. He had returned to Paris, apparently worried sick that the riders would not be able to make it up the climbs and his brainchild would lose its credibility. It was left to

cyclists. Its tacky souvenirs – key-rings, badges, free samples – lead to feeding frenzies among the roadside fans. In the same year, Desgranges began offering prizes for the first riders to cross the great mountains, and in 1933 he founded the "King of the Mountains", which rewards the best climber over the whole race. The basic elements of today's race were all in place.

Desgrange and his journalists sold the Tourmen as supermen – "the most courageous champions since antiquity" – and he put superhuman obstacles in front of them. The mix was a simple one: the public could relate to the effort of racing a bike, while admiring the

Steinès to wait close to the top of the day's final climb, the Aubisque, to see if anyone would make it along the vertiginous goat-track along the side of the mountain, where, it was feared, mountain bears still lurked.

"Our car gave out three-quarters of the way up," he wrote. "I calculated that the riders would be with us in a quarter of an hour. After an hour disaster stared me in the face. I felt that the business delegated to me was going bankrupt. I was sure the Tour was going to plunge into nothingness." The first rider, François Lafourcade, was bombarded with questions about where the others were, but could not answer.

The second, Octave Lapize, was "on foot, leaning on his machine rather than pushing it. His shattered eyes revealed immense distress and he was yelling insults. 'You are murderers. Yes, murderers.'" Desgrange and Steinès took note and the following year they sent the riders over the 2,600-metre (8,000-foot) high, 34-km (21-mile) long Galibier pass in the Alps.

The human as well as the superhuman side of the three-week soap opera also proved irresistible. With so many variables – men, machines, the open road, the elements – there was no knowing who would be singled out by Fate on any given day. In what other event is there a prize for the most unfortunate competitor?

In the early days, broken bikes were the biggest problem, and it was not uncommon to see riders losing vast amounts of time as the bad roads got the better of their primitive machines. Two early examples make the point. Jean "the Boy" Alavoine, 14 times a stage winner and four times a finisher in the first three overall, completed his first Tour in 1909 by carrying his bike for 10 km (6 miles) to the line, and was said to have punctured 46 times in the 1919 race alone.

En route to victory in 1928, the Luxembourger Nicolas Frantz broke his bike between Metz and Charleville and rode on a ladies' bike for over 90 km (55 miles). He lost 28 minutes in the process, but already had so big a lead that he kept the yellow jersey.

THE ILL-FATED "OLD GAUL"

The Tour's most notorious victim of mechanical incident by far remains "the Old Gaul" Eugène Christophe, in 1919 the first man to wear the yellow jersey, but never a Tour winner. Descending the Tourmalet in the 1913 Tour, he was knocked off by a car, and broke his forks.

With his bike on his shoulder, he ran down the 13 km (8 miles) into the little town of Saint-Marie de Campan, and laboriously set about making a new set of forks from plain tubing in the local blacksmith's, shaping the metal and making holes to hold his wheel. The repair lasted four hours, and all that time race officials, including Desgrange, watched over him to make sure he received no outside assistance.

There was something about Christophe and his forks: he was robbed of victory in the 1919 race by another fracture, in northern France, and this time found a small bike factory in Valenciennes to make the repair, losing two and a half hours. In 1922, it happened a third time, while he was descending the Galibier, and he was forced to borrow a bike belonging to the priest in the village of Valloire.

PHILIPPE THYS

Thys was the first man to win the Tour three times, a record that lasted 35 years; he would surely have been the first to win five if the Great War had not postponed the Tour. Nicknamed "le Basset" ("the Low Slung One"), because of his crouched riding position, he led the 1914 race from start to finish. When he was fined half an hour the day before the finish for failing to show the referees his broken wheel after an accident, he still had enough time in hand to win.

A calculating man, who would wait for ever for signs of weakness in his rivals, he was said to have a habit of getting up in the middle of night, and going out on his bike to watch the dawn break each morning.

NATIONALITY	Belgian
DATES	8 October 1890–8 September 1983
NICKNAME	le Basset (the Low Slung One)
PROFESSIONAL	1912–27
MAJOR WINS	
1913	Tour de France.
1914	Tour de France.
1917	Paris–Tours; Giro di Lombardia.
1918	Tours–Paris.
1920	Tour de France.

The 1913 incident was what endeared him to the public, however, because the race officials added a further three minutes onto his time when he broke the rules by allowing a small boy to pump the bellows of the forge while he used both hands to shape the metal. It wasn't just fate against the man, but the system.

Over 80 years later, the officials were just as heartless and nitpicking. When the great Miguel Indurain lost the Tour in 1996 at Les Arcs in the Alps, he ran out of energy on the final climb on a chilly, rain and hail-soaked day, and pleaded with the following service cars for a bottle of energy drink or something to eat. He was given a bottle by a rival team but this was against the rules, and he paid the price with a 20-second penalty. High up in some cyclist's Paradise, Christophe probably had a wry smile on his face.

THE DRUDGERY OF THE DOMESTIQUES

Also among the factors the Tourman has to contend with is cycling's feudal team structure, with one or two leaders supported by a group of devoted pedalling assistants, the "water-carriers" or *domestiques*. The French term also means "housemaid", and their duties vary from collecting bottles of water from the team cars behind the race to pacing the leader back to the group if he punctures. They make the tempo if a dangerous break escapes, they shelter the leader if the wind blows from the side, and they push him along as he answers nature's call on the move. Much of the suffering in the Tour is on behalf of a superior who is invariably paid far more than the mere underling.

To be a domestique can involve heart-rending sacrifice, but earns public sympathy. In 1934 the little climber René Vietto earned his place in Tour history by performing a U-turn on the descent of the Col du Portet d'Aspet in the Pyrenees, and riding back up the hill to give a wheel to his leader, Antonin Magne.

Vietto had lost time on the first stage of the race with a puncture, then come back in the Alps to win two stages and rise to fifth overall. To add insult to injury he had already had to stop the previous day to offer his bike to Magne. It was partly Vietto's sacrifice that captured hearts and minds, but mainly the photograph of him sitting on a wall during his long wait for his support vehicle to bring him a wheel. This picture of

despair and resignation briefly made him France's most popular cyclist.

Sometimes the domestique has his day, as in 1994 when the biggest rider in the bunch, the hulking Italian Eros Poli, conquered Mont Ventoux ahead of the climbers. Most slip back into obscurity, like Roger Walkowiak, the completely unexpected winner of the 1956 Tour. One or two, like Claudio Chiappucci, turn into unlikely stars.

Chiappucci was thrust into the limelight in 1990 when the favourites all decided to save their teams' strength on the opening stage, letting "Chiappuccino" build a 10-minute lead, which meant he clung onto the yellow jersey until the penultimate stage. He even had the temerity to attack the double winner Greg LeMond on the toughest mountain stage in the Pyrenees, on the day when it was widely assumed he would be relieved of the yellow jersey. To prove it was all more than a fluke he went on to win a rainlashed Milan–San Remo the following year, and provided doughty opposition for Indurain in 1991 and 1992.

Cycling's feudal system is partly explained by the risk a team runs if it has more than one leader. They will build their own little team within the team, and fratricidal war breaks out. This is one reason why national teams no longer contest the Tour: during the 1950s infighting was rife in the Italian and French teams in particular, as managers attempted to direct sworn rivals like Fausto Coppi and Gino Bartali, or high-strung stars like Jacques Anquetil and Roger Rivière.

The cohabitation of Hinault and LeMond in the La Vie Claire team in the 1985 and 1986 races best illustrates the dangers. In 1985, LeMond was made to give up what he saw as a winning opportunity, to enable the Breton to join the select group of five-Tour winners. He did so on the understanding that Hinault would help him win the following year.

Hinault's response was to break away on the opening mountain stage, winning the yellow jersey, to LeMond's annoyance. Hinault, "the Badger", acted the devoted team mate in the Alps, where the pair finished hand in hand at l'Alpe d'Huez, but LeMond was convinced to the very end – and remained convinced eight years later – that his team mate was looking for

RIGHT Roadside repairs were something of a habit for the "Old Gaul", Eugène Christophe. This puncture in the 1925 was small stuff compared to the run of broken forks which cost him two Tour wins.

a chance to sneak past him for a sixth win. When his forks broke, the first thing on his and his family's mind was sabotage. "The Badger", meanwhile, just dismissed it all as American insecurity.

THE TOUR TAKES ITS TOLL

Bikes are miniature works of art now, so crashes have taken over as the most unpredictable factor. Open wounds, bruises, and road rash have always been the usual complaints, but it is common for riders to finish stages with broken bones, most often in their wrists, and sometimes their collarbones, in the forlorn hope that they can continue the next day. Not many have had to go as far as Honoré

Barthelemy, who finished eighth in 1920 with a broken shoulderblade and a dislocated wrist, or the notoriously accident-prone Alex Zulle of Switzerland, who began the 1997 Tour with a broken collarbone pinned together, in the vain hope that it might get better.

Few Calvaries match that of Pascal Simon, eldest of a cycling family of four brothers from the Champagne region, all of whom either won stages or wore the yellow jersey in the Tour. Tall and shy-looking, Simon took a decisive lead on a scorching day in the Pyrenees in the 1983 race, only to crash the day after and break his left shoulderblade.

He struggled on in agony for a further five days, with his four-and-a-half-minute advantage being whittled away, before abandoning in tears. It was an inevitable

ABOVE Djamolidin Abduzhaparov (left) flies down the Champs-
Elysées with the greatest of ease in 1991. Olaf Ludwig (centre with
head down) is put off his stride, and the stage will fall to Dimitri
Konychev, just to Ludwig's right.

often by simple miscalculation, as in 1991 when
Djamolidin Abduzhaparov, the thunder-thighed Uzbek,
weaved head-down into a two-metre (six-foot) plastic
Coca Cola can and performed a face plant on the
Champs-Elysées tarmac.

Abdu, the "Tashkent Terrror", was wearing the
green jersey, so, to fulfil the condition that he had to
finish the stage to win the jersey, he was carried
over the line in a groggy, bloodied mess before being
taken to hospital. He later received the jersey in a
ceremony in October, which smacked of "thanks
for the spectacle", and where his crash was shown
several times in slow-motion.

Disaster is a split-second's inattention away, as at
the Parc des Princes in 1960 when a track official got
too close to the 22-times stage winner André
Darrigade as he sprinted for the line. He paid with his
life. At Armentières in 1994, the culprit was a
gendarme, who decided to take a photograph of the
finish from his privileged vantage point on the finish
line, but did not realize that the figures in his
viewfinder were about to collide with him. Ironically,
Abdu had his head up this time and avoided the mass
of bikes and bodies – Laurent Jalabert's face still
bears the scars – and sailed past for the win.

Sometimes the Tour ends careers. The 1960
favourite Roger Rivière broke his back and never raced
again after falling into a gorge in the Auvergne –
rumour has it under the influence of amphetamines –
while in 1955 the "Bald Mountain", Mont Ventoux, did
for the elegant, flamboyant Ferdi Kubler, winner of the
Tour five years earlier. "Watch out Ferdi, the Ventoux
isn't a mountain like the others," he was warned. "Ha,
Ferdi's not a rider like the others," he replied, and
went full-pelt up the mountain. On a day of searing
heat, Kubler implored the spectators to push him, fell
off three times on the descent, was seen riding the
wrong way down the road, and called a press
conference that evening to announce his retirement.

Such farcical moments are rare, and tempered by
more sober memories. Halfway down the hairpinned,
wooded descent of the Col du Portet d'Aspet in the
Pyrenees stands an elaborate marble monument of
wheels and wings. Just up the hill on 18 July 1995, in
a crash that initially seemed just like any other, the
Barcelona Olympic road race champion Fabio
Casartelli piled into a great stone block at high speed
and died soon afterwards of massive head injuries.

end as he stood no chance of getting to Paris in yellow,
but, his team-mates in the Peugeot squad suspected,
his daily displays of ultimately purposeless heroism
made better publicity for the cycle-maker than if he had
simply withdrawn in the first place. Simon, however,
was never the same again.

For sheer terror, for the viewer if not the participant,
nothing matches the pile-ups that happen as the pack
sprints for the finish line in a weaving mass moving at
70 kph (45 mph). Sometimes they are caused by
riders colliding as they compete for road space, more

The peloton was in a state of shock the following day, and there was no race. Instead, they simply rode at the speed of a funeral procession through the great rock circus of the Aubisque before permitting Casartelli's team-mates in the mostly American Motorola squad to ride ahead at the finish in Pau. Now, the memorial is surrounded by mementos left by cycling fans, and the Italians in the peloton who knew Casartelli stop to pay their respects when the race passes. Companions in daily danger, like coal miners or deep-sea fishermen, they know it could easily have been one of them.

The Tour has had other victims: Tom Simpson's memorial stands close to the top of the moonscaped summit of Mont Ventoux, the "Giant of Provence",

where he collapsed and died on 13 July 1967, a victim of heatstroke exacerbated by the use of amphetamines and alcohol. The mementos under the relief of Britain's greatest ever cyclist are the same mix as on the Casartelli monument, and a steady stream of amateur cyclists pedal painfully up all summer to remember Simpson and look at the view.

KINGS OF THE MOUNTAINS

If the bunch sprints that tend to dominate the first week's racing merely whet the appetite, the time trials and the mountains are the Tour's main course. Since

the 1930s, the Tour has tended to be a contest between the time triallists, who can produce the concentration and sheer power necessary to dominate against the watch, and the climbers, usually minute, often stick-legged, typically with the ability to accelerate effortlessly up the great passes.

The Tour's greatest riders are those who can dominate both domains, using their sheer power to ride the opposition off their back wheel, as the first man to win five Tours on the trot, Miguel Indurain, did to devastating effect. Fausto Coppi would ride most of the mountain stages on his own, like a great extended time trial.

Jacques Anquetil, the greatest time triallist ever, was also capable of winning the two greatest mountain stages in the 1963 Tour. Eddy Merckx, nonpareil of the sport, broke away on the Tourmalet pass in the Pyrenees for his best Tour stage win at Mourenx in 1969, prompting the headline "Merckxissimo", while Bernard Hinault based his Tour wins around time trial supremacy, yet was twice King of the Mountains.

The contest between time triallist and climber is what produces the spectacle, the cut and thrust, the Tour's most memorable moments. The invulnerable Merckx never looked so vulnerable as in 1971 when the slender Spaniard Luis Ocaña destroyed him in the Alps en route to Orcières-Merlette. It led to the greatest act of defiance of the Belgian's entire career 48 hours later, when he attacked with his team-mates from the moment the flag dropped, descending from the ski resort like there was no tomorrow, and racing to Marseille with Ocaña and his men in hot pursuit for 250 km (155 miles). Ocaña crashed heavily in a thunderstorm in the Pyrenees two days later and withdrew, but that did nothing to lessen Merckx's reputation.

A climber unleashed is a rare and wonderful sight, not merely for the speed with which he can pedal up mountains that would be steep to walk up, but

because of the sense of history. Claudio Chiappucci's quixotic, doomed attempt to unseat Indurain across four mountain passes into Sestriere in his native Italy in 1992 was more than an echo of Coppi's great escape to the same finish 40 years earlier.

Similarly, Marco Pantani's attack on the rainsoaked Galibier to win the 1998 race, with the yellow jersey Jan Ullrich trailing far behind, again had Tour followers casting their minds back 40 years, to the original "Angel of the Mountains", the little Luxembourger Charly Gaul, and his tour-winning escape on a dank, chilly day in the Chartreuse Massif above Grenoble. For Jan Ullrich, who lost nine minutes and the Tour, read Raphael Geminiani, and 12 minutes.

LEFT The 2002 Tour scales the Col de la Madeleine on the stage between Les Deux Alpes and La Plagne, won by the Dutchman Michael Boogerd.

RIGHT The "Eagle of Toledo", Federico Bahamontes, takes wing. Perhaps the greatest mountain climber cycling has ever seen, he won the Tour's King of the Mountains prize seven times in 10 starts, but was just as capable of quitting the race on a whim, as he did in 1957.

LOUISON BOBET

"Certain people are born with a disability: Louison came into the world with a mad desire to win," was Jean Bobet's summing up of his brother. The elegant Louison, with his brylcreemed hair and his private aeroplane, was also the epitome of Breton grit, probably forged in early life, working from before dawn in the family bakery, and still finding time to excel at table tennis and football.

In his second Tour in 1948, he was reported to have quit the race in San Remo due to a painful boil on his foot, but won the next stage into Cannes. His hat trick of Tour wins – two of them forged on the scree slopes of the Izoard, where a plaque stands in his memory – was the product of pure guts,

a triumph over the boils on the crutch that affected him through his career.

TRUE GRIT

The same quality won him his world title in 1954 in the German town of Sollingen. Bobet had escaped with the Swiss Fritz Schaer when he punctured on the last lap. He had to do a U-turn, go back to the pit area for a spare wheel, and somehow closed a one-minute gap on Schaer with a few metres to spare.

His final Tour win, in 1955, came in spite of a gaping wound in his "saddle" area; when operated on at the end of the year, it took 150 clips to patch up

the blood vessels. Yet Bobet still found the strength to attack alone over Mont Ventoux, in burning sun, to take the lead.

Although Bobet was also an accomplished Classics rider – the first Frenchman to win the Tour of Flanders – nothing became him so much as his final appearance in the Tour de France in 1959.

He was ill, and was left behind by the bunch on the 2,770-metre (8,000-foot) high Col de l'Iseran in the Alps. He forced himself to the top, so that it could not be said that he could not get up the mountain; on climbing into a journalist's car, he asked to borrow a hat. "I don't want anyone to recognize me. I'm ashamed to abandon."

NATIONALITY	French
DATES	12 March 1925–13 March 1983
NICKNAME	the Baker of Saint Méen
PROFESSIONAL	1947–61
MAJOR WINS	
1950	French national championship.
1951	French national championship; Milan–San Remo; Giro di Lombardia.
1952	GP Nations.
1953	Tour de France.
1954	Tour de France; World Road Championship.
1955	Tour de France; Tour of Flanders; Dauphiné Libéré.
1956	Paris–Roubaix.
1959	Bordeaux–Paris.
OTHER RESULTS	1950: Tour de France, third and King of the Mountains. 1957: World Road Championship, silver; Giro d'Italia, second. 1958: World Road Championship, silver.
	Tour de France: four stage wins; 34 days in yellow jersey. Giro d'Italia: two stage wins.

Very occasionally, the Tour is won on the flat, most notoriously in 1951, when the Swiss Hugo Koblet – nicknamed "le pedaleur de charme" for his perfect style in the saddle – launched what has been known ever since as the "coup d'Agen" – the great Agen attack. Defying all logic, Koblet attacked in the rolling hills of the Dordogne, and raced alone for over 135 km (85 miles), with the cream of 1950s Tours – Coppi, his great rival Gino Bartali, and the triple winner Louison Bobet – trailing in his wake. The reward, 2 minutes, 35 seconds, was minimal in proportion to the length of his effort, but the psychological advantage it earned him won the Tour.

A CLASH OF TITANS

Since World War II, and the start of the modern cycling era with decent bikes on relatively well-surfaced roads, the Tour has tended to follow an implacable physical logic. The stronger the cyclist, the more quickly he recovers from each day's effort, and the more slowly his body deteriorates. As a result, it usually follows that the man who is strongest in the first key stage, be it time trial or mountain, will eventually win. If he is the strongest after the initial warm-up of between seven and 10 days on the flat, he will usually be the strongest after 20 stages.

The Tour offers most excitement when this rule does not apply. The greatest Tour ever, the suspense-filled 1989 race, pitted two previous winners who were slightly below their best, Laurent Fignon and Greg LeMond, against a third, Pedro Delgado, who gave himself a seven-minute handicap by missing his start in the opening time trial. Fignon and LeMond swapped the yellow jersey five times, LeMond winning it in the opening time trial at Rennes and the mountain time trial to Orcières-Merlette, while Fignon twice took it from him, in the Pyrenees and the Alps.

For two weeks, the pair were never more than 50 seconds apart, and the race came down to the grand finale, a time trial ending on the Champs-Elysées. In an Indurain, Hinault, or Armstrong year it would have been just another demonstration of strength, but

LeMond and Fignon turned it into pure theatre. The American finished first; two minutes later when the yellow-jersey-clad Fignon arrived, his 50-second lead had evaporated.

LeMond had won by just eight seconds and, to complete the story, it was one of the greatest comebacks ever seen in any sport, not merely cycling. Two years earlier he had come within seconds of death, losing pints of his blood when accidentally shot by his brother-in-law while they were hunting wild turkey. He was still carrying lead shot in his vital organs when he won the 1989 race.

There were echoes of previous titanic battles: Bernard Hinault's race-long fight against the Dutchman Joop Zoetemelk 10 years earlier, which ended with the pair finishing together ahead of the main field on the Champs, and Jacques Anquetil and Raymond Poulidor's epic combat of 1964. The Tour had seen final-day upsets – Jean Robic's attack en route to Paris

LEFT Marie-Louise Bobet, commonly known as "Louison", rides alone through the Casse Deserte on the Col d'Izoard in the Alps en route to Tour win number two in 1954.

LAURENT FIGNON

One episode sums up the bespectacled Parisian's career. After retirement, he met a company director to clinch a deal, and was greeted with the words "Ah, you lost the 1989 Tour by eight seconds." "Humph," said Fignon, "I won it twice." That dramatic 1989 defeat overshadows two great Tour wins, which include his crushing 1984 beating of Bernard Hinault, with five stage wins en route. The press called him "the Ogre".

Fignon is a studious-looking veterinary sciences graduate, famously blunt about his profession, and often at odds with the media. He also suffered some bizarre turns of ill-luck – a broken bottom bracket when on course to win the 1982 Paris–Tours, a tapeworm in the 1988 Tour de France, and a crash in a tunnel in the 1990 Giro. None hurt more than Greg LeMond's miracle on the Champs-Elysées.

NATIONALITY	French
BORN	12 August 1960, Paris
NICKNAMES	the Professor; the Ogre
PROFESSIONAL	1982–93
MAJOR WINS	
1982	Criterium International.
1983	Tour de France; French national title.
1984	Tour de France.
1986	Flèche Wallonne.
1988	Milan–San Remo; Tour of the EC.
1989	Giro d'Italia; Milan–San Remo; GP Nations.

ABOVE Wearing the leather-strapped crash hat that earned him the
nickname "leatherhead", Jean Robic attacks during the first post-
war Tour, 1947, on the Lyon–Grenoble stage.

in 1947, Jan Janssen's shock time trial win in 1968 – but nothing to compare with 1989. The organizers have resisted the temptation to stage another time trial finish in Paris, for fear of anticlimax.

SCANDALS AND SKULDUGGERY

For all the rapturous public reception to the first Tour, the second race was close to being the last. Racing at night, on lonely roads, with only one official – Desgrange's factotum Géo Lefèvre – to watch over them, the riders were vulnerable to sabotage and intimidation, and the opportunities for cheating were endless. Nails were continually placed on the roads to obstruct riders and, early on, cars driven by men wearing blindfolds threatened Garin and the 1903 runner-up Pottier and tried to run them into the ditch. At the top of the Col de la Republique, outside Saint Etienne, the riders were met by a crowd bearing clubs and yelling support for the local rider, Fauré, and an Italian, Gerbi, was badly beaten. The official cars were

RAYMOND POULIDOR

Genial and bumbling, "Poupou" was the most popular man in France during the 1960s, initially as the underdog in his head-to-head duels with Jacques Anquetil in the Tour de France, later for selflessly helping others win the race, such as Roger Pingeon in 1967. Poulidor could win major races, but was over-reliant on brute strength in the Tour. He still had the tenacity to finish third at the age of 40 in 1976, and at one point it was estimated that he would be first choice as a dinner guest for almost half the French population, but the title of his best-selling autobiography perfectly summed up his career: *Glory without the Yellow Jersey.*

NATIONALITY	French
BORN	15 April 1936, Masbaraud-Merignat, Creuse
NICKNAME	Poupou
PROFESSIONAL	1960–77
MAJOR WINS	
1961	Milan–San Remo; French national title.
1963	Flèche Wallonne; GP Nations.
1964	Vuelta a España; Super Prestige Pernod Trophy.
1966	Dauphiné Libéré.
1972	Paris–Nice.
1973	Paris–Nice.

forced to pull out revolvers and shoot in the air to drive off the mob. In Nîmes a couple of days later, in spite of a massive police presence, a crowd of 150 attacked the race, outraged at the disqualification of the local rider, Payan. Again, revolvers were drawn and used.

Garin joked that "if I'm not assassinated before I get to Paris, I'll win," but he and the rest of the top four finishers were eventually disqualified for a wide variety of offences, including taking pace behind cars, taking short cuts, swapping race numbers, and collusion with fellow competitors. Henri Cornet, who finished fifth, was declared the winner, and remains the youngest Tour victor. "The Tour is finished," wrote Desgrange in despair, "killed by its own success, by the blind passions it has unleashed."

The race went on, but skulduggery of varying degrees has been ever-present. Three cyclists in the 1906 race were disqualified for taking a train. In 1911 the race leader, Gustave Garrigou, had to be disguised with a wig and dark glasses to get through Rouen, for fear he would be lynched by supporters of the local Paul Duboc, who had been given a bottle of poisoned water. Even as late as 1950, the entire Italian national team walked out in protest – with Fiorenzo Magni wearing the yellow jersey – after Gino Bartali was attacked by spectators in the Pyrenees.

When superhuman demands are made of mere men, it is hardly reasonable to expect them always to behave like angels, and by and large the public's sympathy is with the cyclists as they attempt to get round the implacable officials. The rules have been draconian in the past. Fines were levied from riders who did not spend the night in their allotted hotels, and as recently as 1991 a Swiss cyclist, Urs Zimmerman, who suffered from a fear of flying, was disqualified for choosing to travel in his team car rather than in the official plane during a lengthy transfer.

The riders went on strike on his behalf and he was reinstated. That was a mere ripple compared to their protest at Valence d'Agen in 1978, when they brought a stop to a new, if lucrative, strategy by the organizers. They had realized that if the cyclists were made to race three short stages in a day, that would triple revenues from the stage towns. The riders could not stomach the early morning starts and walked across the finish line in Valence, led by Bernard Hinault, who became involved in a heated exchange with the town's mayor. The mayor backed down, and the pugnacious Hinault remained the "boss" of the bunch for the next seven years.

Strategies for getting round the rules or stealing a march on the opposition can border on the farcical. The Belgian Sylvère Maes won the 1934 race by taking the side gate over a level crossing while the chasing bunch were forced to wait for a freight train. Jean Robic – known as "Biquet" ("Little Goat") – would have a bottle containing 5 kg (10 lb) of lead handed up to him at the top of a mountain so that he could descend more quickly.

Perhaps the cheekiest incident came in 1960, when the peloton stopped to meet General de Gaulle

LEFT The Tour's doctor, Pierre Dumas, in black T-shirt, fights vainly to save the life of Tom Simpson on Mont Ventoux in 1967. He had already felt the pills in Simpson's pockets, and knew a scandal was about to erupt.

ABOVE Marco Pantani sits (in the foreground) as the riders strike during the "Tour de Farce" of 1998. Eleven months later, Pantani would himself be at the heart of a major drugs controversy.

in his summer home in Colombey-les-Deux-Eglises, and the lowly Pierre Beuffeuil took advantage to catch up after a puncture, and then sneaked past to win the stage. For sheer cunning, however, Anquetil takes the biscuit for faking a broken brake cable so that he could change onto a lighter bike at the foot of the Col du Forclaz in 1963. Bike changes were only permitted in case of mechanical incident, so as he stopped the mechanic ran up and snipped through the cable, under the eyes of the referee.

Such tricks are frivolous compared to the Tour's biggest bugbear, which is the riders' reliance over the years on drugs to help them on their way. Prior to the

death of Simpson, there were no limits and little stigma attached to the use of stimulants, mainly amphetamines, which were often used in quantity. There were incidents, such as when the Breton Jean Mallejac collapsed and came close to death on the Ventoux in 1955, but Simpson's death in 1967 was what finally focused minds, and daily drug tests were brought in in 1968.

Since then there has been a regular occurrence of positive tests, in spite of the fact that the most common and most efficient drugs have tended to be undetectable – steroids in the 1970s, cortisone and testosterone in the 1980s, and the blood-boosting hormone erythropoietin (EPO) in the 1990s. Roughly every 10 years there has been a scandal involving a big name. 1967 was Simpson; in 1978 the Belgian Michel Pollentier took the yellow jersey at l'Alpe

d'Huez, only to be discovered with an elaborate tubing contraption containing someone else's urine attached to his penis.

In 1988 it was again the *maillot jaune*, Pedro Delgado, who tested positive for the steroid-masking drug Probenecid, but was let off, as the substance had not been included on the International Cycling Union's banned list. A decade later, however, saw the biggest scandal of them all, when the Festina team masseur Willy Voet was stopped by customs en route to the Tour with a huge cargo of EPO and growth hormone, kicking off what was to become the "Tour de Farce".

Festina, the number-one team in the world, led by France's most popular cyclist, Richard Virenque, were sensationally thrown off the race, which descended into chaos as the gendarmes began investigating another five squads under French laws banning the provision of performance-enhancing drugs. They arrested riders and managers for questioning, and descended on the race en masse to search hotel rooms and team cars. The riders responded by sitting down and refusing to race on two stages, in an intriguing echo of their protest when the first random controls were carried out in 1966.

During their second strike, between Albertville and Aix-les-Bains, it seemed as if Desgrange's words of 1904 would finally come true and the Tour would not go on, until the race director Jean-Marie Leblanc and the 1996 winner Bjarne Riis persuaded the riders to get to that day's finish, and so to Paris. It was a close-run thing. The Festina saga shook the Tour to its core, but has at least had the merits of focusing minds on its unpleasant underbelly.

THE FANATICAL FOLLOWING

Much of the Tour's enduring appeal is the proximity and interaction between its stars and the public, who remained faithful to the race even after the revelations of drug-taking. They did, however, express their displeasure, by painting slogans on the roads such as "No to EPO", and even by baring their bottoms at the Tour organizers as the riders went on strike.

The fans are sometimes eccentric, like the German bike inventor Didi Senff, who has followed the last 10 Tours dressed up as the devil, complete with toasting fork and dangly tail. They are frequently vocal, and, in the case of the Dutch who congregate on l'Alpe d'Huez, often drunk, but the Tour's crowds are rarely intimidating. The last unpleasant incident dates back to 1975, when a stressed-out middle-aged Frenchman punched Eddy Merckx in the kidneys on top of the Puy de Dome. The atmosphere is that of a vast picnic rather than a football match.

Now, the fans tend to limit their intervention in the race to passing bottles of water and giving the backmarkers a helping push in the mountains. Sometimes they do get too close for comfort, as

FEDERICO BAHAMONTES

"In the mountains, it was accepted that Bahamontes would attack. Always. The mountains were his domain," said one fellow pro of "the Eagle", who set a record for King of the Mountains wins in the Tour – only equalled by the Belgian Lucien van Impe.

He won the 1959 race, claims the organizers rigged the 1963 Tour against him, and he is celebrated for breaking away up a mountain in his first Tour in 1954, stopping at the top, and eating an ice cream while waiting for the field to catch up. The truth is more prosaic, he says – he broke his back wheel, and was waiting for his mechanic.

NATIONALITY	Spanish
BORN	9 July 1928, Santo Domingo-Caudillo (Toledo)
NICKNAME	the Eagle of Toledo
PROFESSIONAL	1954–65
MAJOR WINS	
1954	King of the Mountains in Tour de France.
1957	Vuelta a España.
1958	Spanish national title; Vuelta a España; King of the Mountains in Tour de France.
1959	Tour de France and King of the Mountains.
1962	King of the Mountains in Tour de France.
1963	King of the Mountains in Tour de France.
1964	King of the Mountains in Tour de France.

Giuseppe Guerini of Italy found out in the 1999 Tour when a youth wielding a camera knocked him off as he rode to the stage win at l'Alpe d'Huez. Fortunately he was going uphill at 16 kph (10 mph) and the only damage was to his concentration.

These days it is the political demonstrators who tend to take advantage of the Tour's openness. The Basque separatist group ETA have twice blown up vehicles in the race convoy, in 1974 and 1992 – when the British television company Channel Four were on the receiving end. A different group of Basque extremists, calling for the release of political prisoners, pulled off a considerable coup in the 2000 Tour by dressing up in race clothing at Courchevel in the Alps, and joining in the final few hundred yards of the stage alongside the stage winner Marco Pantani and the yellow jersey Lance Armstrong.

The French "agriculteurs" turn up most years, with varying levels of disruption – they caused the 1990 race to be led on a diversion around a roadblock in deepest Poitou by a local on a moped – and striking steelworkers stopped a stage in 1982. That, however, is a small price in an event that goes to the people, and the cyclists tend to accept it. The triple winner Lance Armstrong is the exception: he was sufficiently worried about his own safety to bring two burly bodyguards to the 2001 race, and consulted the organizers about security in the 2002 race following the terrorist attacks of 11 September 2001.

THE TOUR TODAY

Desgrange gave up organizing in 1933, and *l'Auto* mutated into *l'Equipe* after World War II, but the Tour's father would not find the race completely unfamiliar today. It travels abroad every other year and has occasionally started outside France, although plans to take it to America in the 1980s were quietly dropped. Britain was visited in 1994, Ireland hosted the start in 1998. The "Euro-Tour" in 1992, visiting every EU country bordering France to celebrate European Monetary Union, had to miss out the Pyrenees, and was not considered a great success.

The prologue time trial, a brief race on the first day to decide the pecking order and a way of getting an extra day's racing, was introduced in 1967. In 1975 Jacques Goddet, son of Desgrange's head of finance Victor and the man who had taken over both the race and *l'Auto* in the 1930s, added the final element in today's race when he obtained permission for it to finish on the Champs-Elysées. Both are now permanent fixtures.

The biggest change came during the 1980s, with the arrival en masse of cyclists from outside the European heartland. The English had been in the Tour since 1934, but with limited impact apart from Barry Hoban's eight stage wins. Suddenly, in the 1980s, the Tour opened up, with Phil Anderson of Australia wearing the yellow jersey in 1981; Sean Kelly of Ireland taking the points jersey in 1982; the arrival of

CHRIS BOARDMAN

A track and time trial specialist who transferred his talents to the road relatively late in his career, Boardman became virtually unbeatable in stage race prologue time trials. He broke the record for the fastest stage in the Tour de France in his debut prologue victory in Lille in 1994. Famously "clean" in the drug-ridden 90s, legendary for his obsessive dedication to training, and unfairly accused of constantly consulting his pulse monitor at every turn, Boardman suffered from a bone-wasting condition later in his career, which ended with a narrow beating of Eddy Merckx's hour record.

NATIONALITY	British
BORN	26 August 1968, Hoylake, Wirral
PROFESSIONAL	1993–2000
MAJOR WINS – ROAD	
1993	GP Eddy Merckx.
1994	World time trial title.
1996	Criterium International; GP Nations.
	Tour de France: prologue winner 1994, 1997, 1998.
MAJOR WINS – TRACK	
1992	Olympic 4,000 m pursuit: hour record 52.270 km.
1994	World 4,000 m pursuit.
1996	World 4,000 m pursuit; hour record 56.375 km.
2000	Hour record 49.441 km.

RIGHT Greg LeMond climbs in the 1989 Tour, a race where he struggled in the mountains, yet triumphed by a tiny margin in the final time trial.

GREG LEMOND

During the 1990 Tour de France, the Z team mechanic, Julien de Vriese, had a crisis. Greg LeMond's brand-new carbon-fibre bike had been stolen, or so he assumed when he could not locate the sleek black machine in the team's equipment truck.

In tears, a panic-stricken De Vriese sent a junior mechanic speeding down the motorway towards Belgium to collect a spare – until he realized that LeMond had taken the bike up to his hotel room to make sure it came to no harm during the night, and had to call his errand boy back.

In its mix of meticulousness and absent-mindedness, the episode perfectly sums up LeMond. He was then en route to his third Tour win in the five years in which he took cycling into the 20th century thanks to a single character trait: his refusal to do things by the European cycling book.

SALARY HIKE

Cycling was a low-rent sport in 1984, but when he joined the La Vie Claire team, LeMond won the first million-dollar cycling deal; his salary rose to $5.5m over three years after his 1989 comeback. He would travel with his own chef, his own portable air-conditioning unit, and went truly against cycling's puritanical grain by insisting his wife Kathy and his children should join him at races.

LeMond's return from near death to win the 1989 Tour popularized aerodynamic triathlon bars; he also pioneered the now ubiquitous Oakley sunglasses, helmet radios, and titanium frames, and experimented with suspension forks in Paris–Roubaix. As the first American cycling star, LeMond globalized the sport by turning the US media on to the Tour. Lance Armstrong is noticing the benefits today.

There remains one imponderable about LeMond: what would he have achieved without his April 1987 shooting accident? It robbed him of his best years and the best of his ability, and would end his career. The man himself believes that without it he could have won five Tours.

NATIONALITY	American
BORN	26 June 1961, Lakewood, California
PROFESSIONAL	1981–94
MAJOR WINS	
1982	Tour de l'Avenir.
1983	Dauphiné Libéré; World Road Championship; Super Prestige Pernod.
1985	Coors Classic.
1986	Tour de France.
1989	Tour de France. World Road Championship.
1990	Tour de France.
1992	Du Pont Tour.
OTHER RESULTS	1982: World Road Championship, silver. 1984: Tour de France, third. 1985: Tour de France, second; World Road Championship, silver; Giro d'Italia, third.
	Tour de France: five stage wins; 22 stages in yellow jersey. Giro d'Italia: one stage win.

an entire team of Colombians in 1983; Robert Millar's King of the Mountains victory in 1984; and Greg LeMond's first Tour win in 1986. The picture was completed when a team of Russians rode in 1990.

By the end of the 1980s, the Tour had suddenly turned into a sprawling behemoth. It left vast traffic jams in its wake. Corporate guests were everywhere. The number of vehicles speeding along the route in front of the race was getting out of control, and the number of cyclists had expanded to around 200. The newly international field meant the press corps had grown from a handful to close to 1,000, while the huge expansion of worldwide television coverage had brought thousands of technicians and vehicles to the race. To keep sponsors happy, 16 separate prize presentations took place after every stage.

The new fear was gigantism – that the Tour would simply grow too large for its own good. The expansion coincided with a management crisis, as Jacques Goddet's half a century at the helm came to an end. After an interim year, 1988, marked by the drugs scandal involving the winner Pedro Delgado, the former journalist and Tour cyclist Jean-Marie Leblanc took over, his brief to make the race more coherent as the 21st century approached.

Leblanc's task has been managing the race's growth rather than putting a lid on it. It is more smoothly organized, more corporate, and the interminable prize presentations have been pared down. However, he looked powerless when the 1998 race spiralled out of control after the Festina drugs bust, and he was reduced to threatening and pleading with the riders to keep the race on the road.

Drastic measures to reduce the number of race vehicles travelling along the route were only taken after the death of a child by the roadside during the 2000 race, and the stage distances have been cut to liven up the race. Leblanc is set to retire after the centenary Tour in 2003, and it seems likely that afterwards, for the first time ever, the race will not be run by a journalist. For a race conceived by a newspaper editor to boost circulation, born in a newspaper office, and delivered by journalists, that will be change indeed.

RIGHT In the cauldron: Lance Armstrong, in yellow, and Marco Pantani are dwarfed by the fans and the motorbikes as they scale Mont Ventoux during the 2000 race.

NATIONALITY	French
DATES	8 January 1934–18 November 1987
NICKNAME	Master Jacques
PROFESSIONAL	1954–69
PROFESSIONAL TEAMS	1954: La Perle. 1955–61: Helyett. 1962–4: St Raphael. 1965–6: Ford France. 1967–9: Bic
MAJOR WINS	
1953	(independent): Grand Prix des Nations.
1954	GP des Nations.
1955	GP des Nations.
1956	GP des Nations; hour record 46.159 km.
1957	Tour de France; Paris–Nice; GP des Nations
1958	Four Days of Dunkirk; GP des Nations.
1959	Four Days of Dunkirk.
1960	Giro d'Italia.
1961	Tour de France; Paris–Nice; GP des Nations; Criterium National; Super Prestige Pernod Trophy.
1962	Tour de France.
1963	Tour de France; Vuelta a España; Paris–Nice; Dauphiné Libéré; Criterium National; Super Prestige Pernod Trophy.
1964	Tour de France; Giro d'Italia; Ghent–Wevelgem.
1965	Bordeaux–Paris; Dauphiné Libéré; Paris–Nice; Criterium National; GP des Nations; Super Prestige Pernod Trophy.
1966	Liège–Bastogne–Liège; Paris–Nice; Tour of Sardinia; GP des Nations; Super Prestige Pernod Trophy.
1967	Tour of Catalonia; Criterium National.
1969	Tour of Basque Country.
OTHER RESULTS	1959: Tour de France, third; Giro d'Italia, second. 1961: Giro d'Italia, second. 1966: Giro d'Italia, second; World Road Championship, silver.
	Tour de France: 16 stage wins; 51 days in yellow jersey. Giro d'Italia: three stage wins. 65 time trial wins. 158 professional wins.

JACQUES ANQUETIL

Some images of sport remain etched in a nation's consciousness. For the French, cycling will always evoke the sight of Jacques Anquetil and Raymond Poulidor shoulder to shoulder, elbow to elbow, on the slopes of the Puy de Dome in the 1964 Tour de France. "France's equivalent of the Stanley Matthews Cup Final," wrote Geoffrey Nicholson in *The Great Bike Race*. "Siamese twins in suffering," said Poulidor.

This was Anquetil's finest moment, epitomizing the approach that made him the first man to win five Tours: gain time in the time trials and hang on like grim death in the mountains. Anquetil was perfectly capable of outclimbing the climbers on his day but his strong suit was racing against the clock – he won 65 time trials during his career, including the time trial Classic Grand Prix des Nations nine times – and he exploited it to the full. It was a tactic Indurain, Hinault, and Armstrong would use in future Tours.

A BATTLE FOR RESPECT

His calculated approach meant the public respected rather than loved the strawberry grower's son from the little town of Quincampoix, just outside Rouen. Anquetil led the 1961 Tour from start to finish, but the organizer Jacques Goddet derided him as a "dwarf" – as opposed to the "giants" of the road who preceded him – in an editorial, and even after that 1964

LEFT "Master Jacques" at his best, climbing in the yellow jersey en route to his second Tour win in 1961. Three more Tour victories would follow.

Tour win, he was whistled by part of the crowd at the Tour finish in the Parc des Princes.

So the high-cheekboned, slick-haired "Master Jacques" had to try to race with panache. He outclimbed "the Eagle", Federico Bahamontes, to win the two key mountain stages in the 1963 Tour, from Pau to Bagnères de Bigorre in the Pyrenees, from Val d'Isère to Chamonix in the Alps. And in 1965, at the prompting of his team mate turned manager Raphael Geminiani, he produced his most audacious feat.

For total defiance of sporting logic, there can be no match for Anquetil's back-to-back victories in the Dauphiné Libéré stage race, and the Bordeaux–Paris "Derby of the Road", the now-defunct 560-km (350-mile) motorpaced Classic lasting 15 hours. The Dauphiné, eight days in the Alps, finished at 5 p.m.; the "Derby" started at two the next morning.

Anquetil flew from the Alps in a government jet, with the permission of General de Gaulle himself, snatched an hour's nap en route, fought his way to Paris in bone-chilling rain against riders who were properly rested, and won, having covered 2,500 km (1,500 miles) in nine days.

A precocious talent, who broke Fausto Coppi's hour record at the age of 22, Anquetil built up his time trial speed suffering like a dog behind a motorbike driven by his trainer André Boucher – 80 km (50 miles) at 64 kph (40 mph) in which he was not allowed to yell "slow down" – but he was notoriously unwilling to forego life's little pleasures merely to win bike races. "Diet?" he said once. "No fouler

swearword can be said in my house." Lobsters, champagne, and whisky were his favourites, although sometimes the contents of the glass would be poured down the sink once the journalists had left the house.

The rivalry with Poulidor was real enough. On one occasion in 1967, he was drinking whisky at 3 a.m. with Geminiani, having pulled out of the next day's Criterium National one-day race with a cough. "Let's toast Poulidor's victory tomorrow," said "Gem". Anquetil was not amused, told his wife Janine to "set the alarm for seven o'clock", and duly won the next day.

UNCOMPROMISING

Off the bike, he was independent-minded, admitted the use of drugs, campaigned against the introduction of dope tests, and attacked those he called hypocrites, the people who said it was possible to race 200 days a year without using amphetamines. His domestic life verged on the incestuous; he had children by both his wife Janine's daughter from her first marriage, and her daughter-in-law.

Later in life, he was to worry about the drugs he had used and developed a morbid fear of death, refusing to go to bed for fear he might not wake up. Instead, he would prowl his estate in Normandy, watching the creatures of the night, before stomach cancer finally carried him off. Even on his deathbed, Anquetil could not forget their rivalry, even if it was with a touch of irony in his final words to "Poupou": "I'm sorry Raymond, you're going to finish second again."

MILAN—SAN REMO

Cycling's annual rite of spring takes place on the third Saturday in March. There is a special nervousness about the field as they prepare for the race in the shadow of the Milan's great cathedral. They ignore the cries of encouragement from Italian cycling fans, some dressed in team replica kit, others in the green wool Loden coats that wealthy Milanese wear until May each year. The tension is palpable, and understandable. Milan—San Remo is when professional cycling starts for real after the winter break and the gradually intensifying round of early spring training races, which climax with two eight-day events, the Paris—Nice "Race to the Sun" and, in Italy, the Tirreno—Adriatico, "Race of the Two Seas". They are merely warm-up events for this, the race the Italians call "la Primavera" (Spring) or "la Classicissima" – the Classic of Classics.

LEFT One of Italy's greatest landmarks, the marbled splendour of the Duomo in the centre of Milan, gives a spectacular send-off to the 1990 Milan—San Remo, which will be won in some seven hours by the Italian Gianni Bugno. Spring has arrived, and the professional cycling year has begun in earnest.

MILAN – SAN REMO

FOUNDED TO PUBLICIZE A FADING RESORT ON THE LIGURIAN RIVIERA KNOWN ONLY FOR GAMBLING, THE RACE NICKNAMED "SPRING" HAS TURNED INTO THE EVENT EVERY ITALIAN CYCLIST DREAMS OF WINNING.

Alone of all Europe's great bike races, the course of La Primavera remains virtually identical to that traced out in 1907 by the organizers from *La Gazzetta dello Sport*, who still sponsor the race after almost a century. That is why it remains the longest of the one-day Classics, a throwback to cycling's origins in the Belle Epoque at almost 300 km (190 miles).

The roads have improved, but the Classic of Classics still runs down the flat roads past the great Charterhouse of Pavia, crossing the Apennines on the gradual ascent of the Turchino pass. Then there is the plunge down to the outskirts of Genoa and the old Roman coast road through Alássio and Imperia to San Remo, the last sizeable Italian town before the French frontier at Ventimiglia.

There have been minor additions, but that in essence is the course Milan–San Remo covered in 1907, a year after a disastrous car race on a similar route via Acqui Terme, close to the Turchino, in which only two cars made it to the finish. The race organizers were not certain the cyclists would fare any better, so the Giro di Lombardia winner Giovanni Gerbi was sent out to reconnoitre the route.

Gerbi was one of the favourites for the first race, together with the Frenchman Gustave Garrigou. The pair escaped together, but approaching the finish they began arguing about who should make the pace, and they were caught by Gerbi's Bianchi team-mate Lucien Petit-Breton. With Gerbi holding Garrigou back in the finish sprint, Petit-Breton won, and his team was relegated from second to third. "A splendid success, with great animation as the winner was awaited," noted the Catholic weekly *L'Armonia*.

Petit-Breton's real name was Lucien Mazan – "Breton" was a pseudonym he had adopted because his father did not approve of his bike racing. He would go on to win the Tour de France that year and the year after – the first man to win the race two years in a row. He was also to be one of several cyclists killed during World War I. En route to the Ardennes front in 1917, he was mown down by a lorry driven by a drunken peasant.

In the early years, its March date meant that Milan–San Remo was frequently hit by foul weather. The first race was run off in freezing rain, but the worst conditions were in 1910, and the man at the centre of events was Eugène Christophe, the same "Old Gaul" whose front forks had a habit of breaking at the most inconvenient moment possible in the Tour de France.

The riders left Milan in bitterly cold weather, but initially were more bothered by the mud on the flatlands around Pavia, where they could only ride along the road's edges, dodging around the stones that marked the route every 20 metres. As they climbed the Turchino it began to snow. Christophe got to the tunnel at the top on foot and took the lead as the riders who had escaped earlier on abandoned one by one due to the cold. However, befitting his status as cycling's unluckiest man ever, things deteriorated from there as he descended the pass.

In 1922, he told the magazine *Le Miroir des Sports*, "The snow was 20 centimetres deep, more in places. I kept putting my feet down, ran with the bike, walked, until I could ride no further. Then I ran, but I had to slow down. A bit further on, I got stomach cramps. Holding my bike in one hand, and my belly in the other, I leaned up against a rock by the roadside. The cold had paralysed me: I could move my head from left to right and right to left a little, and that was all."

As he lay there, thinking how much money he would lose if he did not get to San Remo first – not realizing that he was about to die of exposure – a man passed. "He didn't stop," recalled Christophe, who shouted "Signor, signor, casa, casa" ("Mister, mister, house, house"), as that was all the Italian he knew. He was dragged rather than guided into shelter.

While warming up in the cottage, in fact a small inn, drinking rum and hot water by the wood stove and doing exercises to restore the circulation to his limbs,

ABOVE RIGHT Five members of the BresciaLat team (in blue jerseys) with a lone domestique from the ONCE squad, in yellow, control the pace in the 1997 race. The final hills – the Cipressa and Poggio – are not far away.

Milan
START

Pavia

KEY
— route
mountains

Turchino pass
Takes the race over the Apennines from the Lombardy plains to the Ligurian coast, with the steep diversion to the summit of Bric Berton a recent addition to toughen up what is basically a long grind with a hair-raising descent to the outskirts of Genoa. Only occasionally is the winning move formed here, as in Claudio Chiappucci's rain-lashed victory of 1991.

Genoa

L i g u r i a n   S e a

Savona

THE ROUTE

Uniquely among all the great bike races, the route of Milan–San Remo is in essence the same as when the race was founded 90 years ago. As the 2002 race shows, first comes a flat, fast run across the Lombardy plains, where wind can split the race, to the foot of the Apennines. Then comes the ascent of the Turchino pass – once a dirt track, now a well-surfaced main road – and the high-speed descent to the outskirts of Genoa. The final phase has the clear blue waters of the Mediterranean as its backdrop, with little ascents over the headlands along the coast to break the rhythm before the decisive climb of the Poggio and the heart-stopping hairpinned downhill into San Remo.

Poggio di San Remo
Coming just before the finish, with only the tight hairpins of the descent and the flat final two kilometres into the town centre remaining, this was the traditional location for the winning attack until the mid 1990s, but since Laurent Jalabert's win in 1995 the tendency has been for the race to be decided in the streets of San Remo.

Cipressa
There is a desperate battle for first places in the field before this steep, hairpinned little hill through the olive groves outside Imperia, as it invariably sees the bunch split for the first time as the course cuts briefly inland, and more victims are claimed in crashes on the dangerous descent back to the coast.

Capi
Three little hills – Capo Mele, Capo Cervo, and Capo Berta – are the first test of the cyclists' legs in the final phase. These are merely short rises over a series of small headlands as the race winds along the Ligurian coast, but they are climbed after almost six hours in the saddle, and the distance tells.

Poggio di San Remo

Capo Verde

San Remo

Alássio

Capi

FINISH

Cipressa

Imperia

Riva Ligure

San Remo

"the Old Gaul" kept his eyes fixed on the road outside. He made sure he got a pair of long trousers from the innkeeper and left after 25 minutes, ignoring the Italian's demands that he stay in the warm.

Other riders had passed by – or rather four "bags of mud", as he told *Le Miroir* – but he overtook them and won. The second rider, Luigi Ganna, who won the first Giro d'Italia two years later, was disqualified for clinging on to a car, so second place was given to Cocchi, who was one hour and 10 minutes behind Christophe. Only two other riders finished. His ordeal had lasted 12 hours, and it took its toll. Christophe spent a month in hospital recovering from hypo-thermia, and it was the best part of two years before he raced properly again.

Unlike the other Classics – some of which retain only their start and finish towns, others a distinctive climb or two or an association with a certain area – all that has changed in Milan–San Remo since the years of Christophe and Petit-Breton is the addition of three small deviations from the route to add in new climbs. The reasoning has always been the same: as road surfaces have improved, it has proved harder and harder for the field to split apart. Hence the climbs, which provide an opportunity for the non-sprinters to try to make their escape.

First, and most famously, 1960 saw the introduction of the Poggio, a loop up off the coast road over a little hill on the outskirts of San Remo. The Cipressa, just outside Imperia, followed in 1982, and 2001 brought the Bric Berton, a steep offshoot of the Turchino, which was impassable that year due to a landslide. The road was reopened but the Berton was retained.

What was largely an exercise in stamina and good fortune in the early years has turned into a tactical battle of considerable subtlety since the 1960s. The race is only rarely won on the Turchino or the Cipressa; instead, the key point is the Poggio, snaking up in a series of hairpins through the glasshouses above the coast to a little village on a ridge. It is preceded by 48 km (30 miles) of desperate struggle for position at the front of the bunch, down the coast road, over the little headlands, the Capi, and the Cipressa. Every cyclist's mind is on the Poggio, and the need to be in the first 10 in the string as it turns off the coast road.

"You're fighting all the time, and there are crashes everywhere," says double winner Sean Kelly. "Everyone gets so nervous, because they know that if you have 100 metres' lead at the top of the Poggio, you'll win." "You could put the finish line at the top," says another rider. "You have to keep in the first 20. If you get behind, you are among the domestiques who let gaps open. In a few seconds, you can lose heaps of places." The battle is most intense approaching the Cipressa, as the descent back to the coast is dangerous; there are frequently crashes, and there is little time to regain any ground before the Poggio.

French and Belgian cyclists dominated the early years, but with the advent of World War I, Milan–San Remo closed in on itself. Few foreigners came to compete until 1938 when the organizers realized that their race was becoming stifled and began encouraging the *stranieri* (foreigners) to make the trip. In the 40 years before Louison Bobet won the 1954 race, only one non-Italian, the Belgian Joseph Demuysère, succeeded in breaking the stranglehold of the Italian *campionissimi* – the champions of champions – men such as Gaetano Belloni, Costante Girardengo, and Alfredo Binda in the 1920s, and Gino Bartali and Fausto Coppi in the 1930s and 1940s.

RIVALRY AMONG CHAMPIONS

The Italian campionissimi have often tended to let their personal feelings get the better of them. Down the years, defeating the big rival has often been more important to them than actually winning the big race. Binda lamented in later years that he had been so focused on getting the better of Girardengo in 1927 that he let the "unknown" Pietro Chesi gain a decisive lead, and reacted too late; but that did not stop him doing the same thing five years later. The only difference was that he was watching a new rival, Learco Guerra, and the beneficiary was Alfredo Bovet.

Such great rivalries are a cornerstone of Italian cycling tradition, a constant over 60 years, partly based on real antagonism, partly manufactured by the press with its love of *polemica* – the war of words – between the two *campioni*. For Binda and Girardengo in the 1920s, read Bartali and Coppi in the 1940s and 50s, Francesco Moser and Giuseppe "il Beppe" Saronni in the late 1970s and early 80s, and Marco Pantani and Michele Bartoli in the late 1990s.

Moser was one of the few ever to articulate in plain Italian the pre-eminence of the need to get the better

ABOVE A definitive victory for Fausto Coppi, Italy's greatest ever cyclist, in 1948. The photographer has strayed too close to the action, and the race referee on the motorbike is waving to him to get out of the way.

of the rival, and hang the race. Approaching San Remo in 1981, he and Saronni were in the leading group when the elegant, long-haired Belgian Fons de Wolf broke away. Moser refused to assist Saronni in the chase, and the Belgian won. "Il Beppe" complained bitterly, but Moser responded, "I'm not paid to help Saronni. Yes, I rode to make him lose."

After four near misses, the stocky, pugnacious, pouting Saronni would win two years later wearing the jersey of world champion. Moser was already a legend by 1981 after his unique hat trick of victories in Paris–Roubaix. His "Classic of Classics" came in 1984, his year of grace following his hour record in Mexico, and his discovery of Professor Conconi's blood transfusions.

La Primavera is an obligatory victory for any Italian cyclist with pretensions to the status of campione or campionissimo. There is a moment of passage for all of them, and since 1960 it has usually come when they attack on the Poggio, leave the bunch trailing behind, and whizz through the hairpins on the tricky descent back to the coast road, with glory just a couple of kilometres away.

"ARRIVA COPPI!"

The reign of the greatest of them all, Fausto Coppi, truly began in 1946, the first race after World War II, with probably the most dominant Milan–San Remo win of all time. Coppi was in front soon after the race left Milan, and he was alone by the time the race reached the tunnel at the top of the Turchino pass.

Pierre Chany described the scene in his book *Arriva Coppi* (*Coppi is Coming*). "The Turchino tunnel is modest, only 50 metres long, but on March 19, 1946 it took on an exceptional dimension. It was six years

ABOVE The decisive moment of the rainsoaked 1991 race: Claudio Chiappucci, leading in white jersey, has sensed that the Dane Rolf Sorensen is weakening on the Poggio climb, just before the finish.

long, and darkness reigned in its interior because the peace had not yet meant the return of electricity. There was a rumbling inside, and an olive car emerged, lifting as it went a cloud of white dust. A second car, another and another ...

"'Arriva Coppi! Arriva Coppi!' repeated the crowd. And he arrived, very quickly ... thin legs, disproportionately long, a short torso, head sunk into his shoulders, and a mouth seeking air, a paradoxically harmonious ensemble. The 'heron' in Italian colours, perched on his invisible saddle, had scattered the race to the four winds."

Coppi would win in San Remo with 14 minutes' lead on the next man, after being in front for 250 km (160 miles). It was, wrote Chany, the start of the modern era of cycling: with his radical attitudes to training and diet, Coppi would transform his sport in the next six years.

All the Italian campioni have been here. Felice Gimondi was mobbed by the crowds on the Via Roma when he finally won la Primavera in 1974, alone at the age of 31 when it seemed his best years were behind him. Claudio Chiappucci's 1991 victory, meanwhile, transformed him from the domestique who got lucky in the 1990 Tour into something altogether more substantial.

"El Diablo", as he was later known, broke away on the descent from the Turchino in horrendously wet and dangerous conditions, and then, with his eyes shining through the murk and the dirt, he wore out his breakaway companions one by one along the coast road. Finally, only the Dane Rolf Sorensen was left, and he fell back on the Poggio, leaving Chiappucci to ride alone into San Remo in the manner of the greats.

Italy's finest one-day rider of the 1980s, Moreno Argentin, never won in San Remo, to his lasting regret.

As world champion, he was hyped to the heavens by the press before the 1987 race. *La Gazzetta dello Sport* still runs the event, so it has every interest in whipping up stories and polemica concerning the home stars. Argentin could not take the pressure, and quit the race claiming that an anonymous phone call to his hotel room during the night had disrupted his sleep.

Five years later, Argentin had his chance to take the win that would have made his career complete, and he blew it. In textbook style, he attacked on the Poggio, crossing the summit with a few seconds' lead, and embarked on the descent with victory in his grasp. Behind him, however, Sean Kelly of Ireland had decided that, even at the age of 36, it was worth risking everything on that last downhill.

At this point, it's worth mentioning that the descent into San Remo is not simply a matter of sitting back and freewheeling. It is, the double winner Laurent Fignon told me, "a series of sprints. You brake at the last moment, you don't necessarily take the corners quickly, then you get up speed quickly again and sprint down the straights."

As well as testing a man's courage, the descent tests how well that man can concentrate after seven hours in the saddle, culminating in the hectic sprint for the Poggio. Kelly had mental energy, and to spare: flying into and out of every corner, he gained on Argentin metre by metre, and finally latched onto him as they entered the streets of San Remo.

Argentin looked round and could not believe his eyes when he saw who was on his wheel. Kelly duly won the sprint a minute later, but, in fact, his victory had been assured from the moment Argentin caught sight of him. In essence, the race came down to who was prepared to take the bigger risks on the descent when they had a sniff of victory. Argentin was not; Kelly was – and there can be no better illustration of the difference between a great of the sport, and a lesser campione.

La Primavera is not always ruled by the campioni. Sometimes they take their eyes off the ball. In 1982, the Italian *tifosi* – the fans – gathered on the Poggio could not believe their eyes when a bespectacled, awkward-looking cyclist called Marc Gomez came up ahead of Saronni, Moser, et al. They assumed he was Spanish; in fact, he was a first-year French professional riding his first Classic. So modest was he that the year before his wife had to persuade him that

turning professional was in his best interests. The campioni and their teams had let him and another Frenchman, Alain Bondue, gain far too much ground after escaping immediately the flag was dropped on the outskirts of Milan; they mounted a chase, but it was too little and too late. Bondue fell on the descent from the Poggio into San Remo; Gomez savoured his moment of glory. In 1987 the campioni made the same mistake, and it was a solid Swiss domestique, Erich Maechler, who triumphed while "the stars just sat back and watched", as the Italian magazine *Bicisport* said bitterly.

The year 1990 offered the most curious spectacle, however, as the race split apart on the flat plains between Milan and Pavia, with 122 riders in the front group. A host of stars such as Kelly and Fignon were left behind while chatting at the back of the bunch and were unsure how to cope with the situation – as the bulk of their domestiques were in front. The result was a race run at record speed, almost 46 kph (28.5 mph), and victory for the Italian Gianni Bugno, of whom more later.

"SUPERMARIO"

For an Italian, Milan–San Remo remains the race of dreams. As a small boy, Mario Cipollini was taken to the Turchino to shelter under his father's coat as the snow fell while he waited for his brother Cesare to race up. For Cipollini, the fastest sprinter and the most charismatic character in cycling in the 1990s, la Primavera became the ultimate goal, where victory beckoned, but something always happened to stop him winning.

He could win the bunch sprint, but in 1994, that was not enough, and Giorgio Furlan finished just ahead. In 1993, after Maurizio Fondriest's lone win, the crowds invaded the finish line, holding up the race director's car just long enough for the chasing group, which included Cipollini, to pile into the back in a heap of broken bikes and bruised bodies. In his rage at the near-disaster, Cipollini picked up his bike and hurled it through the car's back windscreen.

In 2001, at his 13th attempt, he again finished second, this time to Erik Zabel. He would never win the Classic of Classics, it seemed. That is, until 23 March 2002, when Zabel fell off before the Cipressa, and from somewhere, "SuperMario" found the strength to hang on over the Poggio before winning the sprint on the Via Roma – for first place this time, at 35.

Cipollini is a mix of the spiritual and the extremely earthy, by turns coarse and suave. On the Poggio, he said, while suffering to stay in touch, he had been supported by the spirit of the recently deceased television commentator Adriano de Zan, a central figure in Italian cycling. And before the race, "work, work, work, nothing but that", including the ultimate sacrifice for this most macho of cyclists: "a long period of sexual abstinence".

Others have prepared in different ways: before his 1977 win, the Dutchman Jan Raas studied film of Merckx to prepare for his escape down the Poggio descent. Gianni Bugno listened to the music of Mozart to steady his nerves. That eliminated the vertigo that had always meant he was left behind coming down from the mythical hill until the victory of 1990, the launching pad for a career that would include leading the Giro from start to finish, and two world titles.

CHAMPIONS OF CHAMPIONS

Three names have dominated la Primavera: Eddy Merckx and Costante Girardengo, who between them have won it 13 times, and Erik Zabel of Germany, who managed four wins in five years between 1997 and 2001, finishing second in the unusual year, 1999, to Andrei Tchmil – a Moldavian naturalized as a Belgian.

Merckx's seven wins frame the era in which he dominated world cycling. Nineteen sixty-six was "the Cannibal's" first major professional victory, with his elbows apart and a delighted grin on his face in the final sprint on the Via Roma – a photofinish in which he was just ahead of Adriano Durante. He was only 20. It had the same resonance as Coppi's 1946 win: afterwards, cycling would never be the same again.

For his 1976 win he was metres in front of Jean-Luc Vandenbroucke, who was subsequently disqualified after a positive drug test. It put him ahead of Girardengo's six victories, but Merckx said, "it was dazzling rather than reassuring. For the rest of the year, what with health problems and odd things going wrong, I realized just how much I'd demanded of my body for so many years." He would never win another major race.

The man most likely to equal Merckx's record is Zabel. Cycling at the start of the 21st century is as different from the Merckx era as that was from Girardengo's time: the sport is far less predictable. The general improvement in standards means that there are 20 or 30 riders in with a chance of winning most one-day races, so it is infinitely harder for any one rider to dominate a single Classic. Winning Milan–San Remo four times in five years is in fact a less likely feat than winning the Tour de France four times, because there is more competition.

Zabel, however, is unique in several ways. The finish favours him. Between 1985 and 1994, the race finished on Corso Cavalotti, close to the foot of the Poggio; since 1994 it has moved back to the traditional place, Via Roma, which is about a kilometre further away. This makes it harder for riders who

COSTANTE GIRARDENGO

Girardengo was the first "campionissimo", champion of champions, dominating Italian cycling between 1919 and 1925, in spite of the diminutive stature that earned him the nickname "the Novi Runt". After Girardengo's crushing win in the Giro d'Italia in 1919, with seven stage wins out of ten, the runner-up Gaetano Belloni admitted, "I'll never be a campionissimo, but the names of a few pretty girls will be etched on my heart", and the term instantly became Girardengo's nickname instead of "Gira".

In the 1920s, Girardengo was said to be more popular than Mussolini and it was decreed that all express trains should stop at the station in his home town, an honour normally only awarded to heads of state.

NATIONALITY	Italian
DATES	18 March 1893–2 February 1978
NICKNAMES	il Campionissimo; the Novi Runt
PROFESSIONAL	1912–36
MAJOR WINS	
1913, 1914, 1919–25	Italian national champion.
1918, 1921, 1923, 1925, 1926, 1928	Milan–San Remo.
1919, 1921, 1922	Giro d'Italia; Giro di Lombardia.
1923	Giro d'Italia.

ABOVE Erik Zabel wins the bunch sprint which decided the 2001 race, with Mario Cipollini (red jersey, white sunglasses) in second place. Cipollini's frustration at losing to Zabel lasted only a year: he returned to win in 2002.

escape on the Poggio to avoid being swept up before the finish, and to make a mass sprint between all those who survive the final climb more likely.

The profile of Milan–San Remo as it currently stands suits Zabel perfectly. He is a slightly better climber and has a little more stamina than the other sprinters, who tend to be ruled out by the distance and the hills. Thus, even if they can hold on, they feel the cumulative effort more than he does. He is among the most professional of today's cyclists, meticulous in his preparation over the winter, and his Telekom team have invested heavily in domestiques to assist him in the sprint, notably Mario Cipollini's former henchman Gian-Matteo Fagnini, who guided Zabel to perfection for his 2001 win.

His string of victories has been taken in bunch sprints from groups of various sizes without a single rider or group of riders being able to gain any advantage on the Poggio. His dominance has raised the inevitable question: is Milan–San Remo getting too easy? It may just be that it is time for another little adjustment to the course, the introduction of another hill close to the finish to stop it becoming too predictable.

ERIK ZABEL

A product of the old East German sports system and initially regarded as unmotivated by his coaches, Erik Zabel is a prolific sprinter. His house in his home town of Unna contains the trophies and jerseys he has won, along with 13 of the bikes he won them on, and a cupboardful of shoes he won them in.

In 2001 he took the record for winning the Tour de France points competition with his sixth victory on the trot and, like the previous five times, he appeared on the podium with his son Rik – named after Rik van Looy – who has grown taller with each of his dad's green jerseys.

NATIONALITY	German
BORN	7 July 1970, Berlin
PROFESSIONAL	1993 to date
MAJOR WINS	
1994	Paris–Tours.
1996	Points jersey in Tour de France.
1997	Milan–San Remo; Points jersey in Tour de France.
1998	Milan–San Remo; German national championship; Points jersey in Tour de France.
1999	GP Frankfurt; Points jersey in Tour de France.
2000	Amstel Gold Race; World Cup overall; Points jersey in Tour de France.
2001	Milan–San Remo; Hew–Cyclassics; Points jersey in Tour de France.

EDDY MERCKX

Every sport has its reference point – Pele, Muhammad Ali, the Don, Senna. Eddy Merckx is the two-wheeled equivalent, a colossal figure whose records in individual races can be equalled, but whose dominance over five years at the start of the 1970s will never be repeated. Indeed, it is hard to find a parallel in any sport.

Bernard Hinault and Miguel Indurain matched Merckx's feat of winning five Tours de France, and Lance Armstrong may do the same. Merckx, however, is above such comparisons and will remain so. No cyclist will ever again compete in so many races per year with such an incredibly high strike rate.

For once, the statistics do not lie. Merckx took 54 victories out of 120 races he started in 1971. In the 21st century for a cyclist to race over 100 days in a year is seen as excessive, and 20 victories is considered a magnificent achievement. At his peak, between 1969 and 1973, he won 250 times in 650 starts. He is the most competitive cyclist ever to grace the planet.

A RUTHLESS COMPETITOR

No race was too small for Merckx. "Whenever someone waved a flag, Merckx would sprint for it," said Barry Hoban, who was among those who tried to beat him, and very occasionally managed it. "If Merckx went 10 days without a win, he would get fed up," said his masseur, Guillaume Michiels.

Take a period of just over nine weeks in 1973. Beginning on 3 April, Merckx won four major Classics in 19 days: Ghent–Wevelgem, Amstel Gold Race, Paris–Roubaix, Liège–Bastogne–Liège. A four-day break, then the Vuelta a España: overall victory with six stage wins along the way. Another four-day break, then the Giro d'Italia. Merckx

led from start to finish, with another half-dozen stage wins.

Or you could look at the following year. Another nine-and-a-half-week burst between May and July tells the same story of insatiable appetite: overall wins in the Giro d'Italia, Tour of Switzerland, and the Tour de France, including a record eight stage wins in the latter. Racing against Merckx meant constant frustration for his opponents, and often simply looking foolish. In the 1971 Midi Libre stage race one defeated rival, Christian Raymond, christened Merckx "the Cannibal" after he left the bunch half an hour behind on the opening stage. The name stuck.

He began young. As a child playing in a building site with his friends, he started a climbing race up a crane, and was found 20 metres above the next youth. Aged three or four, he told me, he was already nicknamed "Tour de France" by his neighbours because of the amount of time he spent on his bike. As an adolescent he tried boxing, football, tennis, and basketball before settling on cycling.

Merckx is more than a list of victories. He stands out because of the way he would crush the opposition with the ruthlessness of a heavyweight boxer. "He always does more than what is necessary to win. He is not content with mere glory," wrote the Tour de France organizer Jacques Goddet.

His need for every victory to be as decisive as was physically possible was born of a lack of confidence, of basic insecurity, he told me. "When you're alone in a one-day race, you're certain to win. In a stage race, you're never certain of winning – you can always

RIGHT Fine young cannibal: Eddy Merckx announces himself to the world by winning the world amateur championship in Sallanches, France, in 1964. He would rule the cycling world for the next dozen years.

NATIONALITY	Belgian
BORN	17 June, 1945, Meensel-Kiezegem, Brabant
NICKNAMES	Big Ted; the Cannibal
PROFESSIONAL	24 April 1965–19 March 1978
PROFESSIONAL TEAMS	
1965	Solo-Superia
1966–7	Peugeot
1968–9	Faema
1970	Faemino
1971–6	Molteni
1977	Fiat
1978	C&A
MAJOR WINS	
1964	(amateur): World Road Championship.
1966	Milan–San Remo; GP Cerami.
1967	World Road Championship; Milan–San Remo; Ghent–Wevelgem; Flèche Wallonne.
1968	Giro d'Italia and Points and King of the Mountains; Paris–Roubaix; Tour of Sardinia; Tour de Romandie; Tour of Catalonia; Tre Valle Varesine.
1969	Tour de France and Points and King of the Mountains; Milan–San Remo; Tour of Flanders; Liège–Bastogne–Liège; Paris–Nice; Paris–Luxembourg; Super Prestige Pernod.
1970	Tour de France and King of the Mountains; Giro d'Italia; Paris–Roubaix; Ghent–Wevelgem; Flèche Wallonne; Tour of Belgium; Coppa Agostoni; Belgian national championship; Super Prestige Pernod.
1971	World Road Championship; Tour de France and Points; Milan–San Remo; Het Volk; Liège–Bastogne–Liège; GP Frankfurt; Giro di Lombardia; Tour of Belgium; Tour of Sardinia; Paris–Nice; Dauphiné Libéré; Midi Libre; Super Prestige Pernod.
1972	Tour de France and Points; Giro d'Italia; Milan–San Remo; Liège–Bastogne–Liège; Flèche Wallonne; GP Escaut; Giro di Lombardia; Fleche Brabançonne; Giro dell'Emilia; Super Prestige Pernod.
1973	Giro d'Italia and Points; Vuelta a España and Points; Het Volk; Ghent–Wevelgem; Paris–Roubaix; Amstel Gold Race; Liège–Bastogne–Liège; Paris–Brussels; Tour of Sardinia; GP Fourmies; GP Nations; Super Prestige Pernod.
1974	World Road Championship; Tour de France; Giro d'Italia; Super Prestige Pernod.
1975	Milan–San Remo; Amstel Gold Race; Tour of Flanders; Liège–Bastogne–Liège; Tour of Sardinia; Catalan Week; Super Prestige Pernod.
1976	Milan–San Remo; Catalan Week.
OTHER RESULTS	1975: Tour de France, second. World hour record (Mexico City, 25 October, 49.431 km).
	Tour de France: 34 stage wins; 96 days in yellow jersey. Giro d'Italia: 24 stage wins. Vuelta a España: 6 stage wins.
	87 time trial wins. 445 wins in 1,582 races as a professional.

LEFT The cold, the wet, and the cobbles mean nothing as Merckx wins the 1970 Paris–Roubaix. The opposition are far behind, as usual.

ABOVE The "cannibal" is prostrated in the changing rooms after being punched in the kidneys by a fan in the 1975 Tour. He would claim, and win, a symbolic one franc in damages.

have a bad day, no matter how big your lead. The bigger the lead you have, the more [in hand] you have if that happens." And in the races that didn't matter, exhibition races that are fixed for the benefit of the public? "People work to earn the money to pay to see you; you mustn't disappoint them."

Hence the legendary Merckx exploits. The Tre Cime di Lavaredo mountain-top finish in the 1968 Giro d'Italia, fighting his way through a snowstorm to mop up a break which had begun the climb nine minutes ahead. The 136-km (85-mile) lone break through the Pyrenees in the next year's Tour, finishing at Mourenx-Ville-Nouvelle eight and a half minutes ahead of the next man, on a day when he was already in the yellow jersey, and needed only to ride defensively. The 60-km (40-mile) solo in that year's Tour of Flanders, against the advice of his team manager.

"HALF MAN, HALF BIKE"

With the inscrutability of a sphinx, Merckx frustrated fans and press. There was none of Muhammad Ali's bombast in him, no playing to the gallery. Finding pictures of him smiling became a game for the press. "Merckx, a super winner in unprecedented style, walks away, without a trace of fatigue, with nothing to say, just a hint of boredom," wrote the French journalist Lucien Bodard in 1970. "He has robotized himself. There are no aspirations, no sense of destiny. Just an awareness that he is unique, set apart. So he transformed himself into a machine with the utmost meticulousness. He is half man, half bike."

Merckx's finest hour, in every sense, came in Mexico City on 25 October 1972, when he broke the world one-hour distance record. After a full season's racing, he found the mental strength to spend six weeks preparing by riding six times a day on a home trainer wearing a face mask to feed his lungs the same oxygen-deprived air he would breathe at altitude. He set off like a fury, hung on for grim death, and had to be carried from his bike.

The graven exterior hid a genial man with a passion for jazz and football, now an avuncular, portly presence at major races. It also hid the nerves that led him to wake up the night before major races and go downstairs to make sure that his bikes were adjusted perfectly. Nothing was left to chance. The garage in his house at Tervuren, near Brussels, contained 110 spare wheels, and 200 tubular tyres, which he would season for two years. At the 1970 Giro d'Italia, he took 18 bikes, all with components that he had personally perforated with a hand drill to reduce weight.

His nerves and reserve were partly down to the fact that he was a francophone Bruxellois – Belgian cycling is dominated by the Flemish – but were mainly the product of two devastating events. There was the positive drug test at Savona in the 1968 Giro, which he swore was from a spiked bottle, and a horrendous crash in a motorpaced race in September 1969, which killed the motorbike rider, and left Merckx with permanent back pain. He insists he was never quite the same again – but it barely showed in his results.

DEFIANT IN DEFEAT

Nothing became Merckx quite like his defeats. There was the incredible response two days after he had grovelled up the slope to the Orcières-Merlette ski resort in the 1971 Tour, almost nine minutes behind Luis Ocaña: his attack from the moment the flag dropped that led to the race finishing 30 minutes ahead of schedule 250 km (156 miles) later in Marseille.

In the 1975 Tour he was finally defeated by Bernard Thévenet, and two days after losing the lead, he broke his jaw in a crash. He had every reason to go home and lick his wounds. Instead, he stuck in the `race, against the advice of his doctors, only able to consume liquids, and even pulled back a little time on the Frenchman. In competing, he made sure there were no question marks about Thévenet's victory and his own defeat.

NORTHERN CLASSICS

Belgium in March and April equals one thing for the professional cyclist: a string of fearsome and prestigious one-day races in cobbles, mud, wind, and rain. The highlight of the Belgian cycling year is the Tour of Flanders, through the steep little climbs of the "Flemish Ardennes", and it has spawned other Classics: the season-opening "Het Volk" and the distinctive roads of Ghent–Wevelgem, and a string of minor events. The "Ronde", as the Tour of Flanders is known, and the races leading up to it, are an obsession in the Flemish-speaking area of Belgium, the breeding ground of generations of hardmen and hordes of passionate fans.

LEFT The Tour of Flanders peloton comes to grief on the notoriously steep and cobbled climb of the Koppenberg in the 1982 race, despite the unusually dry and sunny conditions. As is often the case, many of the field are reduced to walking.

TOUR OF FLANDERS

NO RACE MEANS MORE TO THE CYCLISTS OF BELGIUM'S FLEMISH-SPEAKING REGION THAN THE TOUR OF FLANDERS, A DAY-LONG ORDEAL OVER COBBLED HILLS AND PATHS, OFTEN IN FOUL WEATHER.

When Johan Museeuw took the yellow jersey in the 1993 Tour de France, he was asked if this was the greatest achievement of his career. No, he said sternly. "As a Belgian rider the highlight of my career will always be my first win in the Tour of Flanders. It is the most important race for every Belgian rider."

The Flemish cycling fans feel the same about the race they call "De Ronde", and that is why they turn out in their hundreds of thousands in April to watch. They arrive at the start in team replica gear to hunt for autographs, and shiver in the cold wind at the top of one of the cobbled climbs before sprinting for their cars and speeding off to the next viewpoint.

In this corner of Europe, throughout history trampled by invading armies from the Spanish to the Germans, local identity is proudly proclaimed. Squeezed between the North Sea, the French border, and the French-speaking industrial heartland of Wallonia to the south, Flanders is small, hard-working, proud, and navel-gazing.

Walloon cycling stars are a rarity; the Flemish dominate the sport in the same way that South Wales dominates Welsh rugby. Eddy Merckx, for the rest of the cycling world the non-pareil of the sport, was a French speaker from Brussels, so in Flanders he never received quite the same adulation that would be accorded a Flandrian contemporary like Walter Godefroot.

THE FLANDRIAN LEGEND

In a war-torn region where the roads are bad and the hills bumpy, being a Flandrian cyclist takes self-sacrifice and acceptance of grim suffering. The history of Flandrian cycling is not so much the story of the Tour of Flanders, and its two offshoots, Ghent–Wevelgem and Omloop Het Volk, as of an entire subculture of hard characters on two wheels.

The story of Alberic Schotte epitomises the Flandrian cycling tradition, an almost monastic cocktail of catholic culture and hard work. Schotte, later dubbed the "Last of the Flandrians", a nickname also given to Johan Museeuw, was a peasant farmer's son.

He was one of six children, and was brought out of the church on the day he took his first communion at the age of 10 to watch the 1930 Tour of Flanders, won that year by the legendary Frans Bonduel. Before turning professional in 1939, Schotte would get up at 3.30 a.m., begin work in a factory in Kortrijk at 5 a.m., and would race after clocking off at 1 p.m.

By the age of 18 he had never seen the sea, never ridden on a train or a bus, and when he went to Paris to join the Mercier team in 1939, he was shocked when the train reversed out of Lille Flanders station – it was going the wrong way! He would ride the Tour of Flanders more than 20 times, winning in 1948, and won two world championships on a bike still fitted with equipment dating back to the 1930s.

There have been honorary or adopted Flandrians. The Irish champion Sean Kelly fitted in perfectly with his dour demeanour, constant awareness of the link between hard work and hard cash, and rock-hard rural upbringing. Kelly spent the first five years of his career racing for Flemish teams, spent most of his 18 years in Europe lodging with a Flemish family, spoke the language and was bitterly disappointed that "De Ronde" always escaped him.

Despite being born in Moldova, the Russian Andrei Tchmil also fitted the picture after being the leader of Belgium's leading squad, Lotto, for nine years. It took time: small, selfish, tree-trunk thighed and tough as nails, Tchmil initially fell foul of the Flandrian fans. They hissed him and brandished placards calling him "Judas" after he refused to assist Museeuw in one world championship, but he acquired Belgian nationality and won Flanders in 2000 with a courageous last-ditch attack along the road into Meerbeke.

RIGHT The bunch splits into two in the 1997 Tour of Flanders to tackle this flat stretch of cobbles, with all the riders keen to minimize the strain on their bikes and bodies by taking to the dusty gutters. The 1996 winner Michele Bartoli of Italy leads the left-hand string.

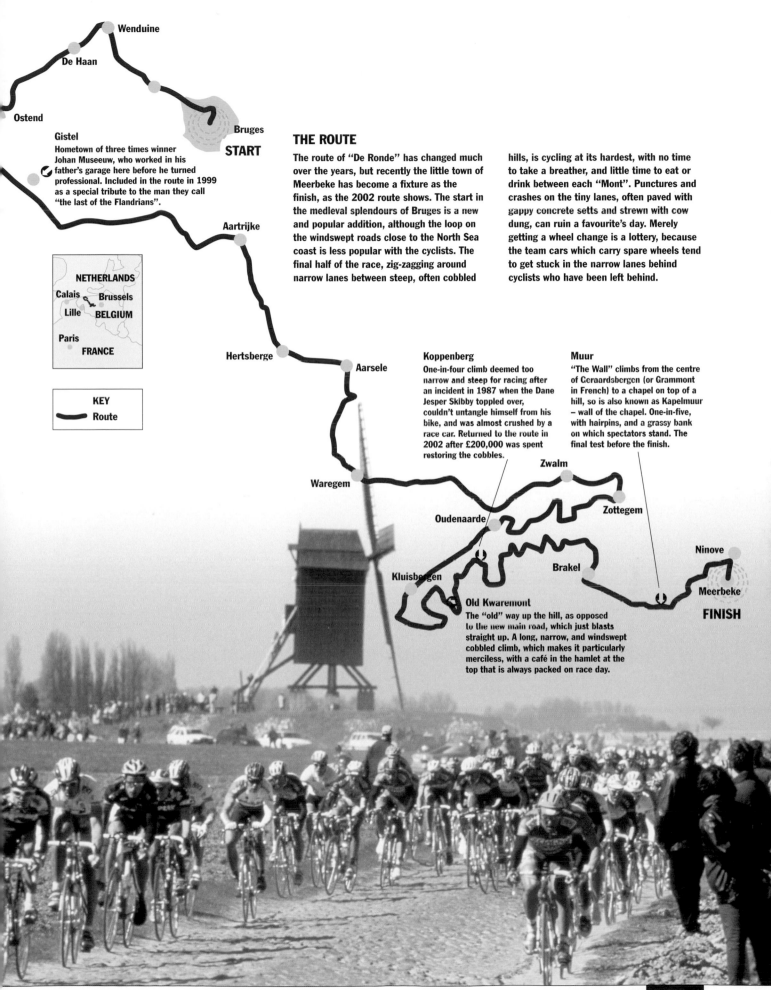

Wenduine

De Haan

Ostend

Gistel
Hometown of three times winner
Johan Museeuw, who worked in his
father's garage here before he turned
professional. Included in the route in 1999
as a special tribute to the man they call
"the last of the Flandrians".

Bruges
START

Aartrijke

NETHERLANDS
Calais   Brussels
Lille   BELGIUM
Paris
FRANCE

KEY
⎯⎯ Route

Hertsberge

Aarsele

Waregem

Kluisbergen

Oudenaarde

Zwalm

Zottegem

Brakel

Ninove

Meerbeke
FINISH

THE ROUTE

The route of "De Ronde" has changed much over the years, but recently the little town of Meerbeke has become a fixture as the finish, as the 2002 route shows. The start in the medieval splendours of Bruges is a new and popular addition, although the loop on the windswept roads close to the North Sea coast is less popular with the cyclists. The final half of the race, zig-zagging around narrow lanes between steep, often cobbled hills, is cycling at its hardest, with no time to take a breather, and little time to eat or drink between each "Mont". Punctures and crashes on the tiny lanes, often paved with gappy concrete setts and strewn with cow dung, can ruin a favourite's day. Merely getting a wheel change is a lottery, because the team cars which carry spare wheels tend to get stuck in the narrow lanes behind cyclists who have been left behind.

Koppenberg
One-in-four climb deemed too narrow and steep for racing after an incident in 1987 when the Dane Jesper Skibby toppled over, couldn't untangle himself from his bike, and was almost crushed by a race car. Returned to the route in 2002 after £200,000 was spent restoring the cobbles.

Muur
"The Wall" climbs from the centre of Geraardsbergen (or Grammont in French) to a chapel on top of a hill, so is also known as Kapelmuur – wall of the chapel. One-in-five, with hairpins, and a grassy bank on which spectators stand. The final test before the finish.

Old Kwaremont
The "old" way up the hill, as opposed to the new main road, which just blasts straight up. A long, narrow, and windswept cobbled climb, which makes it particularly merciless, with a café in the hamlet at the top that is always packed on race day.

JOHAN MUSEEUW

Inevitably, Johan Museeuw has been nicknamed "the Last of the Flandrians". Shy, taciturn, and volatile, the garage-owner's son from Gistel, on Belgium's North Sea coast, is certainly the latest in the line of hard men. His 10 Classic wins over 13 years, plus one epic victory in one of the toughest-ever world championships, on the hilly circuit at Lugano, make him the best one-day racer of the end of the 20th century.

BRILLIANCE BESET BY INJURY

How much better Museeuw's record might be without two horrific injuries will never be known. In April 1999, just after his third Tour of Flanders win, he fell heavily at 65 kph (40 mph) in the Wallers-Arenberg forest in Paris–Roubaix, and was left with an open wound in his knee which went gangrenous. He almost lost the leg, but was back at his best by spring 2000, and with two shows of massive strength won Het Volk and Paris–Roubaix, pointing at his knee to remind the world where he had come from.

Eighteen months later came a crash on his Harley-Davidson, when he was pottering without a helmet near his home, which left him in a coma. Most cyclists would have taken the opportunity to stop there and then, but Museeuw returned to win an epic, slithery Paris–Roubaix in 2002. This time, the gesture was two hands with five fingers – his 10th Classic.

For a hard man, he has a brittle side. Three times, famously, he has threatened to leave the sport – and each has been followed by a key win. In 1991, after falling out with his team manager, he said he was quitting, but came back to win the Championship of Zurich, his first Classic. His world title followed another "farewell", after losing the 1996 Paris–Tours. And his disgust at missing out on a fourth Tour of Flanders in 2002 was closely followed by his third Paris–Roubaix.

NATIONALITY	Belgian
BORN	13 October 1965, Varsenare
NICKNAME	The Last of the Flandrians
PROFESSIONAL	1988–present day
MAJOR WINS	
1990	A Travers Morbihan.
1991	Championship of Zurich; Championship of Flanders.
1992	GP E3; Belgian championship.
1993	Tour of Flanders; Paris–Tours; GP Wielerrevue; Across Belgium.
1994	Amstel Gold Race; Kuurne–Brussels–Kuurne.
1995	Tour of Flanders; Championship of Zurich; World Cup overall; Four Days of Dunkirk; GP Eddy Merckx; Laigueglia Trophy; Circuit of Flemish Ardennes.
1996	World Road Championship; World Cup overall; Paris–Roubaix; Flèche Brabançonne; Belgian championship; Circuit Mandel–Lys–Escaut.
1997	Kuurne–Brussels–Kuurne; Three Days of De Panne; Four Days of Dunkirk.
1998	Tour of Flanders; Flèche Brabançonne; GP E3.
1999	Across Belgium.
2000	Paris–Roubaix; Het Volk; Flèche Brabançonne.
2002	Paris–Roubaix.
OTHER RESULTS	Tour de France: two stage wins.

The local view of cycling goes far beyond the passion of the Italians and the Spanish: it is obsession. The tale of a single climb on the Tour of Flanders route, the Patersberg, amply illustrates this. In 1984 a farmer grew jealous of the profile of the race's most notorious climb, the Koppenberg, which crossed his neighbour's fields. He announced in the papers that he was going to create his own hill. Within 18 months the little strip of cobbles had been laid across the fields, and by 1986 it was on the race route.

THE ORIGINS OF THE RONDE

Intriguingly, in view of cycling's status in Flanders, the region came to the sport later than France, England, and Italy. The Tour of Flanders was founded in 1913 by the journalist Karel van Wijnendaele, a failed racer who was a fan of the first Flemish champion, Cyrille van Hauwaert. He followed Van Hauwaert to established races like Paris–Brussels and Paris–Roubaix, and was inspired to found something similar when he became editor of the daily *Sportwereld* (*Sportsworld*). The paper would eventually merge with *Het Nieuwsblad*, the paper that organizes the Tour of Flanders today.

A field of 37 started Van Wijnendaele's 330-km (206-mile) loop through East and West Flanders, which ended with four laps of the wooden track around a small pond at Mariakerke, the suburb of Ghent which was to be the home of Tom Simpson in the 1960s. One competitor was so exhausted that he fell in the pond, and the spectators were so sparse that there was not enough gate money to cover the prize list. The winner was Paul Deman, a carpet-maker by trade.

The race was run once more before World War I, in 1914, with the finish in the town of Evergem, again on a track, but without the pond. At the outbreak of hostilities, Deman changed profession again, becoming a courier for the intelligence services, carrying coded messages across the country hidden in a gold tooth.

He was caught on his 15th mission, shortly before the Armistice, and would have been shot had peace not been declared on the day of his execution. Cycling

must have seemed a relatively stress-free activity after that, and he returned to the sport after the war, and after an operation on the gastric hernia that had prevented him from doing well in the Tour de France. His final major victory was the Paris–Tours Classic at the ripe old age of 34.

Until the 1930s, the Ronde remained a parochial event because it was run two Sundays before Easter, which often meant a clash with Milan–San Remo and ruled out the best Italian and French riders. A sea-change came in 1948, with the foundation of the competition that was the forerunner of today's World Cup, the Challenge Desgrange–Colombo.

Named after the founders of the Tour de France and Giro d'Italia, this was a season-long points contest run by the organizers of the biggest races: the newspaper *l'Equipe* in France, *La Gazzetta dello Sport* in Italy, and *Les Sports* and *Sportwereld-Het Nieuwsblad* in Belgium. The key development was the payment of travelling expenses to the best placed riders, and a big increase in prize money. Suddenly the non-Flandrians turned up in force at the Tour of Flanders, and the race entered the international arena with Fiorenzo Magni's hat trick of victories in 1949, 1950, and 1951.

Now held on the first or second Sunday in April, the Tour of Flanders acts as the climax of a whole series of Belgian one-day races that begins on the first weekend of March with Het Volk – sponsored by the newspaper called simply *The People*.

The build-up continues through March, after a brief break during the Paris-Nice stage race in France, with Dwars Door Belgie (Across Belgium), Kuurne–Brussels–Kuurne, the Brabantse Pijl or Flèche Brabançonne (the Brabant Arrow), and, most peculiarly, the E3 Grand Prix at Harelbeke, named after the nearby motorway.

The Brabantse Pijl is held in a Flemish-speaking area south of Brussels, and boasts a classic climb of its own, the Alsemberg, which also features in a fading autumn marathon, the Paris–Brussels. The rest of these races, however, are closely based on the Tour of Flanders. In fact, so dependent were they on the big event that in the past, their organizers used to wait for the Flanders route to be announced, before including the same climbs.

The heartland is an area of steep, often cobbled climbs in the range of hills along the rivers Scheldt and Dendre, known as the Flemish Ardennes. In a country

LEFT A familiar and popular sight on the roads of "De Ronde": the present-day legend Johan Museeuw powering over a climb, on this occasion en route to his third victory, in the 1998 event.

divided by language, that is an important statement: the implication is that while French-speaking Wallonia to the south and east may be where the bigger and better known Ardennes are located, Flanders has its own "mountain" range as well, relatively insignificant though it may be.

COBBLED ROUTE

The races loop up and down little hills such as the Old Kwaremont, a thin strip of cobbles across a windswept field. This is where the string of "monts" begins, as well as the intense contest among the field to get to the foot of the Old Kwaremont as if it were the finish, "like a

FIORENZO MAGNI

Thickset and balding, Magni achieved the unthinkable for a "foreigner" in the Tour of Flanders, winning three times in a row – something no home rider has ever managed, and he did it at a time when only one non-Belgian had won the race before.

He achieved something of even greater magnitude in 1952 when he persuaded the Nivea skin cream company to sponsor him. At a time when cycle manufacturers were failing, and were unable to pump money into the sport, Magni brought in cycling's first team backer from outside the industry. Other "extra-sportif" sponsors quickly followed suit, and the result was today's highly financed professional cycling.

NATIONALITY	Italian
BORN	7 December 1920, Vaiano di Prato, Florence
NICKNAMES	the Monza Colossus; the Lion of Flanders
PROFESSIONAL	1941–56
MAJOR WINS	
1947	Tre Valle Varesine.
1948	Giro d'Italia.
1949	Tour of Flanders; Giro di Toscana.
1950	Tour of Flanders.
1951	Tour of Flanders; Italian national championship; Milan–Turin; Giro del Lazio; Giro d'Italia.
1953	Italian national championship.
1954	Italian national championship.
1955	Giro d'Italia.
1956	Giro del Lazio.

string of wild horses", as the adopted Flandrian Allan Peiper put it. If there is a spiritual heart of Flemish cycling, it is the one-in-four climb out of the town of Geraardsbergen, or Grammont, twisting up the hillside to the town's little church. This is the Kapelmuur – the Chapel Wall.

The cobbles are what make these hills special. Nicknamed "kinderkopje" ("children's heads"), they are uneven and often slippery with moss. Thin racing tyres bounce and slide and the inexperienced or nervous will fall sideways. The narrowness of the lanes and the tightly packed field mean that others will follow, and the road will be blocked.

Most notorious of all was – is – the Koppenberg, a 400-metre, one-in-four strip of cobbles leading out of the tiny village of Melden. On its introduction in 1976, the great Eddy Merckx, no less, was reduced to walking up, pushing his bike, and the climb's status was assured. Its status grew when one of the great Flandrians of the 1970s, Freddy Maertens, was disqualified for changing bikes 20 metres outside the zone where it was permitted.

The high verges of the Koppenberg were always packed with crowds waiting for the inevitable crash and the spectacle of dozens of cycling's greats trudging up with their bikes on their shoulders. "A circus", Bernard Hinault called it, and refused to ride the race. Others, such as the wily Frans Verbeeck, saw it as an opportunity and encouraged his team-mates to fall off once he had gone up, to eliminate as many opponents as possible.

The party ended in 1987, when the Dane Jesper Skibby fell off, and as he lay sprawled on the cobbles, still strapped to his pedals, the organizer's car ran over his bike, missing his feet by centimetres. The Koppenberg was taken out of the route and reduced to a footnote, until 1 April 1997, when *Het Nieuwsblad* ran an April Fool story that it was to be tarmacked over and called for a public demonstration against the move.

Two thousand people turned up, including the mayor of Melden, and, given the obvious support for the climb, it was decided to restore it. Cobbles were imported especially from Poland at a cost of £200,000, and the climb was reopened in time for the 2002 race. To underline the importance of cycling to the nation's heritage, the Belgian minister of culture was present.

The sense of place is immutable, almost incestuous. When Achille Buysse became the first man to win the race three times, in 1940, 1941, and 1943, local knowledge was very much on his side: his parents' café was just down the road from the finish in Wetteren. When Johan Museeuw gives a press conference, it is held in a café once owned by the Tour de France winner Sylvère Maes, near his home town of Gistel.

When Museeuw won the race for the third time in 1999, it was on a route that had been changed especially to take in Gistel, not to give him any advantage – it came early in the race – but simply as recognition for his achievements.

Winning the Ronde is not just about the strength of riders like Merckx and Museeuw. Low cunning plays its part, and it gave Britain its only victory in 1961, when Tom Simpson, in his second full year as a pro, was faced at the finish with a stronger and more experienced sprinter in the Italian Nino Defilippis. The response of "Major Tom" was to fake a sprint, feign exhaustion and wait as Defilippis overtook and relaxed slightly, thinking he had won. He then attacked on the Italian's blind side, and won by inches. It was a masterly piece of tactical thinking after seven hours in the saddle.

If the Ronde is worth more than the world championship or the yellow jersey of the Tour de France to the locals, the foreigners rarely get a look-in unless the Flandrians are more occupied with watching each other. Italian winners are tolerated, as they follow in the tradition begun by Magni, who inherited Van Hauwaert's nickname, the "Lion of Flanders", in an ironic reference to the region's symbol. It was not until 1953 that Holland won, thanks to Wim van Est; two years later Bobet became the first French winner.

The cultural divide is simply measured: ask a Flandrian cyclist a question in French and you will be blanked. "De Vlaeminck speaks Italian, a bit of English, a smattering of Spanish … but he regards French as the language of the enemy," wrote Harry Pearson in *A Tall Man in a Low Land*.

There was disgust when the unknown Frenchman Jacky Durand was permitted to race into an unbeatable lead in 1992, as there was when the little round-faced Dutchman Hennie Kuiper snuck away in 1981. Defeat is grudgingly accepted, and so is a winner deemed unworthy of the status of the Ronde: in 1982, when the little-known René Martens stole a march on the favourites after never even managing to finish the race in any of his previous five attempts, the chorus of condemnation began with Merckx and was universal.

ABOVE An adopted Flandrian, Andrei Tchmil, who has had Moldavian, Russian, and Ukrainian passports, but was a naturalized Belgian by the time he took this tight solo victory in the 2000 race.

It was Merckx who had the definitive Flanders victory, his first in 1969. It was a typical day, bitterly cold, with a near gale bending the trees, and pouring with rain. Merckx's ability to win the greatest Flandrian race had been questioned in the Flemish papers, so he went on the offensive early, destroying the field in the second hour of racing.

He was leading a little group of favourites 64 km (40 miles) from the finish when he went to the front to make the pace, and realized they could no longer keep up. As they were left behind, his manager Guillaume Driessens drove up. "He asked if I'd gone mad," recounted Merckx. "I told him where to go, kept going and won." The runner-up, Felice Gimondi, would finish five minutes behind. "The Cannibal" had proved his point.

HET VOLK

FOREIGN VICTORIES ARE A RARITY IN THE OPENING RACE OF THE NORTHERN CAMPAIGN, WITH ONLY SEVEN WINNERS FROM OUTSIDE BELGIUM IN OVER 50 YEARS.

Het Volk, sponsored by the paper whose name means "The People", marks the beginning of the build-up to the key period in every Flandrian cyclist's season: the 8 days in April that take in the Tour of Flanders, Ghent–Wevelgem and Paris–Roubaix.

Het Volk was once called Gent–Gent by newspapers who did not want to give their rival any publicity and just mentioned its route. Now they would have to call it Gent–Lokeren. It is a relatively young race, founded just after World War II, but it has a tradition all of its own: this is when cycling reacquaints itself after the winter break with two of its legendary monuments: the cobbled climbs up the Muur at Geraardsbergen, and the Old Kwaremont.

It is also when professional cycling returns to the northern part of Europe after the February training races on the Mediterranean coast. For the Flandrian cycling fans, it is the first chance in the new year to stand on the windswept hilltops and watch their heroes bounce and grind their way up the cobbles

In a month's time they will return for the race which matters more to them than the world championship itself: the Tour of Flanders. There are other pointers to "De Ronde": Het Volk uses other climbs from the great race, such as the Molenberg and Berendries, and some of the same flat cobbled lanes, like the infamous Paddestraat.

If Het Volk is special because of its place at the start of the calendar, that is not always an unalloyed pleasure. In 1986 the race was cancelled because snow had made the the roads impassable. Often the cyclists have to contend with cold rain, sleet, and bitter winds blowing across the wide Flandrian roads.

The early season date also makes itself felt in other ways. Het Volk has a shorter, easier course than the other Classics, at just 200 kilometres (125 miles), with no major climbs in the finale. There have been years when the race has finished in a bunch sprint, notably in the early 1990s, when sprinters such as the home men Johan Capiot and Wilfried Nelissen and Andreas Kappes of Germany would win. But the wind, the climbs midway through the race, and – often – the weather usually ensure that only the fittest and most motivated of Flandrians fight out the Het Volk finish.

Like its Belgian neighbour Ghent–Wevelgem, Het Volk has suffered in terms of prestige and media attention because of the pre-eminence which has been awarded to the World Cup races, and it now feels like a poor relation compared to the Tour of Flanders. Sadly, it is now a second-string Classic, its distance reduced from 240 kilometres (150 miles) in 1989 to around 200 now, but it remains a vital win for any Flandrian.

LEFT Franco Ballerini leads Rob Harmeling, Edwig van Hooydonck, and Andrei Tchmil in the 1995 Het Volk, on the way to his first victory in almost four years. He would win Paris–Roubaix later that year.

RIGHT The "gypsy" at his best: De Vlaeminck heads towards his second Paris–Roubaix victory in 1975.

ROGER DE VLAEMINCK

Flemish to the core, still living on a farm in his birthplace of Eeklo, and still trying to outride professionals half his age as his 50th birthday approached, "the Gypsy" was, according to Rik van Looy, "the most talented and the only real Classics rider of his generation". De Vlaeminck was the complete one-day rider: a capable bunch sprinter who could win races like Milan–San Remo in a mass finish, and fly over the cobbles of the north thanks to the skill he acquired in bike handling in winter cyclo-cross races.

Paris–Roubaix was his speciality – his four wins have yet to be equalled – but he could also climb to win races like Liège–Bastogne–Liège and the Giro di Lombardia. The only blank in his record is a world championship: in 1976, he was refused a place in the team by his Federation because he had not been willing to defend his world cyclo-cross title the previous spring.

His answer was that of a true champion: three major victories that October: the Giro dell'Emilia, Coppa Agostoni, and the Giro di Lombardia.

AN OUTSIDER

"The Gypsy" was always an outsider: born into a family of travelling clothiers, he was given the nickname at school. Merckx's bitter rival in the Classics, De Vlaeminck was never able to compete with "the Cannibal" for popularity, and a cold war developed between the two men, exaggerated by the press. "When a Belgian daily paper ran a photograph of Merckx entertaining De Vlaeminck at his breakfast table, it was as if the pope had been caught supping with the devil," wrote Geoffrey Nicholson.

Later, both Merckx and De Vlaeminck would unite against another Belgian upstart, Freddy Maertens, to the extent that in one Tour of Flanders, 1976, Maertens and "the Gypsy" let the winning escape disappear up the road, preferring to lose the race rather than risk the other winning. A year later, De Vlaeminck remained glued to the back wheel of Maertens for 100 kilometres (60 miles), before ruthlessly beating him in the finish sprint.

NATIONALITY	Belgian
BORN	4 August 1947, Eeklo, West Flanders
NICKNAMES	the Gypsy; the Beast of Eeklo
PROFESSIONAL	1969–84
MAJOR WINS	
1969	Belgian championship; Het Volk.
1970	Liège–Bastogne–Liège; GP Escaut; Kuurne–Brussels–Kuurne.
1971	Flèche Wallonne; Four Days of Dunkirk; GP E3; Kuurne–Brussels–Kuurne.
1972	Paris–Roubaix; Tirreno–Adriatico.
1973	Tirreno–Adriatico.
1974	Paris–Roubaix; Giro di Lombardia; Tirreno–Adriatico.
1975	Paris–Roubaix; Championship of Zurich; Tirreno–Adriatico. World cyclo-cross champion 1975.
1976	Giro di Lombardia; Tirreno–Adriatico.
1977	Paris–Roubaix; Tour of Flanders; Tirreno–Adriatico.
1978	Milan–San Remo.
1979	Milan–San Remo; Het Volk.
1981	Belgian championship; Tour of Flanders; Flèche Brabançonne.
OTHER RESULTS	Tour de France: one stage win; Giro d'Italia: 22 stage wins.

GHENT–WEVELGEM

TAKING IN SOME EVOCATIVE WORLD WAR I BATTLEGROUNDS AND ONE OF THE MOST DRAMATIC COBBLED CLIMBS IN BELGIUM, THE TOUR OF FLANDERS' LITTLE SISTER HAS A UNIQUE APPEAL OF ITS OWN.

Once close to the Tour of Flanders in prestige, the region's other great cycling Classic, Ghent–Wevelgem, has now fallen far behind. Squeezed into a mid-week slot between the Tour of Flanders and Paris–Roubaix, it has never been allowed a place in the UCI's World Cup, and as they have grown in prestige it has faded. From 275 km (170 miles) at the end of the 1980s, its distance has been cut to 200 km (125 miles) or so.

Like Het Volk, Ghent–Wevelgem was born at the end of the World War II, of rivalry between the newspapers of the region. The Tour of Flanders had worked for *Sportwereld*, so its competitors followed suit – Het Volk with the greatest success, as the race and the paper are now synonymous for cycling fans.

Ghent–Wevelgem was run by the *Gazet van Antwerpen* newspaper. Rather than finishing in Antwerp, as might have seemed logical, it chose the little village of Wevelgem on the main road from Ypres to Ghent, for no better reason than that it happened to be the home of the race's organizer, a rich textile manufacturer called Georges Matthijs.

These days the race starts outside Ghent's stygian Sportpaleis, where the fans come to cheer on the track racers on the wall of death bankings during the winter six-day race, and for the finish, the riders simply ride up Wevelgem's main street.

If the start and finish are fixed, the route of Ghent–Wevelgem has been a movable feast. There were several years during the 1990s in which it made incursions across the Franco-Belgian border to the little hilltop town of Cassel, which boasts a long cobbled drag up to its centre. As a one-off in 1977, Matthijs sent his race south into the Vlaamse Ardennes, up the Kwaremont, the Kluisberg, and the Koppenberg.

It was a blatant attempt to move into the territory of the Tour of Flanders and it failed; the winner, Bernard Hinault, never a man who raced lightly up cobbled hills, said the fact that he had to walk up the Koppenberg was a travesty, and the experiment was not repeated. Now, the race sticks to a course similar to that of the first race, looping north from Ghent to the North sea coast, down the coast through resorts like Knokke and De Panne, and back to Wevelgem from the west.

FORMING EVENTAILS

Two things set Ghent–Wevelgem apart: the wind, and the climb of the Kemmelberg, or Mont Kemmel. Along the coast, the race is battered by whatever is coming off the North Sea. As a result the race often splits into what the French call *eventails* – fans – in which the riders form a single file across the road, each sheltering behind the man in front at just the right angle to gain maximum protection from the wind.

There is a hectic fight for position, as the riders who form the first "fan" have the advantage, and will draw away unless the wind changes. There are often accidents as the riders jostle, and the speed is always high. In 2002, the race leaders and following cars triggered police speed cameras as they sped through De Panne, although the police did not press charges.

There are no such problems on the Kemmelberg, a steep set of cobbles rising to a thickly wooded ridge that dominates the landscape between Dunkirk and Lille. The climb is longer and harder than most of the hills in the Flemish Ardennes, but its two-car width means that crashes are less frequent. The descent is the worst part: vertiginous, paved with massive, uneven cobbles, and terrifyingly slippery in the wet. A crash here in 2002 effectively ended Andrei Tchmil's career.

The Kemmel is currently climbed twice, but it is not close enough to the finish to be completely decisive in the way that, for example, the Poggio can be in Milan–San Remo. Mario Cipollini's victory in 2002, for example, came in a sprint from a small breakaway that he joined after the climb, rather than in a mass finish as in 1992 and 1993.

ABOVE RIGHT Wevelgem, 1992: Mario Cipollini – second from left – prepares to protest after being impeded in the finish sprint by Djamolidin Abduzhaparov, far left. "Abdu" will be disqualified, and "Cipo" will memorably suggest that he returns to Uzbekistan.

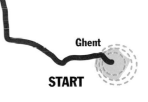

North Sea coast

The windswept roads of Belgium's North Sea coast often cause the field to split into small groups as they speed past popular weekend resorts such as Nieuwpoort and De Panne.

THE ROUTE

The Ghent–Wevelgem route has three features which remain constant, as seen in the 2002 route: the start, the finish, and the cobbled climb of the Kemmelberg. The route has, however, been adjusted over the years, as well as being drastically cut in distance from about 275 km to roughly 200. The run along the North Sea coast is one of the great traditions of the race, where the field often splits into "fans" as the cyclists fight for shelter.

After Mont Kemmel, a recent alteration to the route has pushed the race onto small side roads running parallel with the "Menen Road": these small lanes are narrow, twisting, and windswept, which makes it far less easy for the field to regroup after climbing the Kemmel. This has ended the run of bunch sprints which saw fastmen like Djamolidin Abduzhaparov and Mario Cipollini win in the early 1990s.

Kemmelberg

The decisive point of the race comes on one of the two ascents of the one-in-four cobbled hill, with its views north to the coast and west into France. Now a peaceful place, it was the scene of vicious fighting in World War I, recalled by the giant ossuary with the bones of the fallen.

Menen Road

The final run in to the finish takes the riders down the main road from Menen to Ypres, the "Menen Road" to the front lines of the Ypres salient in World War I.

Ostend

Bruges

Knesselare

De Panne

Ghent

START

Poperinge

Ypres

Wevelgem

Kortrijk

Kemmelberg

FINISH

KEY

—— Route

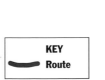

NETHERLANDS

Calais   Brussels

Lille   **BELGIUM**

Paris

FRANCE

NATIONALITY	Belgian
BORN	20 December 1933, Antwerp
NICKNAMES	the Emperor of Herentals; Rik II
PROFESSIONAL	3 September 1953–22 August 1970
PROFESSIONAL TEAMS	
1953–4	l'Avenir
1955	Van Hauwaert
1956–8	Guerra
1958–62	Faema
1963	GBC
1964–6	Solo-Superia
1967–70	Willem II
MAJOR WINS	
1956	Ghent–Wevelgem; Paris–Brussels; Tour of Holland; GP Escaut.
1957	Ghent–Wevelgem; Tour of Holland; GP Escaut; Circuit of West Flanders.
1958	Belgian national championship; Milan–San Remo; Paris–Brussels; Coppa Bernocchi.
1959	Tour of Flanders; Paris–Tours; Giro di Lombardia.
1960	World Road Championship.
1961	World Road Championship; Paris–Roubaix; Liège–Bastogne–Liège; Tour of Belgium.
1962	Ghent–Wevelgem; Tour of Flanders; Paris–Roubaix.
1963	Belgian national championship.
1965	Paris–Roubaix; GP E3.
1966	GP E3.
1967	Paris–Tours.
1968	Flèche Wallonne.
1969	GP E3.
OTHER RESULTS	1956: World Road Championship, silver. 1959: Vuelta a España, third, winner points jersey. 1960: Giro d'Italia, King of the Mountains. 1963: World Road Championship, silver. 1965: Vuelta a España, third, winner points jersey.
	Tour de France: seven stage wins; one day in yellow jersey. Giro d'Italia: 14 stage wins. Vuelta a España: 18 stage wins.
	371 professional wins.

RIK VAN LOOY

The only cyclist to win every conventional one-day Classic, "the Emperor" was to one-day racing in the late 1950s and early 1960s what Jacques Anquetil was to the Tour de France: the undisputed No 1. He remains the archetypal Northern Classic specialist with a powerful riding style, an electric sprint at the end of a long race and the ability to read the wind on the exposed roads of northern Europe.

Initially he was known as "Rik II", as opposed to Rik van Steenbergen, the Belgian Classics champion of the 1940s and early 1950s who was his bitter rival from the day he saw the younger man at a race start and remarked to another legendary Classics man, Stan Ockers, "Who's the young man with the massive thighs?"

THE WHEELBREAKER

Van Looy's legs were unusually muscled: he was known as "the Wheelbreaker", and almost lost a world title, in 1961, when he broke several spokes in his back wheel, which collapsed as he sprinted for the line. Together with Van Steenbergen and Ockers, he marked Belgian cycling's renaissance after the immediate post-war years, considered a fallow period.

Soon, however, Van Looy became "the Emperor". Partly, he earned the name from his dominant riding style – "His biggest joy," says one contemporary account, "was creating panic in the bunch by going to the front and accelerating with colossal power." He also had an extra touch of class – he used to carry a perfumed handkerchief in his jersey pocket.

MASTER OF THE "RED GUARD"

Mainly, however, it was his utterly uncompromising attitude to his teammates that set him apart. Early on, Van Looy realized, from studying Van Steenbergen and Fausto Coppi, that creating a team utterly devoted to his personal needs would go a long way to winning him races, but his attitude to the domestiques of the "Red Guard" he created at the Faema team took cycling's feudal system to its ultimate expression.

Some were recruited specifically for their stamina, others for kamikaze sprinting, but they had to have one thing above all: unswerving devotion to the master. As well as race tactics, Van Looy would decide the gears they used, the time they would go to bed, and the cash they received for their services. One, Edgar Sorgeloos, had to carry a spanner in every race, in case his leader wanted to adjust his saddle or handlebars.

Van Looy was an exacting master. The young Eddy Merckx lasted a year at the Solo-Superia team – there was not room for the two of them. Van Looy did not like his domestiques to finish ahead of him in any race. When one, Julien Stevens, let it be known he was to join Merckx, his appearance contracts and bonuses, arranged by Van Looy, disappeared.

At one time, the Briton Tom Simpson reckoned, if you weren't a friend of "the Emperor", you wouldn't make any money in Belgium. Sometimes, the underdogs bit back: at the 1963 world championship in Renaix, Van Looy was seemingly headed for victory when his team-mate Benoni Beheyt pulled his jersey and robbed him of what would have been a hat trick of world titles.

Van Looy's greatest spring was 1962, when he carried the world champion's jersey to victories in Ghent–Wevelgem, the Tour of Flanders, and Paris–Roubaix. It took him until 1968 to complete his clean sweep of Classics, with Flèche Wallonne, and by then Merckx's star was in the ascendant. Van Looy was eclipsed completely by "the Cannibal's" Tour de France win of 1969; he retired with little fanfare and is now barely ever seen in the cycling world.

LEFT "The Emperor": imperious in his racing style, exacting with his team-mates, clad here in his characteristic red jersey during the 1965 Tour of Spain. Van Looy remains the only cyclist to have won every one of the single-day Classics.

PARIS – ROUBAIX

Once a year, on the cobbled lanes of northern France, cycling goes in search of the time before tarmac. The Queen of Classics is a bike race like no other, the two-wheeled equivalent of horse racing's Grand National. This 220-km (140-mile) slog from just north of the French capital to a little town on the Belgian border is a unique throwback to the sport's pioneering days at the end of the 19th century, when diabolical road surfaces meant that punctures and crashes played a decisive outcome in every long-distance bike race.

LEFT The Belgian Wilfried Peeters is cheered through the toughest section of cobbles, in the Wallers-Arenberg forest, during the dry, dusty race of 1996. That race ended in an unprecedented clean sweep of the top placings for Peeters' team, Mapei-GB: he would himself finish third in the 1998 race, and second in 1999.

PARIS – ROUBAIX

THE MOST PRESTIGIOUS ONE-DAY CLASSIC IS A TRIAL OF STRENGTH, EXPERIENCE, AND SANG-FROID. THE SECTIONS OF COBBLED TRACK AND THE FOUL SPRING WEATHER MAKE IT THE MOST FEARED OF RACES.

During the 19th century, puncturing and crashing were constant risks in cycle races. The roads were smothered with dust in fine weather, creating a muddy skating rink when it rained. It was impossible to ride in the slipstream of an adversary – you would be covered in mud or dust, and would not see the next pothole coming – meaning tactics were almost unheard of. A race was a trial of strength, pure and simple.

The advent of tarmac changed all that. The risks were reduced, making it possible for cyclists to race in a compact bunch, relying on their fellows for shelter until they chose to make their effort according to their individual skill, be it in the final sprint, or on a steep hill.

"La Pascale", as this race is known for its Easter date, takes cycling back to its roots, with the retention of some 50 km (30 miles) of cobbled tracks, or *pavé*. They require a completely different racing style, as Britain's most consistent finisher of the 1990s, Sean Yates, explained in an interview with the magazine *Cycle Sport* in 1994.

"You don't just follow the wheel in front: you have to keep an eye up ahead the whole time because the person might make a mistake," said Yates. "On the pavé you ride a length behind, unless you're really desperate, and then you take the risk of hitting a pothole. You can't make any abrupt movements: you always have to look ahead and predict what you are going to do. If it's a bit wet and you make a last-minute movement, you're down. It's like off-piste skiing through trees: you have to have that wide vision all the time."

A single pile-up blocks the narrow lane: anyone stuck behind loses time and has to waste energy trying to catch up. In 1975 and 2001, for example, a single crash early on cut the field to less than 20. The biggest single pile-up, however, was probably that of 1972 in the Wallers-Arenberg forest, when 40 men went down like dominoes and the great Eddy Merckx went into a tree.

Riding on the cobbles, said the 1990 runner-up Steve Bauer of Canada, "is like sitting on a pneumatic drill". The succession of one cobbled lane after another takes a unique toll. "The pavé is so strength-sapping," said Yates, who states it is harder than a mountain in the Tour de France. "There's no escape. You just start to feel weak. You can feel it as each section goes past, each time it's worse and you end up wondering how long you can hang on for. And when you go, you just stop dead. If you can't keep the big gear going, you go all over the place and you're just knocked out."

The cobbles would have looked familiar to the first winner, the bearded and moustachioed German Josef Fischer, who took some 9 hours, 17 minutes for the distance in 1896, straight up the largely cobbled main road from the Café Gillet, close to the Bois de Boulogne, to Roubaix's velodrome.

LEFT Josef Fischer, winner of the inaugural Paris–Roubaix, was also the first German to start the Tour de France, finishing 15th in the first Tour in 1903 at the age of 38.

RIGHT Gianvito Martinelli gets to grips with the muddy cobbles of the Wallers-Arenberg forest in the 1994 race, widely regarded as the toughest one of that decade. The riders behind him have preferred to try their luck on the grass verge, where there is less chance of a puncture.

FINISH

Carrefour de l'Arbre
The last, and longest, section of cobbles, 4 km (2½ miles) long, is often decisive, as it runs slightly uphill into the beet fields between the villages of Camphin-en-Pévelè and Gruson, to a lonely crossroads with a cafe called "the tree".

The Roubaix Velodrome ⟳
An atmospheric finish, with a lap and a half of the banked concrete oval where the race first finished in 1896 – and afterwards the mud and dust is washed off in the primitive concrete showers.

Arenberg "trench"
This semi-sunken stretch of cobbles, undulating over the dips caused by mining subsidence in the middle of a dank forest, is the toughest on the race, with vast potholes to catch the unwary.

Forêt de Wallers-Arenberg

Chemin des Abbatoirs, and Chemin des Prieres, two of the most evocative names on the route, mark the beginning of the race's finale after a brief tarmacked respite.

THE ROUTE

Of all the one-day Classics, "Hell" is the only one which retains its original finish – on the banked concrete cycling track built by the town's clothiers at the end of the 19th century. Since the late 1960s, however, as cobbled roads became scarcer, the start has been moved 40 miles out of Paris to the former royal hunting centre of Compiègne. This keeps the race to a reasonable length while enabing the organizers to zigzag the route here and there over the cobbled stretches. They begin 100 km (60 miles) in, at the little pigeon-fancying town of Troisvilles, and are numbered like Dante's circles of hell. Most feared are the Wallers-Arenberg forest, just to the north of Valenciennes, and Le Carrefour de l'Arbre crossroads near the village of Camphin-en-Pévèle, close to the finish.

Rue de la Sucrerie, Troisvilles
The "gateway" to hell, first of the cobbled sections that give the race its character. It's a small lane into the fields outside this quiet little town, with a large puddle on the corner: the final kilometres into the town see the field jostle and fight for a place in the first 20, to avoid being held up as crashes block the lanes.

St Quentin

START

Compiègne

ENGLAND
London
BELGIUM
Calais Roubaix
FRANCE
Paris

KEY
▬▬▬ Tarmac
•••••• Cobblestones
▨ Forest

Fischer evaded a bolting horse and a herd of cows en route, while the local favourite Maurice Garin, who was to win the inaugural Tour de France in 1903, finished covered in blood after a collision between a tandem and a triple who were pacing him.

Pacers were normal practice in early one-day Classics, and in the second Paris–Roubaix the riders were paced by three-wheeled motorbikes. Briefly, the race was dominated by "stayers", who specialized in racing behind such Heath Robinsonesque machines, until the practice ended in 1900, after two of them collided and a dozen people were injured.

If all that has changed, the velodrome finish has not. The track came before the race and was essential to its creation. The banked concrete oval was built at the height of Roubaix's industrial prowess, by two mill-owners, Theodore Vienne and Maurice Perez. They wanted to publicize their venture, and, having seen the success of Paris–Brest–Paris and Bordeaux–Paris, decided that a race finishing on their track was the key.

Vienne and Perez suggested the idea to the paper Le Vélo, who sent their cycling editor Victor Breyer to reconnoitre the route. He struggled into Roubaix after two days' cycling in freezing rain, chilled and muddy, derided the notion as "diabolical", and said it should be stopped, before being persuaded to change his mind.

The race duly went ahead, on Easter Sunday 1896, to protests from the local clergy, only assuaged when a special mass was held for the cyclists. The race only truly became established after the second year's event, won by Garin in a nail-biting finish. The Dutchman Mathieu Cordang led onto the track, and slipped and fell, enabling Garin to take 100 metres' lead. Cordang, by far the stronger, fought back powerfully, but the local man held on by two metres.

The velodrome is not the only finish venue in Roubaix that has been used – others have included the soulless Avenue of the United Nations, to please a sponsor; the spectacular, tree-lined Avenue des Villas; and a cinder athletics track – but the race returned to the velodrome in 1988, and it is the heart of the race, if the cobbles can be considered its soul. No other Classic has a finish to compare with it.

Covered in choking dust, or plastered in thick mud, riders enter to a wall of noise from the crowd. They have been watching the race this far on a giant television screen, and the three finishing laps usually turn into a victory parade if the winner is alone. A sprint finish on the velodrome is rare but spectacular, as the crowd can see every pedal stroke right in front of them, and using the shallow bankings to gain speed also calls for skills not needed in any other Classic.

Afterwards, the riders collapse on the grass in the track centre, as Fischer and his contemporaries must have done, before heading to the archaic concrete showers. There, they pour their hearts out to the press as they wash the grime off their skin and out of their wounds. It is an environment perfectly appropriate for this cycling throwback.

THE HELL OF THE NORTH

The finish has changed little since 1896 but the same cannot be said of the route. In the early days, most road surfaces were a mix of cobbles and dirt track, and Paris–Roubaix simply went up the main road from Paris to Lille. It was actually one of the fastest races on the calendar, because of prevailing south-westerly winds. When Fischer won in 1896, it was the first time any long-distance race had reached an average of more than 31 kph (19.5 mph), and as late as 1964, the Dutchman Peter Post set a record average speed for any classic, almost 45 kph (28 mph).

By the early 1960s, cobbled roads were becoming a rarity, and the organizers had moved the start north of Paris, to Chantilly, as they began actively to seek out the cobbled stretches in order to ensure that their race did not turn into a boring procession. They were still able to find one stretch as long as 14 km (9 miles), however, and in 1968 they discovered the now legendary track in the Wallers-Arenberg forest.

The pace of progress was such that by 1977, the cobbles remained on only a few back lanes. The start had to be moved 65 km (40 miles) north of Paris, to the little town of Compiègne, so that the race director, Albert Bouvet, could crisscross the countryside seeking forgotten byways marked with the sign "defective road surface" or "unkept road".

The cobbled sections begin just north of the little town of Troisvilles, after which the route skirts Valenciennes, then zigzags to Roubaix. This is "L'Enfer du Nord" ("the Hell of the North") as the race was christened by a French journalist – with echoes of Breyer's original "diabolique", after World War I when the race's finale crossed a landscape of shell-holes and trenches, ruined villages, dead animals, and blasted trees, with barely a made road to its name.

The road names are sometimes homely ("Sugar Mill Lane"), sometimes ominous ("Prayers' Lane", "Abattoir Lane"). They have differing characters: a terrifying downhill swoop on slippery blue cobbles near Valenciennes; the undulating, dead straight stretch through the dank Wallers-Arenberg forest; and the decisive uphill drag across bare fields outside the village of Gruson to the lonely café at the crossroads known as "Carrefour de l'Arbre".

The lanes are numbered, in descending order: No. 27 is the "Rue de la Sucrerie" ("Sugar Mill Lane") outside Troisvilles, where a vast puddle on the corner

OCTAVE LAPIZE

Cycling will never know what "Curly" might have achieved had World War I not cut his life short. On the outbreak of the conflict, Lapize was France's dominant champion, with hat tricks in Paris–Roubaix, Paris–Brussels, and the French national championship, and a historic win in the 1910 Tour.

That year, Lapize won both the Tour's first two high mountain stages through the Pyrenees, and was the first Tourman to conquer the Aspin, Peyresourde, and Tourmalet. On the Aubisque his tirade at the man who devised the route, Alfonse Steinès – "assassins, assassins"– is a part of Tour legend.

Deaf, but still precocious, Lapize won his first Paris–Roubaix at just 20, abandoned the 1912 Tour de France complaining that his fellow competitors were ganging up on him, and took a legendary win in Paris–Tours in 1911 after chasing for 144 km (90 miles) following a puncture. His death, in an aerial dogfight, robbed France of one of her greatest champions.

NATIONALITY	French
DATES	24 October 1887–14 July 1917
PROFESSIONAL	1909–14
NICKNAME	le Frisé (Curly)
MAJOR WINS	
1909	Paris–Roubaix.
1910	Tour de France; Paris–Roubaix.
1911	Paris–Tours; Paris Roubaix; Paris–Brussels; French national title (also 1912, 1913).

amuses the spectators; No. 1 is a short stretch of perfect cobbles within Roubaix named after Charles Crupelandt, winner in 1912 and 1914, decorated in World War I, and refused a racing licence after it for offences which have never been clearly defined.

Most of the pavé lanes rarely see any traffic apart from tractors towing trailers of manure or sugar beet, but on one day each year they come alive, thronged with cycling fans bearing banners, and echoing to the sound of television helicopters and team support vehicles. In a wet winter, they are flooded by the run-off from the beet fields, and sometimes, as happened in 2001, they have to be pumped out before the race can come through.

New motorways, lines for the *train à grande vitesse*, and the simple desire of villagers to have smooth roads still threaten the cobbles, but there is now an active movement that campaigns for their preservation as part of the region's cultural heritage and encourages local councils to maintain the cobbles rather than letting them slip into disrepair before replacing them with tarmac.

The mix of cobbles and spring weather means Paris–Roubaix is relished by the fans and the harder cyclists, but feared by those riders who don't really want to be there. That daredevil of the 1990s, Fred Moncassin, would grumble if he woke up in his hotel in Compiègne and the weather was fine on race morning. In contrast, two young Americans, Roy Knickman and Thurlow Rogers, looked out of their hotel window one Easter Sunday in Compiègne in 1987 and saw snow. They decided on the spot that Europe was not for them and caught the next flight to the US.

If Paris–Roubaix has always inspired the French press to wax lyrical, trotting out adjectives such as "infernal", "apocalyptic", and "accursed", it has inspired other artists as well. The definitive cycling film, the Dane Jorgen Leth's *Sunday in Hell*, is based around the 1976 race. That year's battle between Eddy Merckx, Roger de Vlaeminck, and the Flandria team of Freddy Maertens and Marc de Meyer is captured in slow motion, close-cropped images of the cyclists' bodies and bikes bouncing over the cobbles amid massive dust clouds to a heroic soundtrack.

Ten years after Leth's work, a situationist artist living in Roubaix, Mahddjoub Ben Bella, painted an entire section of cobbles in the race finale a patchwork of pink, blue, yellow, and white. It took 16 tonnes

of paint, specially mixed with sand so that the riders would not slip.

French television now devotes massive resources to covering the race: fixed cameras on the most celebrated cobbles, a fleet of motocross bikes to carry cameras across the pavé, and several helicopters. In the freakishly muddy race of 1994, however, they were defeated by the elements: not a single camera motorbike was working with 65 km (40 miles) to the finish. None had made it through the mud.

THE QUEEN OF CLASSICS

Paris–Roubaix is called "the Queen of Classics", and she is suitably capricious in dealing out her favours. The Belgian Johan Museeuw lost the 1994 race, run

through a sea of mud after a snowstorm at the start, when an experimental bike broke as the Russian Andrei Tchmil attacked. He chased an agonizing 100 metres behind Tchmil for kilometres.

In 1996, Museeuw was the winner, in bizarre circumstances. Close to the finish, he escaped with two team-mates in the Mapei team, and the team manager, Patrick Lefèvre, called the sponsor in Milan to determine who should win. Three years after this slightly tarnished victory, he crashed heavily in the notorious "Trench", a dead-straight, slightly downhill section through the Wallers-Arenberg forest that undulates with subsidence from coal mines (it is close to the mine where Zola set his novel *Germinal*).

Dirt from the cobbles entered the gash in his left knee, which the doctors plastered without cleaning thoroughly. Gangrene set in, and he came close to amputation of the leg, and liver failure. A year later, he won again, and as he crossed the line in Roubaix, he pointed defiantly down at the knee. In 2001 he guided his team-mate Servais Knaven to victory, and a year later, at the end of a slippery battle with the American George Hincapie, he joined the select few to triumph three times in "Hell".

Museeuw's fate is typical. What Paris–Roubaix gives with one hand, she takes away with the other. After his victory of 1924 the great Henri Pelissier effused, "Just for once I have experienced the kind of Paris–Roubaix you can normally only dream about. Superb weather, a tail wind, and not a puncture. On days like this, cycling is such fun." A year later he made his effort too soon after the start. He was struck down by hypoglycaemia – the "bonk" as English cyclists call it – close to the finish, and was reduced to begging bread from the spectators by the roadside.

There are other hazards. There is the immediate risk of falling on the cobbles of course, but the cars and motorbikes that follow the race are also a huge danger on the narrow cobbled sections, where a single cyclist on the deck can cause a traffic jam that gets in the way of riders who are trying to fight their way back to the front of the race.

Every year has its victims. In 1994, the double winner Marc Madiot broke his pelvis on a high-speed downhill stretch of cobbles and never raced again. In 2001, it was the turn of the Olympic medallist Philippe Gaumont, dragged to the roadside with a smashed femur as his fellows sped past down "the Trench".

The cyclists themselves understand the unique nature of this race. Franco Ballerini, the 1995 winner, says of the race which was his passion: "You have to love her, respect her, understand her, approach with caution, and only then perhaps she will choose you."

VICTORY AND DEFEAT

Sometimes, victory in Paris–Roubaix is given and taken away, and it has nothing to do with the cobbles. Crowds on the Avenue des Villas in 1927 watched Joseph Curtel win by a tyre's-width from Georges Ronsse, and carried him on their shoulders in triumph – until the finish judge ruled that Ronsse was the winner. There was a minor riot and the hapless official came close to being lynched. Two years later, Ronsse was the victim: he slipped on the final bend on the cinder track at Stade Amédée Provost, broke his front wheel, and lost to Charles Meunier.

In 1992, Ballerini suffered the same fate as Curtel. He towed the Frenchman Gilbert Duclos-Lassalle to the velodrome, assuming that he was exhausted. "Gibus" used his track-racing skill to gain a few metres in the sprint, Ballerini fought back to within a few centimetres, passed the Frenchman on the line, and threw his arms in the air. He was duly announced the winner, and performed a triumphant lap of honour, only interrupted when the judge troubled to look at the photo finish film.

"Gibus" had won. "Ballo" was broken-hearted, and swore he would never get on a bike in anger again. He was back the following year, however, when the race was run off in a mudbath, and he fell off four times and punctured five times. "One less crash or puncture and I would have won," he lamented. He came back in 1995 and 1998 to win the race, and rode it in 2001 as his final event before retirement, crossing the line in the velodrome wearing a T-shirt that read "merci Roubaix".

The judges, it seems, can be as cruel as the pavé. As he drove me between two stages of the Paris–Nice race in 1990, Roger Lapébie told how he was deprived of victory 66 years before. "I was with the leaders when I punctured six miles from Roubaix. There was no one with a spare wheel, so I borrowed a bike from a lady who was spectating.

"A little further on, I changed to a men's bike from another spectator. I caught the riders I had been with, and won. Then another rider complained, and the judges looked at my bike. There was no seal on it – it had to have that, to prove it was the same bike I had started the race with. I had broken the rules, I was disqualified, but I always considered it a victory."

The most bizarre finish to Paris–Roubaix, or to any Classic for that matter, came in 1949, when the leading trio were sent the wrong way as they entered the velodrome by a judge who was directing the cars in the race convoy. The three had no idea where to go, and two of them ended up coming back onto the track through the press box.

André Mahé won the sprint, while behind, the chasing group was led in by the Italian Serse Coppi, the brother of the campionissimo, Fausto. Coppi and his brother lodged a protest, on the grounds that Mahé had not covered the correct route. Five days later, their claim was thrown out by the French Cycling Federation.

That should have been the end of it, but, with their greatest cyclist throwing his weight behind his younger brother, the Italian Cycling Federation appealed to the governing body of cycling, the International Cycling Union. Their ruling did not come until November, seven months after the fiasco, when Serse was declared joint winner with Mahé, by which time the result was virtually meaningless.

Over the years, the cyclists devised little tricks to combat the pounding of the pavé. Some put extra tape on their bars, some insert thick foam padding between the tape and the bar, and others favour cyclo-cross

ABOVE **The year is 1967, but the risk of crashing is ever-present. Riders pick themselves off the road, and, in some cases, out of the fields by the road. On the extreme right, the wheel of a motorbike can just be seen: these are as vulnerable on the cobbles as the cyclists.**

type brakes, with wide clearances so that the mud won't clog the calipers. They have used thickly padded shorts, saddles, and gloves, and machines with longer than usual forks to absorb the vibrations. The Canadian Steve Bauer tested a bizarre position sitting way back over the rear wheel – "the stealth bike" – in 1994, while it was Johan Museeuw's experiment with rear suspension the same year that caused his bike to break and lost him the race.

The biggest innovation came in 1992, when Greg LeMond and his team-mates unveiled special front forks using oil damping, based on the forks used by mountainbike racers and motorcyclists. It caught on, and at one point in the mid-1990s, a stroll round the team hotels the night before the race would reveal half a dozen different kinds of front suspension, in some cases put on the bike simply to get a picture in the papers rather than to improve performance.

The 21st century, however, has seen a reversion to the belief that tyres are what matter. They have to be fatter than normal to absorb shocks, and inflated a little less than usual, and the manufacturers, led by the car giants Michelin and Continental, vie to provide something special for their teams, with Michelin, for example, testing 250 tyres in five different types of temperature and weather to get the perfect pressure.

For the team mechanics, Paris–Roubaix is a special time as well, with piles of spare wheels to be prepared. When suspension forks were being used, specially adapted frames for the bikes had to be obtained and built up. Not that they can foresee every eventuality, such as the broken shoe that the German Steffen Wesemann is convinced lost him the 2002 race.

WINNERS TODAY

Recently, Paris–Roubaix has favoured the older cyclist. Performing well calls for level-headedness in the face of minor disasters like a puncture or a crash, and sang-froid in coping with the vicious fight to be in the first 20 going onto the first section of cobbles at Troisvilles, and that tends to come with age. There are other reasons: the more a cyclist has ridden through "Hell" the better he knows the twists and turns of the lanes, and the sheer strength it takes to churn a large gear over the cobbles is best acquired by many years in the peloton.

Four of the six oldest Classic winners ever have been in Paris–Roubaix: Duclos at almost 38 in his first win, 1992; Museeuw at 37 and a half in 2002; Duclos again at almost 39 for his second win; and the 38-year-old Pinc Cerami in 1960. It took the Dutchman Hennie Kuiper 11 attempts before he triumphed in 1983 at the age of 34.

One champion stands out above the rest as "Mr Paris–Roubaix": Roger de Vlaeminck, the swarthy "Gypsy", whose bike-handling skills and brute strength were honed by riding winter cyclo-cross races. He started the race every year between 1969 and 1982, missing only 1980, and took four victories and four second places, never finishing lower than seventh. That was in 1973, when he rode with 25 stitches in his arm from a crash the week before, and not surprisingly found battering across the pavé a painful business.

That year saw one of the definitive victories: Eddy Merckx's 44-km (70-mile) escape, with the injured "Gypsy" the last man to stay with him. It led

BELOW One Roubaix great, Francesco Moser, leads another, Gilbert Duclos-Lassalle of France, en route to third and second places in the 1983 race. The Italian has adopted the classic position for tackling the cobbles, with the arms acting as shock absorbers.

FRANCESCO MOSER

Tall, aristocratic, and ferociously competitive, Francesco Moser's hat trick of victories in Paris–Roubaix matched Lapize and marked him as a specialist second only to Roger de Vlaeminck. His rivalry with Giuseppe Saronni was a defining feature of Italian cycling in the late 1970s and early 1980s, but his two hour records of January 1984 truly set him apart.

His use of filled-in disc wheels, a plunging frame, and skin-tight cycling kit brought cycling into the aerodynamic age. His victory over Laurent Fignon in the 1984 Giro d'Italia marked the arrival of such aids in time trials but remains dubious due to the cancellation of mountain stages that favoured Fignon. What cannot be denied, however, is "Cecco's" ferocious competitive instinct.

NATIONALITY	Italian
BORN	19 June 1951, Palu di Giovo, Trento
NICKNAME	Cecco
PROFESSIONAL	1974–86
MAJOR WINS	
1974	Tours–Paris.
1975	Giro di Lombardia; Italian national title.
1977	World Road Championship; Flèche Wallonne; Championship of Zurich.
1978	Giro di Lombardia; Paris–Roubaix; Tour of Catalonia.
1979	Paris–Roubaix; Italian national title; Ghent–Wevelgem.
1980	Paris–Roubaix; Tirreno–Adriatico.
1981	Italian national title; Tirreno–Adriatico.
1984	Giro d'Italia; Milan–San Remo.

Jacques Goddet to describe "the Cannibal" as "sublime: he decided everything, led everything and succeeded in everything". *L'Equipe's* headline reflected his domination: "Merckx au-dessus de Merckx" – Merckx better than Merckx.

As well as Merckx, a triple winner, Fausto Coppi was another Tour de France great who descended willingly into "Hell". Coppi produced one of the great solo wins, in 1950, taking the rest of the field by surprise at the feed station, attacking as they all slowed down to collect their bags of food. Raymond Diot, who was second, said simply: "Today I won Paris–Roubaix. Coppi was supernatural." Two years later, Coppi returned to do battle with Rik van Steenbergen. The pair finished together: Coppi knew that Rik I would win the sprint, so he attacked time after time, with Van Steenbergen hauling him back before the final sprint.

A SPECIALIST EVENT

The likes of Coppi and Merckx will not be seen again in "Hell", as the Tour de France has become the be-all and end-all of the cycling year. No Tour winner can take the risk of falling and not making it to the great race, and no Tour winner has ridden Paris–Roubaix since Greg LeMond in 1991. Paris–Roubaix is now an event for the specialists.

However, the risk-taking and the brutal effort it takes merely to finish still fascinate the fans and the cyclists who love the race. Like all the greatest bike races, the Queen of Classics is bigger than the biggest stars. As long as the cobbled roads are there, Paris–Roubaix will remain, in the words of the former organizer Jacques Goddet, "cycling's last folly".

There will always be two ways of looking at this: for Goddet, that was praise; for the man who won in 1981, Bernard Hinault, it simply meant that the race should not exist.

Hinault was not unique in his dislike of the cobbles, but he could say what he liked: his win in 1981, wearing the rainbow jersey of world champion, was one of his finest feats. He punctured twice and crashed three times. His first pile-up came on the tarmac before he even got to the cobbles; after the second, in the Wallers-Arenberg forest, he had to run along the verge, with his bike on his shoulder.

ABOVE "The Emperor", Rik van Looy, enjoys the spoils of victory after the 1965 race. Van Looy was at this stage only the second rider since Octave Lapize to win the great race three times.

Hinault's third crash came when a small black dog jumped out from the crowd and he automatically twitched his handlebars and slipped. He still had the clarity of mind to produce an elbows-out, tactically perfect sprint on the velodrome to beat Roger de Vlaeminck and Francesco Moser, who between them had won the race seven times. Afterwards, Hinault noticed a small white spot on his tyre. He pinched it, and the tyre deflated. Such is the fine line between victory and defeat in cycling's "Hell". It remains one of the great victories, in Hinault's career or anywhere else, but it didn't change Hinault's view that Paris–Roubaix is "un cochonnerie" – a pig of a race.

Others don't see it quite the same way. "There are just three races in the season," said Greg LeMond. "Paris–Roubaix, the Tour de France, and the world championship." "A man's race," said Yates approvingly. "The world championship? But I've just won it," was the verdict of Rik van Looy in 1960. The Frenchman Fred Moncassin felt this about merely finishing: "The next day, my throat is full of dust, I'm spitting it up, and I've got tendinitis in my wrist, but I've won the respect of my fellow cyclists."

NATIONALITY	Irish
BORN	24 May 1956, Carrick-on-Suir, Co Tipperary
NICKNAMES	King Kelly; The New Cannibal
PROFESSIONAL	1977–August 1994
PROFESSIONAL TEAMS	
1977–8	Flandria
1979–81	Splendor
1982–8	Sem/Skil/KAS
1989–91	PDM
1992–3	Festina
1994	Catavana
MAJOR WINS	
1980	Three Days of De Panne.
1982	Tour of Haut Var.
1983	Giro di Lombardia; Paris–Nice; Criterium International.
1984	Paris–Roubaix; Liège–Bastogne–Liège; Tour of the Basque Country; Paris–Nice; Criterium International, Paris–Bourges; Tour of Catalonia; Super Prestige Pernod.
1985	Giro di Lombardia; Paris–Nice; Tour of Ireland; Super Prestige Pernod.
1986	Milan–San Remo; Paris–Roubaix; GP Nations; Paris–Nice; Tour of Ireland; Tour of the Basque Country; Tour of Catalonia; Super Prestige Pernod.
1987	Paris–Nice; Tour of the Basque Country; Criterium International; Tour of Ireland.
1988	Vuelta a España; Ghent–Wevelgem; Paris–Nice; Catalan Week. Super Prestige Pernod.
1989	Liège–Bastogne–Liège; Perrier World Cup.
1990	Tour of Switzerland.
1991	Giro di Lombardia; Tour of Ireland.
1992	Milan–San Remo; GP Luis Puig.
OTHER RESULTS	1980: Vuelta a España, points jersey. 1982: World Road Championship, bronze; Tour de France, points jersey. 1983: Tour de France, points jersey. 1985: Vuelta a España, points jersey; Tour de France, points jersey. 1986: Vuelta a España, third overall and points jersey. 1988: Vuelta a España, points jersey. 1989: World Road Championship, bronze; Tour de France, points jersey.
	Tour de France: four stage wins. Vuelta a España: 14 stages.
	193 professional wins.

SEAN KELLY

An Irish sporting icon, the flagbearer for a whole generation of English-speaking cyclists from around the world, and a legendary hardman: Sean Kelly is all these and far more. His rise from a smallholding in the back lanes of County Waterford to dominate cycling for half a dozen years will remain the stuff of legend.

THE RISE TO THE TOP

Kelly's career began when the Flandria team manager Jean de Gribaldy flew to Ireland to hire him, and met him in a lane driving his father's tractor. In his first season as a professional, Kelly beat Eddy Merckx; when he retired, in 1994, Lance Armstrong was a young world champion.

Initially a sprinter – a daredevil who was disqualified several times for dangerous riding – Kelly's career turned when De Gribaldy persuaded him in 1982 that he could do more. That spring he won the first of a record seven successive Paris–Nice "races to the sun". July brought a mountain stage win in the Tour, and the first of four green points jerseys – a record at the time – and August saw him a few metres from being crowned world champion at Goodwood in England.

Between 1984 and 1989, Kelly was world No. 1, able to dominate any one-day Classic or short stage race through raw power and a measure of cunning. It was a remarkable era: no Irish sportsman in any field had achieved Kelly's status. In a flowering of national passion which lasted only seven or eight years, he and his fellow hero

Stephen Roche could fill Irish roadsides for the Nissan Tour of Ireland, a race devised specifically to showcase the country's two heroes, and Irish journalists flocked to the Tour de France.

Kelly's success was born of his consummate professionalism. "Whenever Sean came back from a race, no matter how late or dark it was he would clean his bike before anything else," recalls Herman Nijs, whose home near Brussels airport was a second home for Kelly. Nijs also recalled how when Kelly first came to live with him, he and his wife could not work out why he went to bed every night at nine o'clock, come what may. Was he writing letters home? Reading a book? One night they peeped through the door – Kelly was sound asleep.

Once, Kelly was at a race with his wife Linda, when she sat on the bonnet of his car, leaving a small mark. As he wiped it away, she complained that two things in his life, his car and his bike, came before her. Deadly serious, he looked straight at her and said "the bike comes first".

COURAGE

Kelly's courage was tested to the limit in the twilight of his career. A bitter 1991 saw him break a collarbone in Paris–Nice, drop out of the Tour de France through illness, and, the bitterest blow of all, lose his brother Joe in a road accident. He fought back to win the Tour of Ireland in an epic, rainlashed stage to Cork, and then took the Giro di Lombardia with a ruthless display of controlled power.

Milan–San Remo, at the expense of Moreno Argentin, followed next March.

KELLY'S LEGACY

The Irishman's retirement in 1994 marked the passing of a certain kind of cycling. Kelly was the last great champion to race a full season, taking in early stage races, a full calendar of spring Classics, the Vuelta, Tour de France, and world championships, all with the same appetite. It was an attitude which went back to the 1950s, now superseded by an era in which cyclists specialize to the detriment of their sport. For example, he was the last cyclist to win Paris–Roubaix and Liège–Bastogne–Liège – the cobbled Classic and the hilly Classic – in the same year: nowadays, few cyclists even start both races.

Kelly left cycling lacking two victories which would have made his career complete: the Tour of Flanders, where he finished second three times between 1984 and 1987, and the world championship. His best chance to don the rainbow jersey came in 1989, when he rode the perfect race on the sodden circuit at Chambery in the French Alps, but chose the wrong gear for the finish sprint and could barely contain the tears after taking the bronze.

To his fellow English speakers, Kelly in his prime was a godlike figure. Robert Millar, the Scot who finished fourth in the 1984 Tour de France, wrote: "I haven't ridden with anyone who has that aura of strength. Iron man isn't enough. He's made of stainless steel."

LEFT "The new cannibal" in his hungry prime en-route to victory in the 1986 Milan–San Remo.

ARDENNES CLASSICS

After the northern triptych of the Tour of Flanders, Ghent–Wevelgem, and Paris–Roubaix, the cycling world's attention immediately turns south-east, to the Ardennes hills of southern Belgium, a rolling range of highland intersected with deep pine valleys where the Nazis launched the Battle of the Bulge, their final despairing offensive westward at the end of 1944.

The Ardennes rarely approach 900 metres (3,000 feet) in height, but the terrain is demanding and inaccessible, and the two Ardennes Classics – Liège–Bastogne–Liège and Flèche Wallonne – have a character all of their own. On these heights, the spring weather can be more severe and snow can be a problem. So too can unseasonal heat.

LEFT Spring blossom, buds on the trees, warm sunshine, and a touch of colour in the countryside as a parade of bright jerseys and flashing spokes passes by.

FLECHE WALLONNE

THE "LITTLE SISTER" OF THE TWO ARDENNES CLASSICS HAS A LOW-KEY CHARACTER OF ITS OWN, AND IS NOW INDELIBLY LINKED WITH A VICIOUS LITTLE HILL BETWEEN LIEGE AND CHARLEROI.

The Mur de Huy is a tranquil back street, twisting up from the banks of the river Moselle, with aubretias and periwinkles tumbling over garden walls between redbrick houses. The Mur ("Wall") feels as steep as the roof of a house, zigzagging through the little town that perches on the riverside between a vast nuclear power station and a brooding medieval fortress.

Liège–Bastogne–Liège's sister race, Flèche Wallonne (Walloon Arrow) has finished on top of this one-kilometre-long monster more times than anywhere else in its almost 70-year history, and, now, it is the "Wall" that sets the opening race in the Ardennes Weekend apart. No other Classic has a hilltop finish; no other tackles its main climb three times.

It is as if the Tour of Flanders ended on top of the other "Wall", at Geraardsbergen – after going over it twice. Since 1983, the Flèche and the Mur have been synonymous: there are other climbs on the route, but the Mur is nearly always decisive. The fans always line its slope two or three deep, as they can see the race pass three times and watch the women's Flèche Wallonne finish before the professional race.

At the top are a church, a recreation ground, and two bars – one of them closed. Appropriately, on what is a hill of pilgrimage for cycling fans and a Calvary for any cyclist who is out of form, four identical small shrines with biblical scenes have been built at the points on the climb where pedestrians would rest, while the finish line is opposite the church's main door.

At the time of the move to the Mur it was said that the climb had been included to ensure victory for the only Walloon cycling champion of the 1980s, Claude Criquielion. "Criq" lacked the explosive power to sprint or to jump away to win on his own, but he could certainly climb.

Hence the snide comments – but on the big day, "Claudie" made a point of breaking away on a climb before the finish, just to prove the cynics wrong. The fact that he was clad in the jersey of world champion, which he had won the previous year in Barcelona, merely added to the prestige of the win.

Since then, the Mur has often been decisive, as in 1995 when Laurent Jalabert outsprinted Maurizio Fondriest, and the following year, when Lance Armstrong disposed of France's Didier Rous to become the youngest ever Flèche winner.

Compared to his current wafer-thin appearance, Armstrong was powerfully muscled, broad-shouldered, and round of face – and probably already harbouring the cancer which nearly cost him his life. Four days later, he could have completed the "double", had he not been foiled – and consequently outraged – by the cunning tactics of the Swiss Pascal Richard.

THE ORIGINS OF THE FLECHE

The Flèche was founded by two journalists on the Brussels newspaper *Les Sports*, Paul Beving and Albert van Laethem. It was first run on 13 April 1936, at a time when Belgian cycling was on a high, following victories in 1935 for Romain Maes at the Tour de France and Jean Aerts in the world oad championships at Floreffe, near the Walloon town of Namur.

The initial course linked Tournai in Flanders with the Walloon capital Liège. Since then, the Flèche has had several different finish towns – Charleroi, the Charleroi suburb of Marcinelle, Spa, and Verviers – but its character has always been the same: a profusion of short, steep hills, which in some years have been the same climbs that figured in the route of Liège–Bastogne–Liège, such as the Mont Theux and the Côte des Forges.

Walloon cycling champions are rare beasts, and it was one of these, the sprinter Eloi Meulenberg, who was expected to win the first race. He rode into Liège with Philémon Demeersman but was knocked over by a motorcycle just metres from the finish. The following year Meulenberg was to win Liège–Bastogne–Liège and the world road title, all before his 25th birthday, but his career went downhill from there.

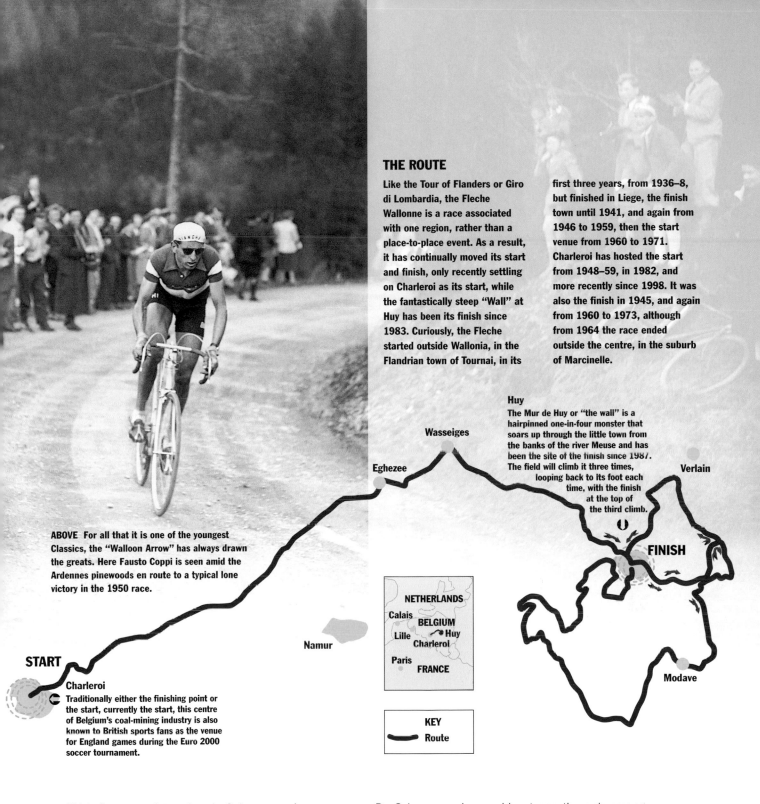

THE ROUTE

Like the Tour of Flanders or Giro di Lombardia, the Fleche Wallonne is a race associated with one region, rather than a place-to-place event. As a result, it has continually moved its start and finish, only recently settling on Charleroi as its start, while the fantastically steep "Wall" at Huy has been its finish since 1983. Curiously, the Fleche started outside Wallonia, in the Flandrian town of Tournai, in its first three years, from 1936–8, but finished in Liege, the finish town until 1941, and again from 1946 to 1959, then the start venue from 1960 to 1971. Charleroi has hosted the start from 1948–59, in 1982, and more recently since 1998. It was also the finish in 1945, and again from 1960 to 1973, although from 1964 the race ended outside the centre, in the suburb of Marcinelle.

Huy
The Mur de Huy or "the wall" is a hairpinned one-in-four monster that soars up through the little town from the banks of the river Meuse and has been the site of the finish since 1987. The field will climb it three times, looping back to its foot each time, with the finish at the top of the third climb.

Wasseiges

Eghezee

Verlain

FINISH

Namur

NETHERLANDS
Calais
BELGIUM
Lille **Huy**
Charlerol
Paris
FRANCE

KEY
Route

START

Charleroi
Traditionally either the finishing point or the start, currently the start, this centre of Belgium's coal-mining industry is also known to British sports fans as the venue for England games during the Euro 2000 soccer tournament.

Modave

ABOVE For all that it is one of the youngest Classics, the "Walloon Arrow" has always drawn the greats. Here Fausto Coppi is seen amid the Ardennes pinewoods en route to a typical lone victory in the 1950 race.

Thirty-five years later, Jos de Schoenmaecker, one of Merckx's most loyal domestiques, experienced exactly the same despair. He had been in front for 160 km (100 miles), and rode up the finishing straight in Avenue Mascaux in Marcinelle alone, unaware that behind him a former milkman, Frans Verbeeck, and the future king of Paris–Roubaix, Roger de Vlaeminck, were in hot pursuit.

De Schoenmaecker could not see the pair among the convoy of cars which was following him, and De Vlaeminck won the sprint. It was no more convincing a victory than his controversial win at Liège the previous year, when he allegedly whistled to his brother Eric as they went into the tunnel at the Rocourt velodrome, and Eric duly held back Verbeeck while Roger began his sprint. Verbeeck cried "foul" again, and it was not until De Vlaeminck's victory of the following year in Paris–Roubaix that Belgium took him seriously.

Italy's king of the Ardennes, Moreno Argentin, made his mark on the Flèche in two ways. His 1991 victory, after a 65-km (40-mile) lone escape in cold rain, with a crash on a slippery corner, was the first part of the only Ardennes "double" of recent years. This consummate Classics rider declared it was "the best win of my career. I could feel the eyes of all the others watching me, and that makes it even better."

Three years later, Argentin won again after the greatest show of strength in any Classic by any team. The nine silvery-blue-clad riders in his Gewiss-Ballan team spent 80 km (50 miles) chasing down a breakaway group, without accepting any help from other squads, and when they reached the Mur with 65 km (40 miles) to the finish, Argentin and his two team-mates Evgeny Berzin and Giorgio Furlan broke away, with Armstrong desperately trying to cling onto their wheels.

The trio rode the last part of the race as if it were an exhibition event, with the entire field powerless in their wake, and finally Argentin, in his last year as a pro, was permitted to win atop the Mur. It was an incredible start to the season for the Italian team, who had already won Milan–San Remo with Furlan. Four days later Berzin would win Liège–Bastogne–Liège in unstoppable style, and he would then go on to defeat Miguel Indurain in the Giro d'Italia.

No one at the Flèche had seen anything to match that day's result, but they began to ask questions later, when journalists spoke to the team's doctor, Michele Ferrari. They asked him about a new "wonder drug", erythropoietin, which boosts the body's red blood cells.

"If a rider uses it, that's not a scandal to me," said Ferrari. "EPO is not dangerous, only its abuse. It's as dangerous as drinking 10 litres of orange juice." He was promptly sacked by Gewiss. It has yet to be proven that Ferrari ever administered the drug to any

BELOW Ardennes king Moreno Argentin leads Evgeny Berzin of Russia and his fellow Italian Giorgio Furlan as the Gewiss-Ballan "blue express train" races far ahead of an impotent bunch to take an unprecedented – and controversial – clean sweep in the 1994 race.

cyclist in his charge, but the comment was a turning point: it perfectly illustrated the mindset that would drag cycling down to the drug scandals of 1998 and 1999 in the Tour and the Giro.

CYCLING'S JEWEL

The Flèche Wallonne truly gained its status as "the jewel of Classics" during the 1940s and 1950s. The 1949 race was a memorable duel between Fausto Coppi and Rik van Steenbergen. "Rik I" had claimed he was racing merely to prepare for Paris–Roubaix, and did not carry either a spare tyre or a even a bottle of water, which meant risking disqualification by taking bottles from cars in the race convoy.

Coppi would later that year become the first cyclist to win both the Giro d'Italia and Tour de France in the same year, and he looked the strongest when he broke away in the finale. Van Steenbergen, however, managed to catch up with him on the long descent into Liège after the cars following Coppi became snarled up on the Côte des Forges, and the Belgian won the sprint.

The campionissimo returned in 1950, and performed the same trick that had won him Paris–Roubaix three weeks earlier. At the feeding station at Spa he left his food bag behind and attacked the field. On the long Côte de Malchamps, he rode effortlessly up to the four leaders, had a drink, poured water on the back of his neck, and sucked an orange, as they tried desperately to hang on to him.

"We'd better hurry up a bit, or the others will be on us," he said to the quartet, but they were unable to hold him. Coppi, determined to avoid the problem with the cars of the previous year, rode the final 100 km (60 miles) alone, and at the finish in Liège he was five minutes in front of the second rider, Raymond Impanis.

Van Steenbergen would return in 1958, wearing the world champion's jersey, but under threat from "Rik II", Van Looy, who had just won Paris–Brussels. Rik I had heard a radio announcer call the younger man "the greatest rider in the world" and began training like a man possessed solely to prove he was still No. 1.

Van Looy, for his part, would take the race in similar circumstances 10 years later, on a day of unusual heat. He was then 36, virtually at the end of his career, and had won every Classic bar the Flèche, where the hills had never suited him. Eddy Merckx was taking over, just as "the Emperor" had taken over from Van Steenbergen, but the Flèche provided the final flourish, and gave him his unique "full house" of Classics.

The rider who remains synonymous with the "Arrow", however, was Pino Cerami, an adopted son of Charleroi who was actually born in Sicily. When he was five, his father, a poor orange-grower, set out to make his fortune in America, but got only as far as France before he discovered that his papers were not in order. He ended up in Charleroi – not the best of bargains, many would say – and worked down a mine.

Pino, meanwhile, took 12 years as a professional before he realized he could win major races; for most of his career he raced in the summer, and worked in the winter in a factory. He was 38 when he attacked on Charleroi's cobbled Rue d'Assaut in front of a delirious crowd to win "his" Flèche in 1960, 41 when he took second in Liège–Bastogne–Liège in 1963, and is remembered by a midweek race in the little town of Wasmuel.

LIEGE – BASTOGNE – LIEGE

"THE OLD LADY", AS CYCLING'S OLDEST CLASSIC IS KNOWN, IS THE HILLIEST AMONG THE GREAT ONE-DAY RACES, OFFERING A SUDDEN, TOUGH, TRANSITION FROM THE SHORT COBBLED CLIMBS OF FLANDERS.

The hills of the "real" Ardennes are longer than those in the "Flemish Ardennes", and their summits are often windswept, but they are rarely cobbled and the roads between them are better surfaced. One rider, the Swiss Tony Rominger, estimated that the total height climbed in Liège–Bastogne–Liège is about 3,600 metres (12,000 feet), roughly equivalent to a moderately hard Tour de France mountain stage.

Although the great Classic riders – Eddy Merckx, Sean Kelly, Fausto Coppi – can win on all terrains, the typical Ardennes specialist is lighter and a better climber than his Flandrian counterpart. "Liège is the best all-round race," believes the four-times winner Moreno Argentin. "By the end, only five or six riders are in with a chance: the strongest."

Cycling in French-speaking Wallonia is less fervently followed than in Flanders. But when cycling was in its infancy, at the end of the 19th century, Wallonia was Belgium's economic powerhouse, while Flanders was its rural backwater. At a time when a bike was worth seven to eight months' wages, Wallonia was where people had the money to buy them, and it was where the earliest Belgian cycling champions came from.

Hence the status of Liège–Bastogne–Liège as the oldest of cycling's "monuments". It is not the oldest race. Paris–Rouen was the first, in 1869, while Milan–Turin, still a major professional event, was first run in 1876. But Liège–Bastogne–Liège is commonly known as "la Doyenne" – "the Old Lady".

THE ORIGINS OF LA DOYENNE

"The Old Lady" was born on 29 May 1892 when 300 people turned up to watch the 33 riders start from Avenue Rogier in Liège. The race was an amateur event intended to be a dry run for a putative Liège–Paris–Liège event, along the lines of the highly successful Paris–Brest–Paris founded the previous year. Liège–Paris–Liège never happened and the rehearsal turned into the main event.

The turning point, Bastogne, was chosen simply because it was the furthest you could travel by train and back from Liège within a day, so that the race officials could man the checkpoint in the Hotel Collin. The winner, local rider Léon Houa, took 7 hours, 48 minutes to finish. He repeated his win the following year, and added Spa–Bastogne–Spa in 1894, which is now in the record books, being the first edition of the race for professionals.

The race was not run again until 1912, when two independent versions were held. Then World War I intervened, so the race disappeared until 1919, followed by another gap between 1925 and 1930. Before 1949 there was only one non-Belgian winner, the German Herman Buse in 1930, but what gave the race its unique quality was the combination in 1950 with the Flèche to form the "Ardennes Weekend". Until the Weekend came to an end in 1964, the two races were run on a Saturday and Sunday, with a special classification for the best in both and the prospect of double prize money drawing the stars.

In the 1980s, however, "the Old Lady" lost her way. The organization was largely amateur and was not up to the job, as was finally realized in 1988 after a horrific crash on the descent into Houffalize.

The little town where the Americans completed their encirclement of the Germans in the Battle of the Bulge, the Côte de Saint Roch, is a key point, the site of the first climb. The bunch were speeding down the main road into town when they rounded a bend and hit roadworks with no warning. In the carnage, 50 riders came down; behind, the American Davis Phinney, who was racing back to the field, went into the rear windscreen of a car as the convoy screeched to a halt. He needed 150 stitches in deep facial injuries.

Liège was taken over by the Tour de France organizers in 1990; the Flèche Wallone followed

RIGHT The peloton is still tightly packed as it tackles the one-in-eight slopes of the Côte de Saint Roch, which begin in front of a tank commemorating the Battle of the Bulge, in the centre of the little town of Houffalize.

FINISH

Ans

START

Liège
The traditional finish on the banks of the river Meuse was abandoned in 1992 for the hill-top suburb of Ans, and recently two other hills within Liège, the two and a half mile Côte de Sart Tilman and the short "wall" up to Saint Nicholas, have been added to toughen up the last kilometres.

KEY

— Route

NETHERLANDS

Calais Brussels

Lille **BELGIUM** Liège

Paris Bastogne

FRANCE

Spa

Côte de la Redoute
The most popular watching point: the longest and toughest hill in the finale, kicking up to one in five over the top, and conveniently situated next to the motorway.

Stavelot

Trois-Ponts

THE ROUTE

The route of the oldest Classic on the calendar has known many changes, but its essence remains the same, as the 2002 map shows: the north–south out and home trip through the steep pine-wooded valleys and high, exposed plateaux of the Ardennes. The pattern of the race tends to be that the initial phase as far as Trois-Ponts and the hills around the Spa–Francorchamps motor-racing circuit is a wearing down process. The intensity always mounts at Trois-Ponts, with the final shoot-out taking place around the Côte de la Redoute – usually the location for the winning break – and the little climbs just before the finish in Liège.

Manhay

Vielsalm

Houffalize–Côte de Saint Roch
A picture-postcard town in the heart of the Ardennes with a tank on its main street as a memorial of the role the area played in the Battle of the Bulge. The Côte de Saint Roch, a steep hill out of the centre, is the first major climb of "la Doyenne", preceded by a hair-raising descent.

Bastogne
The original turning point, for no better reason than that it lies a convenient train ride from the start point in Liège, so the race judges who made sure the cyclists had completed the course could get there easily.

shortly afterwards, and the overall classification was reinstituted in 1993. It is now a very long "weekend" as the Flèche is now held on a Wednesday, with its elder sister on the following Sunday.

If the Northern Classics are about parochial passion, the rivalry between different Flandrian stars, and the maintenance of a great tradition, the Ardennes races have a different tone. Wallonia has produced few great stars, and none to compare with the great Flandrians. Together with the Amstel Gold race, the two races have a less intense, more cosmopolitan feel, and they draw more stars of the great stage races – who prefer to race on smooth roads rather than risking their necks and possibly missing a tilt at the Tour de France or Giro d'Italia.

WINNING THE DOUBLE

The "double", winning Liège and the Flèche in the same year, remains a rare achievement. The Swiss Ferdi Kubler managed the feat twice in consecutive years in the 1950s, Eddy Merckx – inevitably – did the double in 1972, but the most unlikely, and poignant, story is that of Stan Ockers, a diminutive former docker from Antwerp, who did it with two lone wins in 1955.

In the same year, Ockers won the green points jersey of the Tour de France, the Challenge Desgrange–Colombo, which rewarded the most consistent rider of the year, and the world championship, in the Italian wine-growing town of Frascati. What is truly remarkable is that he did it all at the ripe old age of 35.

The following season Ockers was in contention for a second Challenge when he was riding a track race at Antwerp's Sportpaleis. A few riders had escaped. He was leading the chase and looking back to assess his progress when he collided with another rider who had stopped to change a wheel.

He died two days later of a fractured skull; tens of thousands of fans turned out for the funeral of the man nicknamed, ironically, "Stan who never falls". His memorial now stands on the Côte des Forges, a straight,

FERDI KUBLER

Known as "the pedalling madman", Switzerland's first Tour de France winner was a man of impulsive moods, with a nose worthy of Cyrano de Bergerac, and a habit of making peculiar grunting noises and pulling contorted faces when he was under pressure on the bike. He would harangue his rivals in bizarre pidgin French, and offer them large sums in Swiss francs to let him take the wins he wanted.

Behind the eccentricities Kubler was a powerful time triallist, who excelled in hilly races and was able to hang on to the best in the mountains. His Tour win in 1950 was partly a matter of luck: he took over the yellow jersey after Gino Bartali and the entire Italian team quit in the Pyrenees when a crowd threatened "the Pious One". Kubler's first two Tours had been disasters, but he rose to the occasion, fighting off Louison Bobet, no less, in the Alps, and winning the final time trial from Saint Etienne to Lyon.

VIOLENT MOODS

Kubler was a man of violent moods and strange humours. In one hotel during the Tour de France he was heard yelling, in his pidgin French, "De Gaulle chicken! De Gaulle chicken!" The hotelier, fearing that someone was insulting France's leader, rushed into the restaurant to find Kubler poking the bird on his plate with his fork. "It's resisting, it's resisting," he explained.

"The Eagle" was also utterly meticulous in his attention to detail, and demanded before any important race that his bike be placed in his hotel room.

His finest years were 1950 to 1954, when he was three times winner of the Challenge Desgrange–Colombo, which rewarded the most consistent rider of the year. Those years included his unique "double of doubles" in the Ardennes Weekend, which is unlikely ever to be matched, his world road title, and the motorpaced Bordeaux–Paris Classic, which he characteristically started with no specific preparation, but won in an epic battle with the double winner Wim van Est.

NATIONALITY	Swiss
BORN	24 July 1919, Marthalen, Zurich
NICKNAME	the Eagle of Adliswil
PROFESSIONAL	1940–57
MAJOR WINS	
1948	Tour of Switzerland; Tour of Romandie.
1950	Tour de France; Challenge Desgrange–Colombo.
1951	World Road Championship; Liège–Bastogne–Liège; Flèche Wallonne; Tour of Switzerland; Tour of Romandie.
1952	Liège–Bastogne–Liège; Flèche Wallonne; Challenge Desgrange– Colombo.
1953	Bordeaux–Paris.
1954	Challenge Desgrange–Colombo.
OTHER RESULTS	1949: World Road Championship, silver. 1950: World Road Championship, bronze. 1951: Giro d'Italia, third. 1952: Giro d'Italia, third. 1954: Tour de France, second and points jersey.
	Tour de France: five stage wins; 12 days in yellow jersey.

leg-sapping drag where he overtook the Italian Nino Defilippis en route to his 1953 Flèche Wallonne victory.

THE ROUTE

Les Forges, for many years the last hill before the plunge down into Liège, is no longer on the route – it has been replaced by the easier Côte de Sart Tilman and the steep Côte de Saint Nicholas. Les Forges' final great racing moment was when Miguel Indurain sped over the top in the 1995 Tour de France to fly down into Liège, having stolen a march on all his rivals and effectively won his fifth consecutive Tour.

Three of the great climbs are still on the route: the short and steep "Wall", a dead turn out of the village of Stavelot and up Rue de Stockeu, which is followed immediately by its brother, the longer, if less steep, Côte de Wanne. The focal point, however, is the Côte de la Redoute.

La Redoute is long and steepens near the top, before a drag over the plateau on a road surface that some riders say is as rough as cobbles. A plaque near the bottom celebrates the race and its riders. Often, as when Frank Vandenbroucke scored the most spectacular win of his ephemeral career in 1999, it is the launchpad for the winning attack.

In 1985, however, la Redoute showed up the weakness of "the Old Lady". Too many press motorcycles were allowed in by the creaking race organization and they impeded the field just as the key attacks were launched. There was chaos: Phil Anderson of Australia fell into the crowd and Sean Kelly, the previous year's winner, had to be held up by spectators as he toppled over.

Amid it all the winning escape of Moreno Argentin, local boy Claude Criquielion, and Stephen Roche of Ireland disappeared, and they produced a spectacular finale, with Kelly, Anderson, and Laurent Fignon chasing a few seconds behind all the way down into Liège. In the final kilometre, the gap was a mere 150 metres before Argentin took the first of his hat trick of wins.

The battles between Argentin and Criquielion were an intriguing backdrop for half a dozen years. In 1987, "Criq" evaded the Italian with Roche, but the pair then between them produced what the magazine *Vélo* called "the greatest blunder in cycling history".

They raced into Liège together, but then came virtually to a standstill in the final kilometre. Neither wanted to be the leader when it came to the finish sprint, as the rider in the rear position would have the initiative, so they slowed, and slowed, and slowed, allowing Argentin to fly past for his hat trick. They had been going so slowly that Criquielion could see his wife in the crowd. She was listening to the radio commentary and yelled to him that the Italian was catching up, but he ignored her.

Roche recalled, "I was in another world. I was so scared of coming second. I so wanted to win that I completely forgot what was going on behind. I was one of the cleverest racers, I think, but this one completely backfired on me. I could only think of Criquielion. I knew I had to be on his wheel for the sprint, otherwise he would win. It was like a tape recorder in my head, saying 'You have to risk losing if you want to win.'"

The Irishman would go on that year to equal Eddy Merckx's incredible triple of Giro, Tour, and World Road Championship, but that could not make up for the fact that he never won a Classic, and that day remained the biggest disappointment of his career. He and Criquielion did not speak to each other for several years afterwards.

Four years later, "Criq" finished second to Argentin for the third time, as the Italian completed the "double". The race was a formality for Argentin, who caught up his team-mate Rolf Sorensen on the la Redoute climb, together with Miguel Indurain – who was to win the first of his five Tours later that year – and Criquielion. "Criq" led out the sprint on Liège's Quai Mativa more in hope than expectation that he would do more than take second, as he had done in Flèche Wallonne the previous Wednesday.

Argentin's fourth victory put him just behind Merckx, whose five victories included a typical "Cannibalesque" win in 1969, shortly after his legendary Tour of Flanders victory. Some 95 kilometres (60 miles) from Liège he fled the field with his domestique Victor Van Schil, and they built up enough of a lead for Merckx to slow down and wait for his team-mate when he felt the pace on the later climbs.

Two years later, Merckx was no longer quite as insolently dominant, and instead had to rely on his inimitable spirit. He tried something akin to 1969, but solo, breaking away on the "Wall" at Stavelot in bone-chilling mist. "The Cannibal" rapidly gained four and a half minutes, and looked to have won the race, but on the Côte des Forges he was seen rubbing his legs. He lowered his saddle with an allen key while he pedalled

along, and continually asked his manager Lomme Driessens what the time gap was over the single chaser, Georges Pintens. There came a point when Driessens would no longer tell him, so rapidly was Pintens gaining as Merckx faded.

Pintens caught up as "the Cannibal" entered Liège. Somehow Merckx clung on as they climbed to the finish on the Rocourt velodrome on the city's outskirts, and somehow he managed to use his track-racing skill to win the sprint. "I didn't know you could

MORENO ARGENTIN

The consummate one-day rider, and the ultimate Ardennes specialist, Argentin had qualities that rank him among the sport's top Classic-hunters: unmatched strength on steep hills, a scorching sprint, cunning worthy of Machiavelli, and the ability to work out just when to make his winning effort.

Argentin's finest victory was probably his World Championship in 1986. On a chilly day in Colorado Springs, he dominated the final phase of the race to outsprint Charly Mottet, while the next year he earned his third medal in as many seasons.

His Ardennes Weekend double in 1991 marked the zenith of his career. Argentin was never quite the same as a one-day racer after Sean Kelly caught him just as he seemed to have done enough to earn victory in the 1992 Milan–San Remo, the Classic he coveted above all the others.

NATIONALITY	Italian
BORN	17 December 1960, San Donà di Piave, Venice
NICKNAME	il Furbo (the Cunning One)
PROFESSIONAL	1980–94
MAJOR WINS	
1981	GP Prato.
1982	GP Prato; Matteotti Trophy; Giro di Romagna.
1983	Italian national title; Coppa Sabbatini.
1984	Sicilian Week; Giro del Veneto.
1985	Liège–Bastogne–Liège; Tour of Denmark.
1986	World Road Championship; Liège–Bastogne–Liège.
1987	Liège–Bastogne–Liège; Giro di Lombardia.
1988	Giro del Veneto.
1989	Italian national title (Giro dell'Appennino).
1990	Tour of Flanders; Flèche Wallonne; Coppa Sabatini.
1991	Liège–Bastogne–Liège; Flèche Wallonne.
1994	Flèche Wallonne.

reach such a stage on a bike," he said, for once reduced to the level of a mere mortal.

The Ardennes also witnessed Jacques Anquetil's finest win in a one-day race, in 1966. It was typical of Anquetil: one story has it that he decided to ride Liège–Bastogne–Liège that year because Felice Gimondi was being hailed as the "new Anquetil". According to another version, his team manager told him Raymond Poulidor was riding, and that was enough to get him to the start line.

At the start "Master Jacques" only planned to race for 95 km (60 miles), but he rode away from the field on the Mont Theux, 48 km (30 miles) from Liège, to win by almost five minutes. Afterwards he said simply, "When you are the best, you have to show it," and refused to take a drugs test. "Too late," he told the doctor. "If you can get a sample from the water in the shower, that's where it is." These were more lax days: he was disqualified, but subsequently reinstated.

Anquetil's win came on a day of rare heat, but often the Ardennes' weather is worse than that in the Northern Classics. The 1919 race was described as being held in "Siberian" conditions, while the 1957 event saw riders urinating on their hands to relieve the cold, and seeking shelter and hot drinks in bars along the route. That year's winner, Germain Derycke, was disqualified for having crawled under a level crossing gate, and the victory was awarded to Frans Schoubben, who had come second, before the Belgian Cycling Federation declared them joint winners.

Bernard Hinault's victory of 1980 remains the most dramatic of all. He had already won the race in 1977 on a windy, wet, and chilly day, to prove a point to the Belgian press. They had written off his victory in Ghent–Wevelgem five days earlier with the words "in the land of the blind, the one-eyed man is king", referring to the fact that some of the big names had not started Ghent–Wevelgem. The proud Breton duly fought off Belgium's finest en route to Liège: Merckx, Freddy Maertens, Roger de Vlaeminck, and André Dierickx.

The 1980 race was completely out of the ordinary, however, a "fantastic and phantasmagoric" day, in the words of the cycling historian Pierre Chany. The race was run in a blizzard, and only 60 riders were left after just 65 km (40 miles) – the other 100-odd had already quit. Hinault himself wanted to give up, but was persuaded to go as far as the feed station in Bastogne by a team-mate, Maurice le Guilloux. It was after the

ABOVE "Listen, Michele ..." The most successful manager in cycling history, Italy's Giancarlo Ferretti, calms down his leader Michele Bartoli as "Miki" prepares to outwit Laurent Jalabert and Alex Zülle to win the 1997 race.

race headed back towards Liège that matters usually got serious, so Le Guilloux knew that if he got his leader that far, he would probably find fresh motivation.

"Cyrille Guimard told me to remove my racing cape because the real race was about to start," Hinault said later. "Until then I hadn't really paid any attention to the race, but now my teeth were chattering and I had no protection. I decided the only thing to do was ride as hard as I could to keep myself warm."

Hinault rode the last 90 km (55 miles) alone, winning on the Boulevard de la Sauvinière, Liège's main street, by over nine minutes – the biggest winning margin in the race in the post-war era.

It took "the Badger" three weeks to get proper movement back in two fingers in his right hand, and two joints remain numb to this day. Of such feats are born legends, and legendary races.

RIGHT Stephen Roche of Ireland is left trailing far behind at the finish of the 1982 Amstel Gold as Jan Raas wins the race for the fifth time in six years. Roche's complete lack of a finish sprint would also cause him to lose Liège–Bastogne–Liège on two occasions.

The studious-looking Classic hunter was a key part of the great TI-Raleigh team of the late 1970s and early 1980s. Raas made the Amstel Gold race his own in the late 1970s, winning five times, and is now the mastermind behind Holland's leading pro team, Rabobank.

CUNNING

He was a demon sprinter, and cunning with it. The last Tour stage win of his career in 1984 was typical, as he sat on the wheel of the Frenchman Marc Madiot in the final kilometres into Bordeaux, refusing to cooperate before taking the sprint easily. The French were outraged – but Raas had won.

Two of Raas' most outstanding demonstrations came on home soil, in the 1979 world road title at Valkenburg, where he out-sprinted Dietrich Thurau of Germany. A year earlier, he won the Tour de France prologue time trial when the race began in Leiden, only to be refused the yellow jersey because heavy rain had made the cobbled town-centre roads dangerous, and the stage was turned into an exhibition. To prove his point, he won the next day's stage, and won the yellow jersey as of right.

Jan Raas and Raleigh became synonymous once the manager Peter Post had persuaded him to turn professional. "Basically what happened was that Post managed to get all the best Dutch riders of the period – Gerrie Knetemann, Henk Lubberding, Roy Schuiten and Bert Oostebosch – and the team spirit was incredible."

With Raas acting as manager on the road, the men in red, yellow, and black were virtually unbeatable in team time trials in the Tour de France in the late 1970s and early 1980s. They won 11 of the 23 stages in the 1980 race, including seven in a row.

The partnership turned into bitter rivalry in 1984 when Raas took half a dozen Raleigh men to form the Kwantum team, turning manager in 1985 when a serious back injury from a crash in the 1984 Milan–San Remo continued to plague him.

NATIONALITY	Dutch
BORN	8 November 1952. Heinkenszand, Zeeland
NICKNAME	None
PROFESSIONAL	1975–85
MAJOR WINS	
1976	Dutch national title.
1977	Milan–San Remo; Amstel Gold.
1978	GP d'Automne*; Amstel Gold; Paris–Brussels.
1979	World Road Championship; Tour of Flanders; Amstel Gold; Tour of Holland; GP E3.
1980	Amstel Gold Race; GP E3; Kuurne–Brussels–Kuurne.
1981	GP d'Automne; Ghent–Wevelgem; Het Volk; GP E3.
1982	Paris–Roubaix; Amstel Gold; Across Belgium.
1983	Dutch national title; Tour of Flanders.
OTHER RESULTS	Tour de France: 10 stage wins; 3 days in yellow jersey.

* The GP d'Automne, also known as Blois–Chaville, temporarily replaced Paris–Tours between 1974 and 1987.

AMSTEL GOLD RACE

A WEEK AFTER LIÈGE–BASTOGNE–LIÈGE, THE CLASSICS MEN MOVE A LITTLE WAY NORTH INTO THE DUTCH ENCLAVE OF LIMBURG FOR THE RACE WHICH BRINGS DOWN THE CURTAIN ON THE SPRING CAMPAIGN.

Holland's only Classic belies the notion that the Netherlands are entirely flat. Tucked into the enclave of Limburg, with Belgium and Germany on three sides, and starting and finishing in Maastricht, just down the river Moselle from Liège, the Amstel Gold race includes about 30 little climbs.

Amstel is not technically an Ardennes Classic, but from 2003 has become more tightly tied to its two sisters from up the Moselle valley, after which it will alternate with the two Ardennes Classics, so that in alternate years the "Doyenne", Flèche, and Amstel will take place over seven or eight days.

The "bergs" are not as long as the drags of the Ardennes, and none matches the Mur de Huy for steepness, but for physical and mental effort it is a tough test, as the first organizer Herman Krott intended. "My priority was to make the race 'heavy'," he told me. "I wanted just one rider to be left at the finish."

Krott ran many of Holland's criterium races in the 1960s, and Amstel were among the companies who bought advertising board space on his crowd barriers. In 1964 Krott persuaded them to back an amateur team, and in 1966, when a new marketing manager arrived at the company, Krott "drove him crazy" and secured their backing for the Classic he had always wanted named after their latest brew, Amstel Gold.

He wanted to start the race from Amsterdam, but the police turned him down, on the bizarre grounds that only cars were allowed to use the major bridges across Holland's great rivers. So he started in the town of Breda, and went right across southern Holland to Meerssen, a massive 300 km (190 miles). Jean Stablinski of France won the first race in just under eight hours.

Meerssen remained the finish until 1991, when it was moved to Maastricht. The heart of the race, however, remains the Cauberg climb, a one-in-seven pull out of the little town of Valkenburg, three times a venue for the World Road Championships. There have been incursions into Luxembourg and Belgium, but the current race director, the former TI-Raleigh

professional Leo van Vliet, is determined to have an all-Dutch course.

Krott believes the greatest Amstel in his 30 years as organizer was 1973, when Eddy Merckx took his first win in the race, a typical lone victory on a typical late April day of bitter cold and rain, when the riders went so slowly – pouring hot tea into their shoes to warm their frozen feet on occasion – that they finished in near darkness.

As is so often the case in the Classics, biting cold and lashing rain made for other memorable races. The 1985 race was an emotional farewell for one of the greats of Dutch cycling, Jan Raas' "spectacle brother" Gerrie Knetemann, the former road builder who was world champion in 1978.

Two years earlier he had almost lost his life in a horrific racing crash in Belgium, when he suffered a multiple leg fracture and a severed artery. No one thought he could return to his best, but "Der Knet" escaped with 9 km (5½ miles) to go for a win that, he said, made him happier than the victory 11 years earlier that had launched his career.

In similar weather, and with an impressive show of strength, Bjarne Riis won alone in 1997, after simply drifting to the front of the lead group and upping the pace. This was the only time during the 1990s when a Tour winner won any of the great one-day races, ample illustration of the way the stars of the Tour de France have now sidelined the Classics.

"AMSTEL GOLD RAAS"

In the late 1970s, the Classic was known as the "Amstel Gold Raas", after one rider, Jan Raas, who tended to monopolize it, winning five times between

RIGHT As well as a never-ending series of short, steep "bergs", the narrow, twisting country lanes of Limburg are typical of the Amstel Gold race, the "race of 1,000 corners", as Scotland's Robert Millar once described it.

Elsloo

Beek

Guelle

Ulestraten

Schimmert

Bunde

Maastricht
Start and finish are alongside the river Meuse in the heart of the town made famous for the signing of the 1992 treaty of European union.

Meerssen

Berg en Terblijt

Valkenburg

Bemelen

THE ROUTE

The Amstel Gold race crisscrosses Holland's southern province of Limburg, making the race a fan's delight and a cyclist's nightmare. The climbing starts after just nine kilometres with the 1.1-km ramp of the Slingerberg. It is the first of over 30 small ascents, none longer than 2.1 kilometres, and none with a gradient steeper than one-in-seven: their cumulative effect is what dictates the pattern of the race. The best known is probably the Cauberg, rising out of the town of Valkenberg, where the race will finish in 2004. As well as the hills, the wind plays its part too: these are exposed roads, and the constant changes of direction mean the riders never know where the wind is coming from. Curiously, in view of its difficulty, Amstel Gold does sometimes finish in a bunch sprint, most recently in 2000 when Erik Zabel was the winner.

START

FINISH

Cadier en Keer

Valkenburg
The heart of the race for the fans, who can see it here three times, and usually the decisive point as well, thanks to the presence of a one-in-seven curving climb through the centre of the town, which also hosted the World Road Championships in 1938, 1979, and 1998.

Hulsberg

Heerlen

Voerendaal

Klimmen

Schin op Geul

Ubachsberg

Wijlre

Eys

Simpleveld

Margraten

Gulpen

Eckelrade

Mechelen

Vijlen

St Geertruid

Epen

Vaals

Mheer

Noorbeek

Gemmenich

NETHERLANDS
Calais   **Maastricht**
Brussels
BELGIUM

Paris

FRANCE

KEY – How to follow the route

from	●	follow
from	○	follow
from	○	follow

1977 and 1982. The organizers didn't like this, for while Raas' victories were popular at home, they did nothing for the international standing of the event.

Bernard Hinault's sprint win in 1981 – ahead of Roger de Vlaeminck, with Raas fifth – was welcome, as it proved that not just the Dutch won in Holland. The 1979 race, however, had indicated the opposite, when the Belgian and Italian visitors were outraged after Raas' third successive win.

JOOP ZOETEMELK

Like that other "Eternal Second" and one-time team-mate Raymond Poulidor, Zoetemelk's Tour de France career spanned two decades. His 16 Tour finishes between 1970 and 1986 remain the record. The only year he missed, 1974, was when he was in hospital recovering from a fractured skull.

Zoetemelk's less-flattering nicknames are not really deserved, despite the conservative way he rode the Tour. He would argue that there was no alternative when faced with champions of the calibre of Merckx and Hinault. It was said, perhaps unfairly, that when he got to Paris he was as pale as when he set out, because he would be in Merckx's shadow all the way. He was not alone.

"The Eternal Second" was capable of attacking, as seen in one of the most spectacular Tours ever, his race-long duel with "the Badger" in 1979. He won the Tour in 1980 after Hinault withdrew with a knee injury, but his finest achievement will remain the world championship win of 1985 at Giavera del Montello, at almost 39.

NATIONALITY	Dutch
BORN	3 December 1946, Rijpwetering, The Hague
NICKNAME	the Eternal Second
PROFESSIONAL	1970–87
MAJOR WINS	
1971	Dutch national title.
1973	Dutch national title.
1974	Paris–Nice; Catalan Week; Tour of Romandie.
1975	Paris–Nice; Tour of Holland.
1976	Flèche Wallonne.
1977	GP d'Automne (see note in profile on Raas, p. 95).
1978	Vuelta a España; GP d'Automne; Paris–Nice; Criterium International.
1980	Tour de France.
1985	World Road Championship; Tirreno–Adriatico.
1987	Amstel Gold Race.

Raas broke clear on the Cauberg, and had only to tackle the run downhill to Maastricht. But a phalanx of mainly Dutch press motorbikes were seen dragging him in their slipstream away from the chasers. The manager of Francesco Moser's Sanson team, Waldemaro Bortolozzi, saw the rules of racing being broken in front of him, and yelled to Moser to tuck in behind his car – which is also illegal. Raas' manager, Peter Post, saw him coming and tried to block the car. "The confusion was colossal, the two cars boring and shoving at each other while the riders tried to pass," wrote *International Cycle Sport* magazine.

There were more accusations of skulduggery after Joop Zoetemelk became the oldest Classic winner ever in the 1987 race, which he won at the age of 40. They came from the Briton Malcolm Elliott, who claimed that the Dutchmen in the break, Teun van Vliet and Steven Rooks, had colluded to help their fellow countryman win.

"They were working together. They knew about my sprint," accused Elliott after taking third. Van Vliet confirmed the Sheffield rider's suspicions: "We all attacked in turn, and when Joop went we thought it was better to let him go than see an Englishman win."

Zoetemelk was the last rider to stay with a rampant Phil Anderson when the Australian gave his country its first Classic win by taking the Amstel after a lone break over the Cauberg, riding the final 14 km (9 miles) into Maastricht alone in the teeth-gritted style which had made him the first Aussie to wear the Tour de France's yellow jersey two years earlier.

ARMSTRONG

The Classics are no longer objectives for the Tourmen, but the Amstel has turned into an integral part of the Tour de France preparation of Lance Armstrong, who has ridden every year since 1999. He is never at his absolute best, but took second that year to Michael Boogerd, second two years later to Eric Dekker, and was fourth in 2002 when Michele Bartoli and his Fassa Bortolo team-mate Sergei Ivanov simply proved too strong for the Texan.

RIGHT Not Paris–Roubaix but a stretch of unmade road in the 1991 Amstel. As always, the Dutch teams are to the fore, headed by the blue jersey of Buckler – managed by Jan Raas, no less.

NATIONALITY	French
BORN	11 November 1954
NICKNAME	le Blaireau (the Badger)
PROFESSIONAL	1975–86
PROFESSIONAL TEAMS	
1975–83	Gitane/Renault
1984–6	La Vie Claire
MAJOR WINS	
1976	Paris–Camembert.
1977	Liège–Bastogne–Liège; Ghent–Wevelgem; Dauphiné Libéré; GP Nations.
1978	Tour de France; Vuelta a España; French national title; Criterium International; GP Nations.
1979	Tour de France and points jersey; Giro di Lombardia; Flèche Wallonne; Dauphiné Libéré; Tour de l'Oise; GP Nations; Super Prestige Pernod.
1980	World Road Championship; Giro d'Italia; Liège–Bastogne–Liège; Tour of Romandie; Super Prestige Pernod.
1981	Tour de France; Paris–Roubaix; Amstel Gold; Criterium International; Super Prestige Pernod.
1982	Tour de France; Giro d'Italia; Tour of Luxembourg; GP Nations; Super Prestige Pernod.
1983	Vuelta a España; Flèche Wallonne.
1984	Giro di Lombardia; GP Nations; Four Days of Dunkirk.
1985	Tour de France; Giro d'Italia.
1986	Coors Classic.
OTHER RESULTS	1981: World Road Championship, bronze. 1984: Tour de France, second. 1986: Tour de France, second and King of the Mountains.
	Tour de France: 28 stage wins; 78 days in yellow jersey. Giro d'Italia: six stage wins; 31 days in pink jersey. Vuelta a España: seven stage wins; 16 days in yellow jersey.
	217 professional wins.

BERNARD HINAULT

"THE BADGER"

In 1992 I bought a fluffy badger toy sold in aid of charity during the Tour de France, with a picture of the cyclist universally known as "le Blaireau" (the Badger) – Bernard Hinault, who had endorsed the venture. There was definitely something incongruous about this: the Hinault type of badger would have borne no resemblance to a cute little stripey toy, or the avuncular gentleman from *The Wind in the Willows*.

As Hinault told me, "I was called the badger because it's a devil of an animal to deal with in a tight corner." Think of a badger set upon by dogs and sending them yelping away, and you are getting close to the man. Hinault was the most strong-minded of cycling champions, pugnacious in word and deed, whether he was on two wheels avenging some assumed slight or other, or throwing punches at striking miners who had stopped a Paris–Nice stage.

Hinault was at his best when faced with adversity, with something to prove. His finest win for many was in the 1981 Paris–Roubaix, because he hated the race, and felt he had to win it so that no one could claim he was afraid of it. His world championship at Sallanches in 1980 was a masterpiece of destructive riding, a

series of vicious accelerations up the hairpins of the Domancy hill, sowing mayhem in the bunch. It came after an ignominious withdrawal from the Tour de France, in the dead of night, with a knee injury that refused to go away.

A railwayman's son, Hinault's favourite game as a child was letting the family chickens out to wind up his father. He would be punished severely, but it didn't prevent him from starting again. His first bike was too big, and he had to climb onto a brick to reach the saddle. He rode the machine the 9 km (6 miles) uphill into Saint Brieuc to go to school – and it is said that he claimed he only went because there was the chance of a fight along the way. Greg LeMond's experience in the 1986 Tour showed that the Breton lost none of his ability to play mind games in later life.

COURAGE

Hinault was the most courageous of cyclists, as his 1980 Liège–Bastogne–Liège victory in a snowstorm proved. Adversity brought out the best in him: few will forget the image of his black eyes and broken nose after a finish-line crash en route to his 1985 Tour win. His pride was remarkable. In 1982, he made a point of winning the

bunch sprint on the Champs-Elysées, so it could not be said he had won the Tour without taking a single stage along the way.

A "PATRON"

Hinault was legendary as a "patron", a man who would make the peloton do his bidding or make them pay the price. "The Blaireau was a weird fellow: he frightened me," wrote Paul Kimmage in his book *Rough Ride*. "Sometimes he would attack and the peloton would string out into a long line. Then he would sit up and start laughing, mocking us. He had a godlike aura ... a great champion, but I didn't like him."

FINISHING IN STYLE

A classic Tour-winning time-triallist who could limit his losses in the mountains, nothing became Hinault quite as much as the way he ended his career. He had always said he would quit at 32, so five days before his 32nd birthday he organized a cyclo-cross race near his Breton home, finished 14th in front of 15,000 fans, and never turned another pedal in anger.

LEFT "The Badger" fights the snow and freezing wind to take one of the greatest victories of his career in the 1980 Liège–Bastogne–Liège. Gloves, overshoes, and an extra jersey are his only concession to the weather. Bare legs in this weather testify to his legendary toughness.

GIRO D'ITALIA

If the Tour de France is a multi-national festival, the first great national tour of the cycling year, the Giro d'Italia, is profoundly and proudly parochial. Alone among the three big Tours, the Giro is still run by the original sponsor, the newspaper *La Gazzetta dello Sport*, and it draws millions of cycling's most irrationally passionate fans, the *tifosi*, to the great climbs in the Alps and the Dolomites each year. The greatest architectural monuments of the country have been used as backdrops: Venice's Piazza San Marco, Florence's Ponte Vecchio, and Verona's vast Roman amphitheatre.

LEFT The Giro as it stands in the minds of every Italian fan: the immortal Fausto Coppi, champion of champions, forces the pace ahead of the triple Tour de France winner Louison Bobet through the snowy Dolomites, in front of a passionate crowd.

GIRO D'ITALIA

THE FIRST GREAT STAGE RACE OF THE CYCLING SEASON IS THE MOST TRADITIONAL OF THE THREE MASSIVE NATIONAL TOURS, AND A PERFECT EXPRESSION OF THE ITALIAN MINDSET.

"Look in their faces one by one, eight or ten million Italians who push their faces against the windows of our cars, it is a thing which is only possible with the Giro d'Italia," wrote the journalist Orio Vergani in 1955. "Even if a king or a president of the Republic were to process slowly around the country for 21 days he would see fewer people. Following the Giro is a way of getting to know the Italians, to discover many secrets about their way of life, their tastes, their fanaticisms, their customs."

The Giro boils down to two elements: tradition, and the tifosi. "A whole generation of post-war Italians grew up with memories of summer afternoons clustered around a crackly wireless listening to the heroic deeds of Fausto Coppi and Gino Bartali," wrote the Rome-based Irish journalist Paddy Agnew, adding, "The next generation grew up with memories of their parents telling them about those summer afternoons."

Tradition, a sense of doing what their fathers and grandfathers did, is largely what draws the tifosi to the slopes of the great passes of the Dolomites – the dirt track up the Gavia, the deep snow cuttings of the Stelvio, and the vast rock towers of Lavaredo. They come in their camper vans, official and unofficial fan clubs from obscure towns and villages all over Italy.

They are the most passionate fans in cycling, and the most likely to participate in the race by pushing backmarkers – or in several notorious episodes, the front runners – or yelling abuse. So vicious were the insults hurled at Wladimir Belli in 2001 on one Dolomite pass that he stopped and thumped his abuser – and was disqualified. It was the kind of emotion that could only be seen on the Giro.

Intrigue and the Giro have always gone together, from the moment in August 1908 when *La Gazzetta dello Sport*'s cycling editor Armando Cougnet received a telegram while in Venice on business: "Absolutely essential for the paper you announce immediately the cycling Tour of Italy." The sudden decision was simply explained: a contact in the Atala bike company had learned that their big rival, Bianchi, was to cooperate

in running a Tour of Italy with *La Gazzetta*'s main competitor, *Corriere dello Sport*, and the Touring Club Italiano, which had run the Giro Automobilistico (a touring car event) since 1901.

So when *La Gazzetta* declared that it would run the race it was purely a pre-emptive strike. "It was easy to announce the Giro," Cougnet recalled later, "then the reality hit us: we were broke." Suddenly, at a time when printers and staff did not know if they would be paid at a given week's end, the paper had to find 25,000 lire. Eventually the money came from sources as diverse as the Italian Cycling Association, the Casino at San Remo – and, ironically, *Corriere*, which stumped up 3,000 lire.

The 127 starters were flagged off at 2.53 a.m. on 13 May 1909 in Milan's Piazza Loreto, where Mussolini and his mistress Clara Petacchi would be hanged upside down at the end of World War II. For the next 16 days the crowds gathered daily in the Galleria Vittorio Emmanuele to read the dispatches posted outside Corriere's office, and on 30 May, 50,000 Milanese greeted the 49 survivors, escorted by cavalry, pennants flying in the wind. In shades of the early Tours de France, one rider, Carcano, had been disqualified for taking a train between Rome and Florence.

The survivors were led by Luigi Ganna, a stonemason whose 95-km (60-mile) daily round trip to work had been the perfect preparation for the 2,500 km (1,600 miles) in eight stages via Bologna, Chieti, Naples, Rome, Florence, Genoa, and Turin. The race was decided on points; had it been decided on cumulative time, as is the case today, the winner would have been Giovanni Rossignoli, who would also miss out in 1911.

The pink jersey, or *maglia rosa*, reflecting the fact that *La Gazzetta* is printed on pink paper, was a late innovation, appearing in 1931. Its introduction was

RIGHT Deep in the "heel" of Italy, the Giro "gruppo" tackles the rolling hills of Puglia in 1999. The greatest sprinter the race has known, Mario Cipollini, is keeping close to the front, fourth from the left.

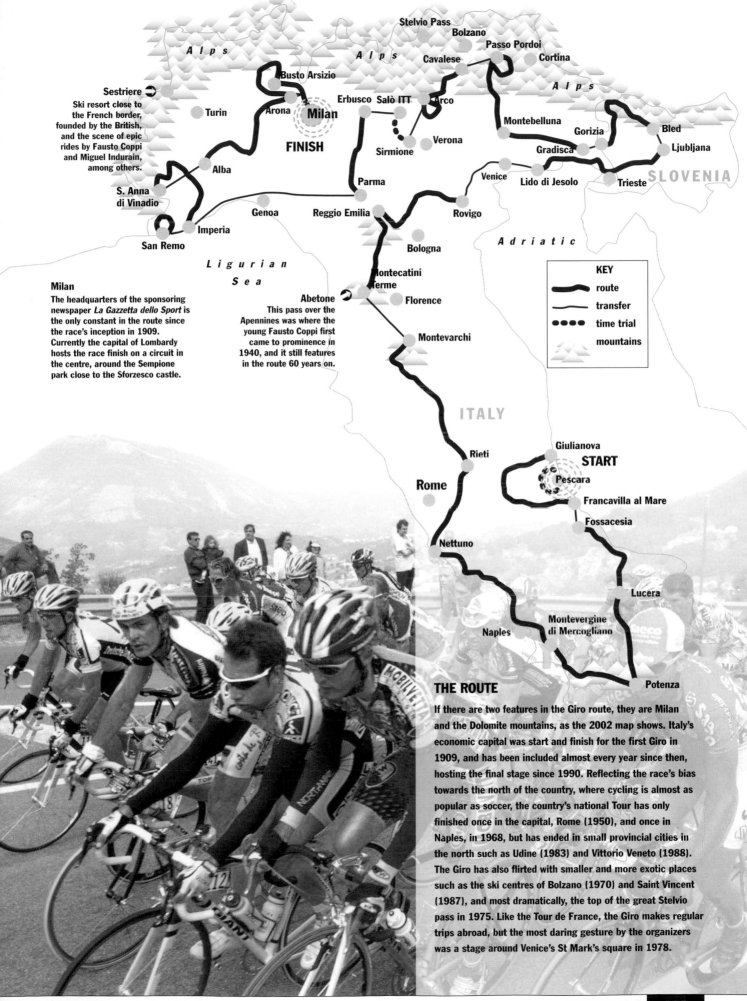

Sestriere
Ski resort close to the French border, founded by the British, and the scene of epic rides by Fausto Coppi and Miguel Indurain, among others.

Alps

Stelvio Pass

Bolzano

Passo Pordoi

Busto Arsizio

Cavalese

Cortina

Alps

Turin

Arona

Milan

FINISH

Erbusco Salò ITT

Arco

Montebelluna

Alps

Gorizia

Bled

Alba

Verona

Gradisca

Ljubljana

Sirmione

S. Anna di Vinadio

Parma

Venice

Lido di Jesolo

Trieste

SLOVENIA

Imperia

Genoa

Reggio Emilia

Rovigo

San Remo

Ligurian Sea

Bologna

Adriatic

Milan
The headquarters of the sponsoring newspaper *La Gazzetta dello Sport* is the only constant in the route since the race's inception in 1909. Currently the capital of Lombardy hosts the race finish on a circuit in the centre, around the Sempione park close to the Sforzesco castle.

Montecatini Terme

Florence

Abetone
This pass over the Apennines was where the young Fausto Coppi first came to prominence in 1940, and it still features in the route 60 years on.

Montevarchi

KEY
— route
— transfer
•••• time trial
⛰ mountains

ITALY

Rieti

Giulianova

START

Pescara

Rome

Francavilla al Mare

Fossacesia

Nettuno

Lucera

Montevergine di Mercogliano

Naples

Potenza

THE ROUTE

If there are two features in the Giro route, they are Milan and the Dolomite mountains, as the 2002 map shows. Italy's economic capital was start and finish for the first Giro in 1909, and has been included almost every year since then, hosting the final stage since 1990. Reflecting the race's bias towards the north of the country, where cycling is almost as popular as soccer, the country's national Tour has only finished in the capital, Rome (1950), and once in Naples, in 1968, but has ended in small provincial cities in the north such as Udine (1983) and Vittorio Veneto (1988). The Giro has also flirted with smaller and more exotic places such as the ski centres of Bolzano (1970) and Saint Vincent (1987), and most dramatically, the top of the great Stelvio pass in 1975. Like the Tour de France, the Giro makes regular trips abroad, but the most daring gesture by the organizers was a stage around Venice's St Mark's square in 1978.

low-key, barely referred to by the paper because Mussolini thought the colour was effeminate, even though it still bore the Fascist insignia.

In spite of the Giro's national status, the Italian Fascist regime between the wars did not adopt the race to any great extent. Mussolini was never seen presenting the pink jersey, for example, although *La Gazzetta* ran propaganda adverts for the Fascists, and the race received between 20,000 and 25,000 lire of subsidy from the government.

The Giro remained Italian dominated until 1950, when Hugo Koblet became the first foreign winner. In 1936, Il Duce's policy of sporting isolation meant there was not a single foreigner in the race. It turned into a dreary succession of bunch sprints for the first eight stages, after which the pink jersey was awarded jointly, for a single day, to Alfredo Bini and Giuseppe Olmo, who could not be separated either on time or points. On a happier note, this was the first Giro when

roadside graffiti appeared bearing the rider's name and the letter W, standing for "eviva" – "long live whoever", beginning a Giro tradition that continues to this day.

CUNNING TACTICS AND "FURBO"

The first Giro was run thanks to inside information from one cycle manufacturer keen to steal a march on a rival, and that has set the tone for a race where dubious deeds have always gone along with competition. The Italians have a word, *furbo*, used, often approvingly, to describe those who get round the rules or use them to their advantage, and there has been a lot of furbismo on the Giro.

The domination of the first campionissimo, Alfredo Binda, in the mid-1920s was outrageous, unmatched by any other cycling great in a major Tour. In 1927 he won nine of the first ten stages, and 12 of the total of 15, while in 1929 he took stages two to nine inclusive. In 1928 he totalled a mere seven out of 12 stages.

What now seems truly outlandish, however, is the conversation Binda recalled with the race organizer Emilio Colombo in 1930. "If you want to prevent me riding, and you want it to stop there, pay me the equivalent of the first prize, six stage wins, and my bonus now," Binda told him, and Colombo duly agreed.

"It was my best Giro," Binda told the French journalist Pierre Chany half a century later. "I didn't just get the prizes without riding, but I took up about 10 contracts on the track in France, Germany, and Belgium. The records say I won the Giro five times, but I consider that I won it five and a half times."

Colombo was not the last Giro organizer to try to affect the overall result, directly or indirectly. In his prime, Fausto Coppi was frequently favoured with massively mountainous routes to suit his particular strength. In the late 1970s and early 1980s, the organizer Vincenzo Torriani included numerous time bonuses at stage finishes, to assist the sprinter Giuseppe Saronni, while his successor, Carmine Castellano, devised routes with more finishes on mountain tops than was usual in 1998 and 1999 Marco Pantani's best years.

In winning his only Giro in 1984, the country's sporting hero Francesco Moser not only had the benefit of the latest aerodynamic equipment when he snatched the pink jersey from Laurent Fignon in the final time trial. He also had the complicity of Torriani, who cancelled a vital mountain stage on the grounds that the road was blocked by a landslide. That was uncertain, but one thing was sure: Moser could not climb, and Fignon would have gained time on him, perhaps enough to win the race.

This was as nothing compared with the events of 1967, which got off to a bad start when Vietnam War protesters blocked the route of the first stage, a midnight race through Milan, which was subsequently cancelled. The tifosi then obstructed the finish at Salerno, this time due to poor crowd control, to the

extent that the finish line could only be distinguished by the banner flying above it.

Worse came in the Dolomites, on the stage to the Tre Cime di Lavaredo. "What happened was scandalous beyond our wildest dreams," wrote René de Latour in *Sporting Cyclist*. "Everyone was being pushed, the Italian favourites so much that they barely needed to pedal. For most of the seven kilometres the riders were pushed from hand to hand as if the service had been organized in advance."

CHARLY GAUL

One of the finest climbers in cycling history, Gaul is a rare star from the tiny province of Luxembourg. Two days in two races two years apart projected Gaul to stardom. First came his 1956 Giro win, when he annihilated the field in a snowstorm over Monte Bondone in the Dolomites, jumping from 24th overall to first in just 12 km (8 miles) climbing.

The second defining day was the stage through the Chartreuse Massif in the 1958 Tour de France, when Gaul told the triple-winner Louison Bobet before the start that he would attack on the Col du Luitel and even named the hairpin bend where he would surge ahead in his graceful style.

A year later Gaul destroyed Jacques Anquetil on the Petit Saint Bernard Pass to take his second Giro, but his career ended in a whimper in the early 1960s, and he was unable to cope with life after retirement. He became a recluse in a hut in a Luxembourg forest. When he finally emerged in the 1980s he was confused and forgetful, and he still seems a shadow of the man who once made mountains look like molehills.

NATIONALITY	Luxembourgois
BORN	8 December 8 1932, Pfaffenthal
NICKNAME	the Angel of the Mountains
PROFESSIONAL	1953–65
MAJOR WINS	
1955	King of the Mountains in Tour de France.
1956	Giro d'Italia and King of the Mountains; King of the Mountains in Tour de France; Tour of Luxembourg; Luxembourg national championship.
1957	Luxembourg national championship.
1958	Tour de France.
1959	Giro d'Italia and King of the Mountains; Tour of Luxembourg; Luxembourg national championship.
1960	Luxembourg national championship.
1961	Tour of Luxembourg. Luxembourg national championship.
1962	Luxembourg national championship.

There were echoes here of the events of 1948, when Fausto Coppi quit in protest at the two-minute fine handed out to Fiorenzo Magni for taking pace behind a car, until De Latour saw "a new scandal, riders hanging on to the backs of cars, commissaires scribbling names in notebooks, a hopeless task because not a single rider was not taking a tow. Gimondi won, not because he was the fastest, but because he had the fastest car." The stage was declared null and void, but the prize money was still awarded.

The Giro's date is fixed in May or June, which has two important effects. The first is the significance of the "double" of Giro and Tour de France wins, as the two races take place within three weeks of each other. It is a feat limited strictly to cycling's greats: Coppi was the first to manage it, in 1949, and repeated the feat in 1952. Anquetil followed in 1964, Merckx in 1970, 1972 and 1974, Hinault in 1982, Stephen Roche in 1987, and Marco Pantani in 1998, while Miguel Indurain, unprecedentedly, managed it in successive years, 1992 and 1993.

The race's early date also means that the weather in the mountains is completely unpredictable. Blinding snowstorms are as common as blazing heat. The legend of Eddy Merckx was born in a blizzard on the Tre Cime di Lavaredo in 1968, when he left Gimondi nine minutes behind in one of the finest mountain climbing feats ever. Charly Gaul's 1956 victory was built in a blizzard on the Monte Bondone, after which he had to be taken into a barn wrapped in a blanket to recover from hypothermia.

Six years later, when a blizzard hit the race, Charly Gaul, "the Angel of the Mountains", was seen walking through the snow, with a spectator alongside him holding Gaul's bike in one hand and sheltering him with an umbrella in the other. That day, 55 of the 109 riders abandoned the race, among them "the Emperor", Rik van Looy, who dived into a farmhouse and straight into a hot bath.

Most epic of all was the crossing of the Gavia pass in 1988. In normal conditions the Gavia is a narrow dirt track, but heavy snow made it virtually impossible for riders to pedal over the top. On the descent, there were many cases of riders urinating on their hands to restore what warmth they could.

The stage assured the first American victory in the Giro for Andy Hampsten, a mild-mannered, bucktoothed boy from Colorado, whose team manager had ordered a car with hot drinks to meet the riders at the top of the climb, and who also had the foresight to give his riders gloves and make them put Vaseline on their legs to keep the cold out.

FELICE GIMONDI

Urbane and aristocratic, Gimondi was one of the many unfortunates whose career coincided with that of Merckx. He was only 22 when he took the 1965 Tour de France, making him the youngest winner of the modern era, and also one of the elite few to win the race on his debut.

Gimondi was not initially selected for that Tour, and only made the cut because other riders fell ill or injured. He actually did not want to start the race, believing he was not yet mature enough for the Tour.

By 1966 he was being hailed as the successor to Jacques Anquetil after winning Paris–Roubaix and Paris–Brussels, but then Merckx came on the scene and Gimondi only won when "the Cannibal" wasn't competing or was having an off-day. He still managed a world title in 1973, and at 33 became one of the oldest riders to take the Giro in 1976.

Gimondi still cuts an elegant figure on the race circuit, working in bike development and public relations for Bianchi, whose bikes are indelibly linked with his career, and that of Fausto Coppi.

NATIONALITY	Italian
BORN	29 September 1942, Sedrina, Bergamo
PROFESSIONAL	1965–78
NICKNAME	None
MAJOR WINS	
1965	Tour de France.
1966	Paris–Roubaix; Paris–Brussels; Giro di Lombardia.
1967	Giro d'Italia; Giro del Lazio; GP Nations.
1968	Vuelta a España; GP Nations; Italian national title.
1969	Giro d'Italia; Tour of Romandie; Giro dell'Appennino.
1972	Tour of Catalonia; Italian national title.
1973	World Road Championship; Giro di Lombardia; Coppa Bernocchi; Giro del Piemonte.
1974	Milan–San Remo; Coppa Agostoni.
1976	Giro d'Italia; Paris–Brussels.

RIVALRY AND "POLEMICA"

If Italian sporting tradition is built around larger than life heroes, so too is its cycling heritage. The confrontations between two great campioni, or campionissimi, are larger than life as well, with the press whipping up polemica, the war of words between the pair.

ABOVE Eddy Merckx is wrapped in a blanket after what would later be seen as a definitive mountain stage victory in the 1968 Giro, in a snowstorm on top of the Tre Cime di Lavaredo in the Dolomites. Merckx destroyed the field in the style which typified "the Cannibal".

The rivalry between Costante Girardengo and Alfredo Binda was the first great set piece, in the 1920s, followed by Binda and Learco Guerra, then Fausto Coppi and Gino Bartali in the 1940s and early 1950s. Francesco Moser and Giuseppe Saronni were the final great protagonists in the 1970s and 80s; the spats between Claudio Chiappucci and Gianni Bugno, and Marco Pantani and Michele Bartoli in the 1990s had a distinctly artificial air about them.

Bartali and Coppi's remains the great rivalry beside which all others are pale imitations. Coinciding as it did with Italy's post-war reconstruction, a time when the bike was the country's main mode of transport, these were the headiest years for the Giro. In 1940 they were team-mates when the young Coppi rode ahead of Bartali, his leader, on the Abetone pass in the Dolomites, to take his first Giro. Six years later, in the first post-war Giro through the shell-torn country, Bartali finished just 46 seconds ahead of the younger man.

The rivalry began in earnest, however, on top of the Falzarego pass in the Dolomites the next year. Bartali was changing gear when his chain became stuck, so he stopped. Coppi promptly attacked, Bartali crashed when his chain became stuck again, and the next 160 km (100 miles) through the mountains were an epic pursuit: Coppi vs Bartali and four others, which Coppi won by five minutes, taking the second of his five Giri.

The 1949 Giro finally settled the question of who was the better man, when Coppi staged the greatest of his legendary lone escapes through the mountains, this time through the French Alps. He rode alone over five great mountains – the Col de Madeleine, the Col

de Vars, the Col d'Izoard, Montgenèvre, and Sestrières – to win in Pinerolo, sealing overall victory by 23 minutes. As he approached Pinerolo the radio commentator Mario Ferretti coined the phrase that was to be forever linked with the campionissimo: "*un uomo solo al comando*" – "one man leading on his own".

At a time when Italy was becoming increasingly secular, the deeply pious Bartali appealed to the Catholic, conservative side of the country, while Coppi, with his highly public adultery and excommunication, stood for the country's newer, progressive, largely urban element. The pair were obsessed with each other. Coppi would not refer to Bartali by name, calling him instead "*l'altro*" – "the other one". Bartali once saw Coppi throw a glass bottle by the roadside, and was convinced it contained drugs, so he noted the place, and went back after the race was over to retrieve the bottle and investigate.

Moser and Saronni had a similar relationship. Moser was still putting Saronni down and belittling his results 10 years after the height of their rivalry when I interviewed him in his home town of Trento. Saronni won the Giro twice, in 1979 and 1983, with a little help from the organizers, who provided generous bonuses – seconds deducted from his cumulative time – at the stage finishes, so he could take full advantage of his searing sprint.

Saronni complained: "I'll never understand the attitude of the public, who insult me every day. Moser's supporters treat me like a dog, and I find their attitude disgusting. Moser provokes them against me by what he says in the papers." And, of course, his outburst in reaction to Moser's provocations in the press was fully reported, prompting an outraged response from Moser – and healthy sales for *La Gazzetta dello Sport*. In 2002, the pair were still locking horns, Saronni blaming Moser for introducing drug-taking to cycling, Moser responding in similar style.

FURTHER FEUDS

The most vicious Giro, however, was that of 1987, the "race of knives under the table", as one *Gazzetta* writer put it. The Carrera Jeans team was jointly led by Roberto Visentini, a volatile playboy from a rich family who had won the race the previous year, and Stephen Roche of Ireland. Given his record, Visentini considered that Roche should act as his domestique, after which the Irishman would get his chance in the Tour de France, but the Dubliner had other ideas.

Roche led the race early on, before Visentini took the maglia rosa from him in the time trial to the Republic of San Marino. Two days later, in the first stage into the Dolomites, to the ski station at Sappada, Roche marked an attack from two lesser riders and found himself in the lead. This left the Carrera manager, Davide Boifava, in a quandary: should he leave Roche in front, which risked him taking the maglia rosa from his Italian co-leader but would mean the other teams had to chase, should he ask him to wait for the bunch, or should he order Carrera's domestiques to chase him, in defiance of any logic?

Visentini would not stand for the first option, so Boifava asked Roche to slow down and wait. The Dubliner refused, so Boifava said the team would have to chase him, producing the famous reply from Roche, "Well, Davide, you tell them to keep something under the saddle [in reserve] because they'll need it later."

"His team-mates didn't want to chase, but Visentini was screaming at them, and the team car came up and told them to chase," recalled Robert Millar, who would go on to finish second in that Giro. "Then they stopped riding [at the front] and it was the most chaotic thing I've ever seen. All the cars were coming up and talking to the teams – 'You ride, you don't ride,

we'll pay, you'll pay.' We [Panasonic] didn't ride because they didn't offer us enough money."

Eventually Roche was brought to heel, but immediately after the race was blown apart by an attack from the world champion Moreno Argentin – he of Ardennes Classics fame. He had a score to settle with Visentini, who had said that Argentin would be two hours behind by the end of the three weeks, so when Argentin saw the maglia rosa in trouble, he had no hesitation in upping the pace.

As they drove up the final climb, the radio reporters repeated the words: "*Roberto Visentini si e litteralmente crollato*" – "Visentini has collapsed." The stress of the whole day caught up with him on the long drag to the finish, and he lost eight minutes in as many kilometres, with not a single Carrera domestique by his side. He was livid when he crossed the line, pointing to the television podium and shouting, "There's a few guys going home tonight."

Only a midnight visit from the sponsor kept Roche in the race: the boss of the jeans company could work out that the Irishman was a more likely winner than the Italian. The team was divided, with the Belgian Eddy Schepers taking Roche's side, as did the French mechanic Patrick Valcke. The rest, all Italians, would help Visentini.

The polemica continued to the finish in Saint Vincent, a week and the whole of the Dolomites away. More to the point, Visentini's home region of Brescia was a short drive from all the mountain passes. Schepers had had to threaten Visentini's fans to keep them away from Roche at the finish in Sappada, but worse was to come.

On the mountains they spat at the Irishman, threw screwed up balls of pink *Gazzetta* at him and brandished pieces of raw meat to show what they wanted to do to him. He rode through the corridor of baying tifosi with Schepers on one side, and Millar on the other. Millar was not his team-mate, but he had served the same apprenticeship at the ACBB amateur club in Paris, and was happy to put one over on the Italians.

And the papers lapped it up, as the pair made their cases through the press. "Visentini talks at the start, Roche answers at the finish," wrote Angelo Zomegnan in *Gazzetta*. Visentini's allegations were outlandish. "Roche has too many allies. All of Fagor [a French team] are working for Roche. He's bought Van de Velde [a Dutch climber] as well. The guys at the top of the standings all attack, then look to see where Roche is," complained the Italian.

"As a rider, Roche is good, as a man I'll say he's shown what he really is: completely two-faced," he moaned in an interview entitled "Visentini: why I hate Roche". "Why?" asked Zomegnan. "One day he smiles at you, the next he shafts you," answered Visentini, adding, apropos of the foreign coterie within Carrera, "They're a right trio, after the stages they get together in a hotel room and have seances." Roche's answer was simple, and explains why the Italian public ended up taking his side: "Roberto fell off in the Tour of the Basque Country [a spring stage race] and hit his head. He sometimes gets the wrong end of the stick." Millar recalled that by the end of the race, Visentini had made himself so unpopular that when Roche punctured close to the finish of a stage, not one rider pointed this out to his arch enemy. Six weeks later, Roche would win the Tour de France, and at the end of the summer, he would equal Merckx's triple of Giro, Tour, and world championship.

The last two great Italian stars, Marco Pantani and Mario Cipollini, sit firmly in this tradition of hype on two wheels. As 2003 approached, Cipollini, the playboy sprinter, was set to equal if not overtake Binda's apparently impregnable record of 41 stage wins. Cycling's greatest ever showman, he had marketed himself as, variously, "the Lion King", "the Fastest Man in the World", "Il Magnifico", and, in the days when he slicked his hair back, "Moussolini". He turned up at Milan fashion shoots and made friends with the footballer Ronaldo.

Cipollini's costumes were equally distinctive. The beginnings were modest: bike, shorts, shoes, and sunglasses to match whatever leader's jersey he was wearing, in contravention of the rules – which led to further publicity for the fines he would receive. By 2001 and 2002 he had graduated to body suits decorated with the body's internal organs, or tigerskin, not to mention an episode on the 1999 Tour de France when his team hired a stripper for a press party. She was called Cleopatra, so "Cipo" dressed up as Julius Caesar.

This last escapade reflected Cipollini's attempts to market himself as a sex god, posing in a publicity shoot for shoes. He was dressed as a sheikh being fed grapes by topless young women, and rode with a photo of Pamela Anderson on his handlebars to boost his testosterone levels. He gave interviews that defied the cycling tradition of sexual abstinence dating back to Binda, Gimondi, and Sean Kelly, including the now legendary quote, "ejaculating costs only 20 calories, no more than a bar of chocolate", yet behind it all was a family man who clearly adored his children and talked at length of the training he had to do to maintain his speed at the age of 35.

Pantani, the diminutive climber from the east coast resort of Cesenatico, was the man all Italy looked upon to attack time triallists such as Miguel Indurain in the Dolomites. His ability to accelerate out of the bunch on a gradient was in the great mountaineering tradition of Charly Gaul and Federico Bahamontes.

His luck, on the other hand, and the *grinta* – grit – with which he overcame it were reminiscent of Coppi. He suffered a broken collarbone in spring 1995, followed that autumn by a collision with a car that left him with a compound fracture in his shin. By spring 1996 he could still barely walk, but in 1997 he took third in the Tour de France and in 1998 managed the Giro–Tour double.

As the Tour descended into chaos, the assumption was that Pantani had saved a disgraced event. By spring 1999 he was Italy's leading sportsman, on a £2m salary, gracing major occasions such as the Ferrari Formula One presentation, and marketing himself as "the Pirate".

DRUGS SCANDALS

Pantani's downfall was dramatic. On 5 June 1999 he was leading the Giro by a street having won all four mountain top stage finishes, including the previous two day's stages. It was two days before the finish of the Giro, and the merchandising companies had the "Pantani wins Giro" T-shirts printed.

Officials of the Union Cycliste took a sample of Pantani's blood, and carried out a test intended to limit use of the banned blood booster erythropoietin. He was well over the limit and had to quit the race,

RIGHT The "Eagle of Toledo", Federico Bahamontes, was one of several of cycling's greatest climbers who left their mark on the Giro. Bahamontes finished 17th in the 1958 race, and also managed eighth in the Tour de France and sixth in the Vuelta that year: a triple to rival that of Marino Lejarreta over 30 years later.

which he did in a scrum of carabinieri. The fans were livid during that day's stage, beating their fists on the roof of the race director's car, yelling abuse, and brandishing insulting placards. The Giro had lost a race leader over drugs before, when Eddy Merckx was found positive in Savona in 1969, but not on this scale, with a national hero involved.

The test did not prove the use of the drug, but it implied it, as a report by the Italian Olympic Committee confirmed later that month. Pantani, hailed after his 1998 Tour victory as "a real champion, a clean one" by the magazine *l'Espresso,* then entered a nether world of almost continuous

court cases as one judge after another tried to prove him guilty of rigging races by taking drugs. He went into hiding, but made a comeback in 2000, turning up sensationally at the start of the Giro in Rome to be blessed by the pope, and winning two stages of the Tour. It was a mere blip, however, and he continued to race with so little success that his future was uncertain by the end of 2002.

By then, the drama and scandal of the Pantani affair had been overtaken by two Giri that shook the sport to its roots. The 2001 race was marked by the "blitz" at San Remo, in which 200 carabinieri and customs police searching for drugs raided in one fell swoop every hotel used by the riders. The result was the cancellation of the main mountain stage, the expulsion of Dario Frigo, the rider lying second overall, and a string of drug bans.

The year 2002 was, if anything, even worse, with the backdrop of a police investigation into a drug-dealing ring in Lake Garda, supposedly linked to the Camorra mafia, and involving members of the Panaria team. The 2000 winner, Stefano Garzelli, won two stages and was set to dominate the race until he tested positive for a diuretic and was sent home amid protestations that he had been framed with a spiked bottle. The same defence, intriguingly, had been used by Merckx in 1969, while Saronni, in 1983, was at the centre of similar claims.

Just as the Garzellia affair was dying away, the 2001 winner, Gilberto Simoni, tested positive twice for cocaine and left the race, although he was later cleared of any wrongdoing after his explanation that he ingested the drug inadvertently in a boiled sweet was upheld. With the two main favourites out, a third, Francesco Casagrande, was disqualified for pushing a fellow competitor off his bike, rendering the whole event virtually meaningless, as the 1999 and 2001 races had been.

Such events could only lead to the feeling that a great national legacy was being squandered by the powerlessness of the organizers and the selfishness of the cyclists. This was a tragedy considering what the race had achieved in its 93 years, and its zenith after World War II; although Italy may have been split

LEFT Mario Cipollini starts the 2001 Giro in a headline-grabbing "X-ray" bodysuit, which, like most of his outfits, earned him vast publicity and a small fine. The "Lion King", or "SuperMario", began winning bunch sprints at the Giro in 1989, and was set to continue into 2003.

between Coppisti and Bartaliani, it simply reflected the power of the event as a unifying force.

UNITING ITALY

It is easy to forget that Italy was unified less than half a century before the first Giro, was twice devastated by world war, and has regions such as Alto Adige and Trieste which have only been incorporated in the 20th century. In that context, a sports event that visited the entire country and brought people together to squabble over the merits of a Tuscan and a Ligurian could only be positive.

The first Giro after World War II, 13 days after the referendum to form a Republic and the elections for the first national assembly, had a particular sense of mission. "It is not true, it is not possible that Italians cannot be united," wrote *La Gazzetta*'s editorial on the

ABOVE The drug scandal that ruined the 1999 Giro: Marco Pantani, Italy's biggest sports star at the time, is escorted from his hotel at Madonna di Campiglio after being thrown off the race 36 hours before the finish. The career of "the Pirate" was over, and the Giro d'Italia would never be the same again.

day of the race. "The Italians know that divided they will perish, united they will rise again.

"The Giro d'Italia is serving a purpose which is greater than the race itself. Neapoletans, Torinesi, Lombards and Laziani, Venetians and Emilians, all Italians, all regions with a single society and a single heart, await the Giro as a mirror in which they can recognize each other and smile."

The 1919 race included stages at the deeply symbolic cities of Trento and Trieste, in an itinerary that included the World War I battlefields of the Veneto and the Carso. "The people along the road," wrote Daniele Marchesini, "and the soldiers themselves still bearing arms to defend our borders, welcome the Giro d'Italia as the symbol of their homeland."

In 1911, on the 50th anniversary of Italian unification, *La Gazzetta* wrote: "It is not only a sporting exercise that engages Italian cyclists from such a variety of regions, in a battle of dialects and personalities on the roads of the south, barely known by the rest of Italy. It is also a true patriotic work, of acquaintance, swiftly turning to brotherhood, greeting, smiles."

Displaying the patronizing attitude that typifies north–south relations in Italy, *La Gazzetta*'s editorialist also hoped that the poorly developed regions of the south would be inspired by its race to "remake their roads, build new factories, gain a desire for self-sufficiency, be drawn closer together, gain *joie de vivre*, improve living conditions and grow rich and fat." All from a bike race.

Even as Italy has grown in national confidence, the Giro has maintained a sense of its unifying mission. It has made a point of visiting every part of Italy, travelling to all the islands around the peninsula – Sicily, Sardinia, even little Elba. In his most dramatic gesture as organizer, the flamboyant Torriani took the race to Italy's most celebrated island, Venice, using pontoon bridges over the Grand Canal to finish a stage in Piazza San Marco in 1978.

The republics within Italy, San Marino and the Vatican, are all visited, while Slovenia hosted a stage in 1994 soon after its independence from the rest of Yugoslavia – a symbol of integration if ever there was one. The first EuroGiro was held in 1973, starting in Belgium and visiting Germany, Luxembourg, and France en route to Italy, and the experiment was repeated, with a Dutch start in 2002, to celebrate the introduction of the single currency.

If the EuroGiro of 2002 was overshadowed by recurrent drug scandals, that simply reflected the greater problems facing Italian cycling at the start of the 21st century. After the 2002 crisis, the race organizers began to show a lack of confidence and the country's flagship sponsor, Mapei, announced it was pulling out. Tradition and the tifosi characterize the Giro, but a third word now has to be used: tarnished.

RIGHT The Giro "gruppo" negotiates a sweeping bend in the Dolomites during the 2000 race.

NATIONALITY	Italian
DATES	11 August 1902–30 March 1976
NICKNAME	la Joconde (the Mona Lisa)
PROFESSIONAL	1922–36
MAJOR WINS	
1925	Giro d'Italia; Giro di Lombardia.
1926	Giro di Lombardia; Italian national title; Giro del Piemonte.
1927	World Road Championship; Giro d'Italia; Giro di Lombardia; Italian national title; Giro del Piemonte.
1928	Giro d'Italia; Italian national title.
1929	Giro d'Italia; Milan–San Remo; Italian national title.
1930	World Road Championship.
1931	Milan–San Remo; Giro di Lombardia.
1932	World Road Championship.
1933	Giro d'Italia and King of the Mountains.
OTHER RESULTS	1926: Giro d'Italia, second. 1929: World Road Championship, bronze. Tour de France: two stage wins. Giro d'Italia: 41 stage wins; 59 days in pink jersey.

ALFREDO BINDA

The second campionissimo, successor and great rival to Costante Girardengo, Binda has a unique place in cycling history: the only champion to be offered money by a major race organizer to stay away, for fear of killing off all interest in the event.

THE GREATEST ROADMAN?

But Binda was also described by the Tour de France organizer Henri Desgrange as the greatest roadman who ever existed, while contemporaries who saw Merckx and Coppi insisted that he was at least their equal. Binda was a devastatingly powerful climber, with a rapid sprint, and one of the finest racing brains ever.

The smoothness of his riding style led the French climber René Vietto to produce this poetic image: "If you put a cup of milk between his shoulders at the foot of a mountain, he would cross the summit without spilling a drop."

What Binda's record lacks is the Tour de France, which his team Legnano had no financial interest in him riding. The one year he started the Tour, 1930, he won two mountain stages, but quit after 10 days, apparently due to a crash, although he said years later that he had been paid so much money to start that he could only do half the race before the organizers' cash ran out.

Ironically, in view of the status he still enjoys in Italy, Binda nearly raced as a Frenchman. His family emigrated from Varese to work in his uncle's plastering business in Nice after World War I, and until he took a contract with Legnano in 1924, he spoke only *nissarte*, the patois of the Nice area.

MULTI-TALENTED

Binda was a talented trumpeter and would give concerts with his brothers, Benito on the saxophone and Albino on the trombone. In his first Giro in 1925, he finished second on the Arenacia track in Naples to Gaetano Belloni, and noticed an orchestra in the track centre. He put down his bike, took up a trumpet, and performed a solo to a standing ovation before heading for the podium.

Binda turned professional simply because the Italian federation could not give amateur licences to emigrés and early in his career he continued to work full-time as a plasterer. But his first year with Legnano in 1925 gave him a win in the Giro d'Italia, which owed much to his forward thinking.

"There was no tarmac in the country," he said later. "I had been warned that the team would not wait for me if I punctured, and in those days, a puncture cost several minutes. To reduce the risk, I put on 500 gramme tyres, while the others used 390 grammes." In a minor miracle, he got through without a single flat.

Binda came second in 1926 in circumstances that spoke volumes about the demands made of the riders in the 1920s, when outside help was forbidden. On the first day, between Milan and Turin, his back brake broke on a descent. His front brake had already failed, so he had the choice between plunging into a drop where he could not see the bottom or falling voluntarily.

He chose the latter, knocked himself unconscious, and lay on the ground for 40 minutes, with an official standing over him to make sure he received no help. Finally, the rain woke him up; the Legnano mechanic had repaired his bike, hiding behind a haystack so no official would notice, and Binda continued, finishing second in the race.

Binda would go on after retirement to manage the Italian national team, masterminding Fausto Coppi's Tour de France victories in 1949 and 1952, and using all his diplomatic skills to make Coppi and his great rival Gino Bartali work together.

UNCOMPROMISING

An uncompromising man, he refused Coppi's wife Bruna permission to accompany the team on the 1949 race. She stayed 24 hours ahead of the team, and didn't even dare telephone her husband. But Binda was merely preaching what he had practised himself. "A real professional should concentrate exclusively on his job," he said at the time. "When I was winning, I permitted myself one sexual encounter a year."

LEFT Crowds on the tree-lined avenues of northern France for the 1925 Paris–Roubaix as Binda makes a rare, and on this occasion unsuccessful, appearance in a race outside Italy. A lone attack proved fruitless, and he was unable to make an impact in a bunch finish contested by a group of 35 riders.

VUELTA A ESPANA

Almost seven decades after the first race was run, Spain's national tour has created itself a solid niche in the country's popular culture. For three weeks every autumn cycling briefly eclipses soccer as the nation's most important sport. Even after each stage, fevered debates between former riders and other armchair experts occupy a sizable proportion of Spanish evening and night-time broadcasting. The next morning, a big local success may even achieve the near unthinkable and push soccer off the front pages of Spain's thriving sporting press. Not even the Tour de France – unless a Spaniard is winning, of course – has the same impact.

LEFT In the natural splendour of Spain's northern hills, the Vuelta leaders enter the mountains.

VUELTA A ESPANA

THE YOUNGEST OF THE THREE MAJOR TOURS HAS A RADICAL POLITICAL PAST, A CONTROVERSIAL HISTORY ON THE ROAD, AND NOW THREATENS TO SHAKE UP THE WHOLE STRUCTURE OF CYCLING RACES.

The Vuelta has its own rich and intriguing history, but as the youngest of all the major three-week races, it still sometimes suffers from an inferiority complex concerning its much more famous elder brothers, the Giro d'Italia and the Tour de France. A change of dates from April to September in 1995 by organizers untroubled by breaking with tradition has produced a radical improvement in the quality of the racing after several years of stagnation, but some foreign teams still tend to treat the Vuelta as a testing ground for their future young stars, or a consolation prize if everything has gone wrong in France in July.

This marked contrast between local and foreign attitudes to the Vuelta is accentuated by the fact that while victory in the Tour or Giro automatically increases a rider's prestige, success in the Spanish race is sometimes undervalued. Ebbing levels of motivation and media interest in cycling after the annual watershed of the Tour de France do not help matters. The old argument that Spanish climbs cannot compare to the Alps or Dolomites is regularly trotted out by the more partisan elements of the foreign media. The level of competition, it is claimed, is far lower than that of the two other major stage races.

From inside Spain, of course, where winning the Vuelta is second only to winning the Tour, success in their top race is given much more importance. As for toughness, the organizers can point to the latest jewel in the Vuelta's crown, the Angliru, a 13-km (8-mile) climb first introduced three years ago, which has steeper sections than any other single ascent used for major stage races in Europe, at some points nearly one-in-four. And there are other great climbs, such as the long drag to the Lagos de Covadonga in the Picos de Europa, home to some of the last wolves in Europe.

There certainly can be no questioning the Vuelta's enduring success amongst the Spanish public – the media interest alone shows that. It's partly explained by Spain's demography and geography. In a country with almost the same land mass as France but roughly two-thirds of the population, stage racing from city to village to town to city across isolated, empty sierras, dry uplands, and the wind-torn mesetas provides the Spanish with a rare sense of their own national unity.

POLITICS AND THE "BASQUE QUESTION"

During the country's 40-year dictatorship under Franco, the General's insistence on maintaining the divisions created by the Civil War as a way of retaining power meant that the Vuelta had a semi-political role to play in uniting the country. But it was a role imposed from above until Franco's death in 1975, and not always a welcome one.

Unlike the Tour or the Giro, the Vuelta a España's added political edge has only disappeared very recently. During the Franco dictatorship, for example, the race would often start and finish in the Basque Country, a convenient means of making the point that the area formed part of the Spanish state, whether the inhabitants liked it or not.

Some of them definitely did not like it. Although cycling was normally off limits for the separatists given the support the sport enjoys in the region, as ETA terrorism began to shake the country in the 1970s cycling could not avoid being drawn into the conflict.

Events reached a head in the 1978 Vuelta, two and a half years after Franco's death, when Basque separatist protesters in San Sebastian scattered tin tacks and put up barricades of timber beams on the two final stages, one a road race, the other a time trial. The first stage was partly cancelled, and the second completely called off, with the previous day's leader, Bernard Hinault, declared the outright winner.

After this debacle, the Vuelta has never returned to the Basque Country and the *Correo Vasco-Diario Español*, a pro-Madrid paper that had organized the

RIGHT Spain's barren terrain and low population density mean that the Vuelta does not attract massive crowds to the roadside, Tour de France style, and much of the riders' day is spent on empty roads.

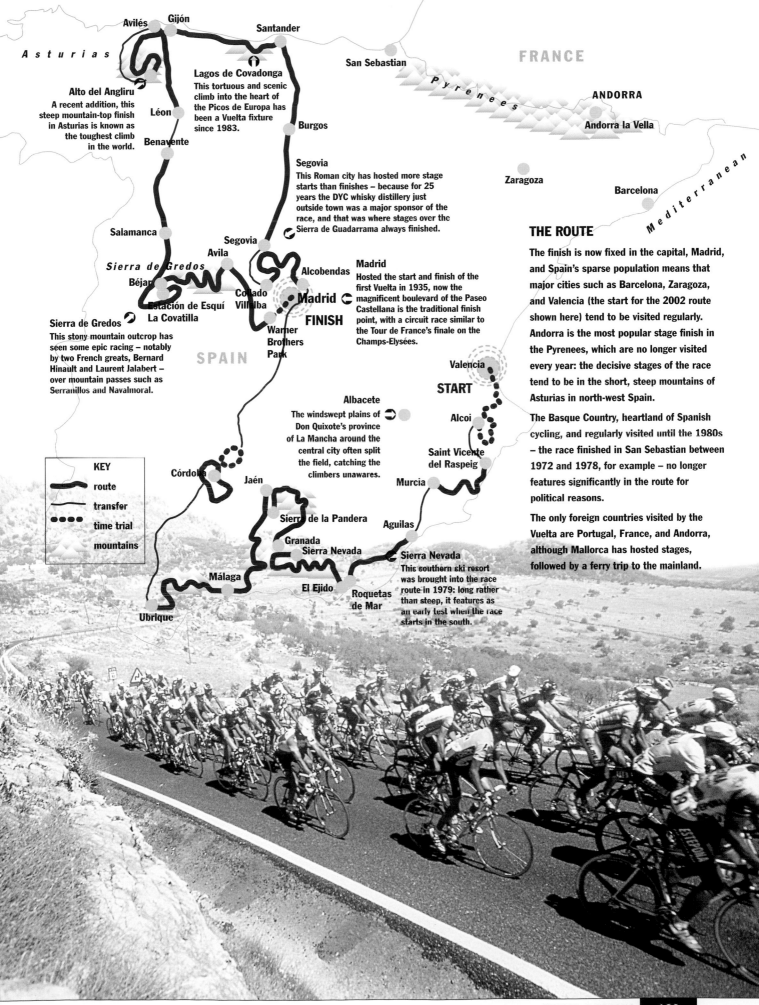

Avilés

Gijón

Santander

A s t u r i a s

FRANCE

P y r e n e e s

San Sebastian

ANDORRA

Lagos de Covadonga
This tortuous and scenic climb into the heart of the Picos de Europa has been a Vuelta fixture since 1983.

Andorra la Vella

Alto del Angliru
A recent addition, this steep mountain-top finish in Asturias is known as the toughest climb in the world.

León

Burgos

Benavente

Segovia
This Roman city has hosted more stage starts than finishes – because for 25 years the DYC whisky distillery just outside town was a major sponsor of the race, and that was where stages over the Sierra de Guadarrama always finished.

Zaragoza

Barcelona

M e d i t e r r a n e a n

Salamanca

Segovia

Avila

Sierra de Gredos

Alcobendas

Béjar

Collado Villalba

Madrid
FINISH

Estación de Esquí La Covatilla

Warner Brothers Park

Sierra de Gredos
This stony mountain outcrop has seen some epic racing – notably by two French greats, Bernard Hinault and Laurent Jalabert – over mountain passes such as Serranillos and Navalmoral.

SPAIN

Madrid
Hosted the start and finish of the first Vuelta in 1935, now the magnificent boulevard of the Paseo Castellana is the traditional finish point, with a circuit race similar to the Tour de France's finale on the Champs-Elysées.

THE ROUTE

The finish is now fixed in the capital, Madrid, and Spain's sparse population means that major cities such as Barcelona, Zaragoza, and Valencia (the start for the 2002 route shown here) tend to be visited regularly. Andorra is the most popular stage finish in the Pyrenees, which are no longer visited every year: the decisive stages of the race tend to be in the short, steep mountains of Asturias in north-west Spain.

Valencia

START

Alcoi

Albacete
The windswept plains of Don Quixote's province of La Mancha around the central city often split the field, catching the climbers unawares.

Saint Vicente del Raspeig

The Basque Country, heartland of Spanish cycling, and regularly visited until the 1980s – the race finished in San Sebastian between 1972 and 1978, for example – no longer features significantly in the route for political reasons.

Córdoba

Jaén

Murcia

The only foreign countries visited by the Vuelta are Portugal, France, and Andorra, although Mallorca has hosted stages, followed by a ferry trip to the mainland.

KEY
— route
— transfer
•••• time trial
⋀ mountains

Sierra de la Pandera

Aguilas

Granada
Sierra Nevada

Málaga

El Ejido

Roquetas de Mar

Sierra Nevada
This southern ski resort was brought into the race route in 1979: long rather than steep, it features as an early test when the race starts in the south.

Ubrique

race from its Bilbao headquarters for over 30 years, threw in the towel. Since then, occasional calls from right-wing orientated press to return to Euskadi (the Basque region) have been politely ignored by the current organizers, the private company Unipublic, who have their offices in Madrid.

It is hard to say what kind of reception the Vuelta would receive now in the Basque Country. In other races in the Basque Country and Catalonia, which has its own nationalist movements, Spanish teams and

FREDDY MAERTENS

In a career of highs and lows, Freddy Maertens' most staggering achievement was the 1977 Vuelta, where he led from start to finish – a picture of dominance that matched anything achieved by Eddy Merckx.

Maertens was no Merckx, but he spent much of his career trying to live up to the standards of "the Cannibal". In 1976 he equalled Merckx's best victory tally – 54 for the year – and equalled his joint record of eight stage wins in the Tour, but after breaking his wrist in a finish line crash at Mugello in the 1977 Giro d'Italia, he was never the same again.

He returned to win the green jersey in the 1978 Tour de France, went AWOL for a couple of years, then suddenly won five stages in the 1981 Tour, plus the world championship. But when he turned up to defend his title the next year, he was found drunk the night before, and his career petered out in a succession of minor teams, hopeless comebacks, and financial disaster.

NATIONALITY	Belgian
BORN	13 February 1952, Nieuwpoort, West Flanders
NICKNAME	the Ogre
PROFESSIONAL	1972–87
MAJOR WINS	
1973	Four Days of Dunkirk.
1974	Tour of Luxembourg.
1975	Ghent–Wevelgem; Paris–Brussels; Tours–Versailles; Tour of Belgium; Four Days of Dunkirk.
1976	World Road Championship; Ghent–Wevelgem; Amstel Gold; GP Frankfurt; Belgian national title; Four Days of Dunkirk; GP Nations; Super Prestige Pernod Trophy.
1977	Vuelta a España and points jersey; Het Volk; Tour of Sardinia; Paris–Nice; Catalan Week; Tour of Catalonia; Super Prestige Pernod Trophy.
1978	Het Volk; Four Days of Dunkirk.
1981	World Road Championship.

riders rarely, if ever, come in for abuse from cycling supporters. Incidents like the one when 1959 Tour winner Federico Bahamontes, insulted by Basques on a Vuelta stage, turned around on his bike and chased them down the road for several kilometres, brandishing a bike pump, are thankfully few and far between. However, it would only take one incident like those of 1978 for the fragile sporting truce to be broken.

Even though Euskadi is avoided, the "Basque Question" still does raise its head on occasion in the Vuelta, which is hardly surprising given that over two-thirds of professionals racing under the Spanish flag come from that region. But mostly it is reflected in relatively trivial ways, as happened in 1999 when Spanish climber José María Jiménez was beaten into second place on the Abantos climb outside Madrid by Basque mountain man Roberto Laiseka.

Jiménez, not a rider renowned for thinking first and speaking later, dismissed his defeat as unimportant because he had been beaten by "somebody who's only half-Spanish". Laiseka then fanned the flames of controversy a little higher by responding he "wasn't half-Spanish, but 100 percent Basque".

A far more serious echo of the 1978 incidents took place in the Vuelta of 1994, when it ventured into the region of Navarre, considered by some separatist movements to form part of the Basque Country. A protest briefly held up one stage, and things could have turned ugly when a *guardia civil* pulled out his pistol and waved it in the air. The protesters retreated under this non-too-civil encouragement but the Vuelta did, too: since then it has not returned to Navarre, either.

THE CIVIL WAR AND FRANCO

But if so much of Spanish life in the second half of the 20th century was shaped by the Civil War, the ensuing dictatorship, and the country's separatist troubles, the Vuelta could hardly be expected to remain completely unaffected.

Furthermore, the race only began in 1935, meaning it barely had time to develop any identity as a sporting event before the Civil War began in July 1936. Following Franco's victory, when the Vuelta returned to Spain's ravaged road system in 1941, the ruling nationalist government – a keen promoter of sport across the board in order to help the population forget minor

ABOVE Police motorcyclists escort the peloton during the 1936 race, won for the second year in succession by the Belgian Gustave Deloor. The Spanish Civil War would put a halt to the event, which did not resume until 1941.

concerns such as the lack of democracy – quickly appreciated the opportunities offered by the Vuelta.

Nor did they beat around the bush. Before the start of the 1941 race, the entire peloton lined up at Madrid's Puerta del Sol – considered to be the geographical and spiritual centre of the Spanish state – extended their right arms and sang "Cara al Sol", the anthem of the Falange, Spain's fascist party. The race might well have been the first government-sponsored sporting event to visit both the former republican and nationalist zones in Spain, but this gesture made clear which side the event supported.

Although the hymn-singing had died out by 1950, the Vuelta's political resonances remained firmly in place. When the race finished in Madrid it was not unknown for El Caudillo himself to shake hands with the Vuelta winner on the final podium. During the dictatorship the more politically minded Spanish riders, when victorious, would actually exchange salutes with the local military authorities, almost always present on the podium.

The relationship was mutually beneficial in some senses, given that had it not been for Franco's Fascist government, the Vuelta would have disappeared after just two editions. Even while World War II raged through Europe, the 1941 and 1942 editions of the newly reborn Vuelta were jointly organized by the newspaper *Gol* and the Obra Nacional de Educación and Descanso – the Spanish Ministry for Education and Leisure – which provided a grant of 25,000 pesetas (£100), a sizable sum in those days.

History repeated itself in 1966 when the organization came close to cancelling the entire race because of cash-flow problems. The Minister of Sport, José Antonio Elola, stepped in at the last minute and provided some much-needed financial support from government coffers. However, it was too late for the big foreign names to be brought in, and for the first time in four years the Vuelta was won by a rider from south of the Pyrenees, Patxi Gabica.

Sometimes, thankfully, the politically tinted moments of the race have become pure Spanish folklore. In 1976, so the story goes, the recently legalized Communist party erected a banner over the Vuelta route. Eddy Merckx, well-known for his unlimited ambitions when it came to winning, sprinted out of the peloton, assuming it was for some kind of prize. This is pure myth, however, as the only Vuelta that Merckx rode was in 1973.

The excellent relationship between the military and the race lingered on for some years after Franco died.

BELOW Jacques Anquetil, five times winner of the Tour de France, relaxes in the 1962 Vuelta alongside his team-mate Rudy Altig of Germany, who would go on to win the event, giving his country its first win in a major Tour.

In 1981 Spaniard José Luis Lopez Cerron dedicated a stage victory he had won by a spectacular 14-minute margin to the victims of terrorism. He promptly received the Order of Military Merit from the Spanish armed forces in recognition of his gesture.

THE VUELTA'S ROCKY RIDE

But if, in the past, the Vuelta was sometimes hijacked by the ruling regime, perhaps that was not so far from its original objective. "Just like in European countries, now we have a national Tour. La Vuelta a España is the incarnation of the country's sense of patriotism," trumpeted the leading editorial of the race's first backer, the newspaper *Informaciones*, the day the Vuelta began on 29 April 1935.

In other circumstances, this might have been a fairly harmless way of describing the launching of a major Tour, but they were dangerously loaded words for the times, given that all over Spain the armed forces' "sense of patriotism" was inducing them to plot against the fledgling Spanish Republic. By describing the Vuelta in these terms, *Informaciones* was clearly indicating which side of the political fence it was on.

Political aims apart, the Vuelta's format was singularly unoriginal and shamelessly imitated the structure of the Tours of Italy and France of the time. Approximately 3,500 km (2,200 miles) long, the 1935 race contained 14 stages and three rest days. Of the 50 riders who started, 29 finished.

Furthermore, if any of the Spanish riders felt they were the incarnation of their country's patriotism, they did little to show it. The first Vuelta was dominated by the six Belgian professionals present, most of whom had at least some experience in major Tours. The half-dozen northern Europeans formed a highly successful combination against the one Spaniard, Mariano Cañardo, to put up any serious opposition.

The race was eventually won by one of the Belgians' number, Gustave Deloor, whose close ally and fellow-countryman François Adam also hit the headlines by insisting on kissing a podium girl when he won the 270-km (170-mile) stage from Sevilla to Caceres. By way of apology, he bowed low and explained to her, "What I did is a custom in our country."

If the country's political conflicts effectively sunk the Vuelta mark one – although they were indirectly responsible for its rebirth in 1941 – the major economic depression caused by the 1936–9 Civil War proved equally damaging. While it was hardly surprising that the race failed to re-emerge in 1940 so soon after the Civil War had finished, its cancellation for a second time in 1943 and 1944, for a third time in 1949, and finally for a four-year period in 1951–4 was invariably due to a persistent lack of funds in a country where after the war the average per capita income had reverted to levels as low as the early 1920s.

The race, itself a luxury, suffered as a consequence. Even before the 1941 Vuelta had begun the Spanish riders had staged a protest over the availability of some top-grade inner tubes that the organization had promised it would provide – but only to half the peloton. Cañardo, the great pre-war local favourite, pulled out in protest.

With hindsight, his departure was understandable: the 32 starters that year suffered terribly on the poor roads, many still unsurfaced, notching up a record 83 punctures between them on the 301-km (188-mile) stage from Verín to Valladolid.

The roads did not improve greatly over the next two decades. In 1946, on a stage from Sevilla to Granada, the race's lead motorcar got hopelessly lost because of fog and a lack of signposts, with three riders following in its wake. One of the trio, Dutchman John Lambrichts, nonetheless somehow won the stage. Then the 1950s Basque cycling star Jesus Loroño, Bahamontes' great rival, captured the feelings of many when he said that "racing in the Vuelta south of Madrid was more painful than climbing the Tourmalet".

There were other minor problems, too – such as World War II. After the Belgians had dominated the first two pre-Civil War editions, reports in the Spanish media show they were baffled and infuriated by the fact that the neutral Swiss were the only country prepared to take part in the 1941 race. The reason for the non-appearance of the expected French and Italian riders was apparently because the authorities feared they would take the chance to avoid the fighting and remain in Spain after the Vuelta had finished.

After the start was delayed in order to give the Swiss time to reach Madrid, a grand total of four (none of them major stars) made it through Vichy France and over the border, with only three completing the course.

The race was therefore controlled by the Spanish, with approximately half of them riding, somewhat confusingly, in identical grey jerseys paid for by the government and complete with Health Ministry logos – presumably just to make sure everybody knew who was behind the Vuelta that year.

While the Vuelta – like Spain itself during the Franco years – craved international recognition rather than being isolated behind the Pyrenees, even after World War II it proved an uphill task. Quite apart from the country's abysmal infrastructure and the problems caused by the war, there was virtually no money to pay the foreign riders' start fees. So for over a decade, the Vuelta remained an almost exclusively Spanish affair.

From 1941 through to 1947, in a total of 103 consecutive stages, no foreigner wore the leader's jersey, which changed colour a bewildering number of times. The *maillot del lider* had started life as a light orange affair in 1935 and 1936, then changed to white in 1941, went back to orange again in 1942, became all-red in 1945, and finally opted for white with a red stripe across the middle from 1946 to 1948 and again in 1950. Only after 1955 did the organizers plump for plain canary yellow, a colour borrowed from the Tour de France, which they retained – with the exception of 1977, when the jersey reverted to orange – for the next 40 years.

Perhaps unsurprisingly, given the conditions in which the race was held, the infrequency and uncertainty with which it was held, and the low level of foreign opposition, Spaniard Delio Rodriguez notched up a record 34 stage wins in the Vuelta, which still stands today. The eldest of five brothers who were all professional racers, Rodriguez won no less than 12 out of a total of 22 in 1941 and then another six in 1945, the year he took the overall.

THE VUELTA GOES INTERNATIONAL

It was only in 1955 that Spain, finally beginning to recover from the so-called *Años de Hambre* (Years of Hunger), could permit itself the luxury of a major Tour once more. For the first time over 100 riders took part, the peloton was divided into teams – including a Great Britain squad of six riders – and the race made a brief excursion abroad, with a stage finish in Bayonne.

Convinced that they would gain more prestige with a foreign winner, the Vuelta organizers then took the bold step of paying out huge sums of "start money" to the big international stars. It proved to be a hit-and-miss system. Fausto Coppi's presence in the 1959 Vuelta was so low-key that the unusual step was taken of asking him to leave – the organizers were keen to save the 11,000 pesetas a day the Italian star's presence was costing them. Coppi politely obliged and quit after 14 stages, while only one of his Italian team-mates actually finished the course.

The first major foreign star to repay the Vuelta's investment in full and win the race was Jacques Anquetil in 1963. "Monsieur Jacques" had a personal score to settle with the race after his domestique, the German world pursuit champion Rudy Altig, had destroyed the Frenchman's chances of victory in the Vuelta in 1962.

The 1963 race started with a 52-km (32½-mile) time trial, which the Spanish teams, on hearing Anquetil would take part, had unsuccessfully tried to have removed from the course. However, the French champion was also favoured by the shortness of the route – a mere 15 stages – and the grand total of four major climbs over the entire course. After winning the first stage by nearly three minutes, the Frenchman then led the entire race, by all accounts a singularly dull affair, from start to finish.

The following year saw the organization ignore the Spanish and bring in Raymond Poulidor and Rik van Looy as the most important stars. However, while "Poupou" fulfilled his sporting obligations by winning the final time trial – a mere 73 km (45½ miles) – and taking the overall, Van Looy, despite leading the event, did not prove so cooperative.

The former world champion's chance to quit came when he crashed and was injured on a dangerous descent on stage five. He was diagnosed with heavy bruising in one shoulder, with the doctor's report stating that "whether the patient continues or not depends purely on his state of morale". But Van Looy's mind was already made up.

Having instructed his hotel to wake him at seven – despite the stage start being after midday – Van Looy abandoned Spain and his overall lead in the race early the next morning by car, his brother-in-law and his favourite domestique, Edgar Sorgeloos, in on the secret. The fact that the organizers fined Sorgeloos

1,000 pesetas for "abandoning without good reason" hardly softened the blow to the race's reputation.

Other non-Spaniards have made a bigger impact in more recent years, as the Spanish teams gained the economic clout to buy in the best foreigners. Laurent Jalabert of France, and Alex Zulle and Tony Rominger of Switzerland dominated the race between 1992 and 1997 riding for ONCE, sponsored by the national lottery for the blind, and Clas, backed by the Asturian milk producers' cooperative.

Most popular of all the imports, though, was Sean Kelly, nicknamed "Casero" (Homeboy), who won a host of lesser Spanish stage races riding for the KAS soft drinks company. He finally took the Vuelta in 1988, in contrast to his painful experience of the previous year when he led the race three days from the finish, but had to abandon after an operation to remove a boil from his groin. The Irishman had claimed that all was well at the stage start, but an observant journalist from the *Marca* newspaper had heard rumours of the most terrible screams coming from Kelly's room and made sure his photographer was there when the race leader quit.

PROBLEMS WITH THE STARS

The Vuelta's problem, then as now, was that it could never be sure whether the foreign stars participating simply regarded the Spanish race as high-level training or whether they would take the money and run.

Sometimes it got even worse than that. In 1966 the Belgian team Libertas abandoned the Vuelta en masse because their sponsor refused to pay the bills for their nightly post-stage junketings. This time the Spanish Federation responded by banning the squad for a year.

Today, 35 years on, similar problems can crop up when it comes to keeping the stars in the race, as happened with Jan Ullrich in 2000 and Marco Pantani in 2001. Despite winning the race in 1999, 12 months later in a rest-day press conference Ullrich took all of seven minutes to announce he was quitting in order to train at home for the Olympic Games.

The fact that the press conference was held in French and German, with no translation into Spanish, merely rubbed in what the local media took to be a barefaced lack of respect. However, after Ullrich missed out on the Tour in 2002, the organizers were

ABOVE Genial off the bike, grimacing on it, Tony Rominger of Switzerland takes his second Vuelta win in the rainy, chilly, 1993 race. Later that season he would threaten Miguel Indurain in the Tour de France.

quick to say that they would be happy to have him back again in 2003.

Pantani's case was even more flagrant. To judge by the massive cheers he received at the team presentation in Salamanca, the 1998 Tour winner was easily the most popular foreign rider present. However, no sooner did the Vuelta reach the Pyrenees, theoretically Pantani's favoured terrain, than the Italian quit – and two of his team-mates went with him.

Unipublic are less prepared to swallow their pride over local stars' indifference to the Vuelta, particularly in the case of five-times Tour winner Miguel Indurain, who steadfastly refused to ride the Vuelta from 1992 to 1995. The reasons for the Spaniard's lack of enthusiasm for his home race were two-fold: firstly, the Giro or week-long stage races in France were better suited for his preparation for the overriding objective of the season, the Tour, and secondly the Vuelta in April was frequently run in cold, rainy weather – and Indurain was notoriously vulnerable to low temperatures.

Unipublic tried everything within their grasp to "encourage" Indurain to race, from insisting that teams sent riders worth a high proportion of their overall UCI points to the Vuelta, to directly putting pressure on Indurain's squad, Banesto. At one point, the question of his non-participation was even briefly debated in the Spanish parliament.

Ironically enough, when Indurain finally decided to take part in the race in 1996, it was under pressure from his team after he had failed to win the Tour that year, and Unipublic's feelings were not taken into account. The results were disastrous. On the race's most important stage, finishing at the mythical Covadonga Lakes, Indurain began losing time on the penultimate climb, the Fito.

By the summit, he was alone, and after riding down to the team hotel at the foot of the Covadonga Lakes, the tall Navarran dismounted, and went inside. Barring one criterium in Valencia in October, it was his last appearance as a professional cyclist before he retired.

Perhaps the one Spanish rider who has managed to give the Vuelta the international sheen it was looking for was Pedro Delgado, the 1988 Tour de France winner. Charismatic, lovably inconsistent – "People like watching me on TV because they never know whether I'll still be in the peloton when they come back from taking a leak," he once joked – Delgado's devastating mountain attacks proved an irresistible draw for the general public. His second Vuelta win combined with the arrival of live television coverage in the late 1980s and an economic boom in Spain. As TV audiences soared, the Vuelta finally became a regularly profitable affair, as it continues to be today.

But Delgado's first Vuelta victory in 1985 remains enshrouded in mystery and shows that the organization was no longer prepared to favour the foreigners against the Spanish – perhaps even the opposite. A late attack on the third last stage alongside Kelme rider Pepe Recio gained Delgado more than six minutes on race leader Robert Millar, more than enough to give "Perico" a hold on the yellow jersey. Millar and his team manager at Peugeot alleged they had never been provided with any time references during Delgado's 60-km (37-mile) attack – something confirmed by the foreign journalists present and firmly denied by the race organization. Other factors operating against the Scot, such as Millar's team-mates being held up at a level crossing while waiting for a train which apparently never arrived, are part of a bizarre succession of events that have never fully been cleared up.

THE VUELTA TODAY

Nonetheless, Delgado's 1985 victory marked the beginning of the Vuelta's modern history. "When I

JAN JANSSEN

Janssen was the first Dutchman to win the Tour de France, and did so without wearing the yellow jersey en route. On the morning of the final stage of the 1968 Tour, a 53-km (33-mile) time trial from Melun to Vincennes, he was lying third behind Herman van Springel and Ferdinand Bracke of Belgium, strong time triallists both, but he managed to win the first long time trial of his career and take the yellow jersey by a mere 55 seconds.

A shock, but only if you ignore the fact that Janssen had won the Vuelta the previous year in the penultimate day's time trial. The race was controlled by his Pelforth squad, with Jean-Pierre Ducasse leading for 10 stages until Janssen took over the day before the finish in Bilbao.

Janssen might also have won the 1966 Tour de France, had his team car radio not broken as the vital break went clear. His world championship, at a rainy Sallanches in 1964, and his Paris–Roubaix of 1967, showed that here was an all-round champion, who was, by his own admission, "burned out by the end of the decade".

NATIONALITY	Dutch
BORN	19 May 1940, Nootdorp, Zuid-Holland
PROFESSIONAL	1962–72
MAJOR WINS	
1962	Championship of Zurich.
1964	World Road Championship; Paris–Nice.
1965	Tour of Holland.
1966	Bordeaux–Paris; Flèche Brabançonne.
1967	Vuelta a España and points jersey; Super Prestige Pernod Trophy; Paris–Roubaix.
1968	Tour de France.

ABOVE The podium in Madrid after Angel-Luis Casero, centre, scored a close victory over "El Nino", Oscar Sevilla, left, on the final day of the 2002 race, with Levi Leipheimer of Germany, right, rising from obscurity to take a surprise third.

started there were just three teams in Spain, most riders had a part-time job in the winter driving lorries or on building sites and the hotels never welcomed teams because the riders got too many towels dirty," Delgado recalls. "Now, at least, cycling and cyclists are valued."

The Vuelta has also realized that its lesser prestige means it is not so tied by tradition as the Giro and Tour. For example, it is the only three-week race to have taken concrete steps in the fight against doping in recent years by radically shortening stage length. Then, in 2000, the yellow jersey changed colour to gold, asserting the Vuelta a España's separate identity.

The race's growing confidence is reflected in its constantly increasing willingness to experiment with the entire concept of stage racing, in what could be the first major adjustment to the sport since Henri Desgrange introduced the current format in the 1920s. Unipublic's latest consultation project is to have 36 teams participating in the first week, in two separate pelotons and two separate races. After seven stages 18 teams would be eliminated and the remaining half will amalgamate for a final fortnight-long battle.

The traditionalists are predictably up in arms at this unprecedented idea, but it says a lot for the Vuelta's current confidence that these are experiments the two older three-week events are unwilling to contemplate. This remains the best possible proof that, despite the sinister links to the Spanish state during the Franco years, the Vuelta is finally making its own way in the cycling world.

NATIONALITY	Spanish
BORN	16 July 1964, Villava, Navarra
NICKNAME	Big Mig
PROFESSIONAL	1985–96
PROFESSIONAL TEAMS	
1985–9	Reynolds
1990–6	Banesto
MAJOR WINS	
1986	Tour of Murcia; Tour de l'Avenir.
1987	Tour of the Mining Valleys.
1988	Tour of Catalonia.
1989	Paris–Nice; Criterium International.
1990	Paris–Nice; San Sebastian Classic.
1991	Tour de France; Tour of Vaucluse; Tour of Catalonia.
1992	Tour de France; Giro d'Italia; Tour of Catalonia; Spanish road title.
1993	Tour de France; Giro d'Italia; Castile–Leon Trophy; Vuelta a los Puertos.
1994	Tour de France; Tour de l'Oise.
1995	Tour de France; World Time Trial Championship; Dauphiné Libéré; Midi Libre; Tour of Rioja; Tour of Galicia.
1996	Olympic time trial championship; Dauphiné Libéré; Bicicleta Vasca; Vuelta al Alentejo.
OTHER RESULTS	1991: World Road Championship, bronze; Vuelta a España, second. 1993: World Road Championship, silver. 1994: Giro d'Italia, third. 1995: World Road Championship, silver.
	World hour record, 53.040 km, Bordeaux, France, September 1994.
	Tour de France: 12 stage wins; 60 days in yellow jersey. Giro di Italia: 4 stage wins; 29 days in pink jersey.
	99 professional wins.

MIGUEL INDURAIN

For half a dozen years, Miguel Indurain's bumbling manner, impenetrable grin, and astounding time trial speed were the focus of the Tour de France each July. In the early 1990s, "Big Mig" became the first cyclist to win the race five times in a row, joining Merckx, Anquetil, and Hinault with barely a glitch, and turning himself into one of Spain's most popular sportsmen along the way.

A COOL HEAD

As an amateur Indurain was a sprinter, a large adolescent who could turn on colossal power when required. His animation, however, was reserved for the bike. "When you came up to him after [a race] and asked him where he had finished, he would just shrug his shoulders and say 'first'," recalled Pepe Barrusso, his first trainer. "As if he would come anywhere else but first."

Indurain always kept his cool. Journalists would count the number of times they had seen him angry – and made it about four in his entire career. In one amateur race, a bottle thrown by a spectator at another rider grazed his head, but he never mentioned it afterwards. At times, his unwillingness to say more than the most banal statement of the obvious frustrated the press. In 1991, one Spanish journalist said: "Even the woman of his life, 20 years from now, will not know who she has spent her nights with."

As with Sean Kelly, Indurain's character was explained by his background. He grew up on the rambling family farm in Villava, a country village swallowed up by the suburbs of Pamplona. One day he rode his bike to the fields to play on his father's tractor. Two tramps stole the machine, and he was bought the first racing bike on which he began competing.

In his best years, Indurain was as devastating on the bike as he was bland off it. In the 1990 Tour he lost 12½ minutes working for his leader, Pedro Delgado, yet was only 12 minutes 47 seconds behind the winner, Greg LeMond. He came back to win in 1991, and in 1992 produced the performance that defined his career, the Luxembourg time trial, when he opened time gaps on the other contenders the size of which hadn't been seen since the days of Bernard Hinault. "Extraterrestrial," said the triple winner Greg LeMond, who could not believe what he had seen that day.

"THE DOUBLE OF DOUBLES"

In 1993 Indurain completed the "double of doubles" – back-to-back Giro and Tour in consecutive years, a feat that will probably never be equalled. By 1994 he was "Big Mig" (an Anglicization of his Spanish nickname "Miguelon"), capable of riding over Mont Ventoux at 21 mph, with his manager in the team car behind pleading with him to slow down for his own good.

LA VUELTA

In spite of Indurain's colossal impact on sport in his homeland, he never made his mark on the Vuelta after being appointed Banesto team leader for the 1991 race, where he was unable to dislodge the surprise winner, Melchior Mauri. He came under pressure to ride the race each year, but preferred to start the Giro as preparation for the Tour.

In 1996, however, he was forced to start the Vuelta by his team managers, who were disappointed with his failure to win the Tour de France. The cracks were opening in the relationship with José-Miguel Echavarri, which had lasted through his career, and he quit the race and the sport on a rainy day in the Basque Country.

He may have been criticized for basing his Tours around the time trials, but Indurain could ride all but the best climbers off their wheels in the mountains as well, and his audacious attack on the Côte des Forges to win the 1995 Tour remains another defining moment. But as the end of his career showed, Indurain was always determined that he would only race his bike on his own terms. "Some people ride to give the fans a thrill, and others ride to win," he told *Cycle Sport* in 1995. "I belong to the second group."

LEFT The most enigmatic of cyclists, Miguel Indurain gazes out from the tear-drop time trial helmet which came to symbolize his impenetrable personality and supreme skill against the watch.

WORLD ROAD CHAMPIONSHIPS

The world road title's place in the racing calendar may be hotly debated, but it retains a unique appeal. This is the only day in the professional cycling year when the stars gather and compete under the flags of their countries, rather than in their sponsors' colours. The result is racing packed with intrigue, and a festival of patriotism, as the fans from the great cycling nations – Italy, Belgium, France, Holland, and Spain – try to outdo each other with displays of flag-waving, chanting, and sign-writing.

LEFT Every Italian's dream: Vittorio Adorni is alone in the lead, wearing the light-blue jersey, on his way to victory in the 1968 world championships, on home soil at Imola. His gold crowned one of the greatest days for a nation obsessed with the "Worlds": five Italians finished in the first six.

WORLD ROAD CHAMPIONSHIPS

THE PRIZE AT STAKE IS UNIQUE: THE RAINBOW-BANDED JERSEY, CHOSEN TO INCLUDE THE COLOURS OF ALL NATIONAL FLAGS, TO BE WORN FOR THE NEXT YEAR.

Traditionally, the world championships were held in August, within a month of the finish of the Tour de France, which meant that the stars of the Tour would be present, and that good weather was guaranteed. But in 1995, the Union Cycliste Internationale decided to move them to an October date, to ensure that the Vuelta a España, which had moved to September, would get a reasonable field, out to gain form for the "Worlds". Now, the professional road race acts as the climax of a week's racing which also includes time trial titles, and championships for junior men and women, senior women, and under-23 men.

The change of date, however, has meant that winning the Tour de France and the Worlds is no longer practical. The last man to win both titles in the same year was Miguel Indurain, who took the time trial title after his fifth Tour in 1995. Now, the Tour stars such as Lance Armstrong tend to have finished their seasons by the time the Worlds come round, which has robbed the event of some of its lustre. More worryingly, the autumn date means that bad weather is often an issue.

The Italians began the moves to found a world championship after World War I, and the race retains a vital importance for them. Merely getting selected for the Azzurri is a target for most Italian pros of any worth. Once the team has been named, acres of newsprint are devoted to speculation about its prospects, and further acres are wasted in lamentation when, as so often happens, the Italians' high hopes are in vain.

An amateur world championship was first held in 1921, at the instigation of the French, Italians, and British, and the professionals entered the fray in 1927. In that year, on the Nurburgring motor-racing circuit, pros and amateurs rode together. The two Italian campionissimi, Alfredo Binda and Costante Girardengo, escaped alone until Binda disposed of the older man and won by seven minutes.

The world championships are never held on a place-to-place course: unlike the great Classics they are on a loop of between 13 and 19 km (8–12 miles), usually with a hill. This requires a special tactical awareness, as the same hills and the same corners have to be negotiated time after time, but it is a dream for the fans: all they have to do is to select their spot, and they can watch the day's action unfold.

Any cycling fan dreams of seeing one of the greats unleashed in front of them, in what is essentially a massive circuit race, and sometimes what they see is simply stupendous. Bernard Hinault's victory at Sallanches in the 1980 championship was one of the best examples. "The Badger" had quit the Tour de France at dead of night with a knee injury, and had a lot to prove, which he did by destroying the entire field with a series of attacks over the Domancy climb in the second half of the race, finishing alone.

Giuseppe Saronni produced the finest sprint of his entire career, positively electric in its sheer power, to take his world title at Goodwood in 1982. Louison Bobet made an epic chase behind the Swiss Fritz Schaer at Solingen in 1954, then attacked to win alone in a state of near exhaustion. When the Marseillaise was played as he was awarded the gold medal, it was the first time the French national anthem had been heard on German soil since before the war.

More recently, Miguel Indurain and Marco Pantani refought the 1995 Tour de France on a hill in Duitama, Colombia, while Lance Armstrong's fourth place at Valkenberg in 1998, on a day of wintry cold, was when his comeback from cancer moved him into the centre of the world cycling stage.

DISPUTES AND INTRIGUE

Intrigue and the world championships have always gone together, which is barely surprising given the conflicts of loyalty that occur every year when professionals are

RIGHT The start of the ninth world professional championship, in 1935 at Floreffe in Belgium. Six hours, five minutes later the home rider Jean Aerts would become the first man to take the rainbow jersey as an amateur and a professional.

made to change their trade-team jerseys for those of their nations. A domestique who rides all year for one master can hardly be expected to race against him on one given day, while there are times when it seems barely reasonable for a domestique to be made to work for a new master who was his sworn rival last week, and will be his sworn rival next week.

Speculation about who has done what for whom and why is a constant. The 2001 world title in Lisbon ended with a dispute among the Italians after Paolo Lanfranchi, who rode for the Mapei trade team, seemed to have chased down Gilberto Simoni, a Saeco man, in the finale, where Mapei's Spaniard Oscar Freire triumphed for the second time in three years. Similar insinuations were made after Vittorio Adorni won the title at Imola in 1968. The strongest rider in the race, Eddy Merckx, rode with Adorni in the Faema team; they had finished first and second in the Giro; and their Italian sponsor was desperate for a home win.

The accusations can be bitter indeed. The Russian Andrei Tchmil was labelled "Judas" by Belgian fans convinced that he should have assisted his trade-team leader Johan Museeuw at the 1993 title in Oslo. Andrea Tafi was vilified in Italy for an attack at the 1996 world title in Lugano which did for the chances of his leader – and trade-team rival – Michele Bartoli. Irish fans maintain that it was the failure of Holland's Steven Rooks to help his trade team-mate Sean Kelly in the sprint at Chambéry in 1989 that lost Kelly his best chance of a world title. Americans still wonder why Greg LeMond chased Jonathan Boyer when he broke away close to the finish at Goodwood in 1982. Such recriminations are nothing new. In 1938 at Valkenberg – the little town in Dutch Limburg that comes alive for the Amstel Gold every year, but which has hosted three controversial world championships – the favourite was Gino Bartali, who was expected to dominate on the Cauberg hill as he had in the Tour de France. But Bartali came nowhere behind the surprise winner Marcel Kint ("the Black Eagle"). He and his team-mates Vicini and Bini abandoned, and afterwards the Italian leader claimed, "Vicini and Bini only came here to make sure that I lost. It's a scandal!"

Even more controversial was the 1946 title, which went to the Swiss Hans Knecht. Kint had looked the likely winner when he broke away with two laps of the circuit at Zurich. But behind, the chase was led by none other than his young and highly talented team-mate Rik van Steenbergen, with Knecht on his wheel. Still more bizarrely, when Van Steenbergen and Knecht caught up Kint, Rik I did nothing to help his team-mate. Finally, just to muddy matters still more, Kint was unable to sprint for the finish because a spectator grabbed his saddle. The only conclusion that Belgian commentators could produce was that Van Steenbergen had been tempted by the strength of the Swiss franc.

The intricacies of who has done what for who require a Macchiavellian mind to follow, and were made more complex by the presence until the mid-1990s of individual stars from weak cycling nations, who might not win themselves, but could make others lose or win. Seamus Elliott of Ireland is the best example. In the 1963 world title at Renaix, he escaped with Tom Simpson, who offered him vast sums of money to work in the break. Elliott refused, claiming that he did not wish to work against his trade-team leader Rik van Looy.

The year before, in Salò, Elliott was effectively part of the French team – because his trade-team leader was Jacques Anquetil. The Dubliner spent the two nights before the race sharing a room with the French team manager Marcel Bidot, and slowed down the chasers behind Anquetil's team-mate Jean Stablinski as he made his escape for victory. Not that the favour was returned – it was later revealed that "Stab" had asked the others to work against Elliott when he had attacked with three laps to go.

National team leaders always have difficulty uniting two trade-team leaders in a common cause, when the rest of the year they are bitter rivals. Inevitably, the problem is felt worst in Italy, where polemica between champions is a way of life. Selecting and managing the national team in the days of Moser and Saronni, Coppi and Bartali called for colossal feats of diplomacy from managers like Alfredo Binda and Alfredo Martini.

Ever the rebel, Jacques Anquetil was adamant that he would have nothing to do with the system. On being told by a delighted French team manager that his arch rival Poulidor had agreed to help him in the 1965 title, he just grunted: "He said that did he? Then he's even more stupid than I thought."

COOPERATION VS RIVALRY

Sometimes, the greats actually enhance their stature by working together. Miguel Indurain was never more noble than when he helped his young Spanish team-

RIK VAN STEENBERGEN

"Rik I" to Van Looy's Rik II, Belgium's great star of the 1940s and early 1950s was a man with a remarkable record, considering that he only saw wins on the road in relation to the number of lucrative appearance contracts they could win him on the track. Unlike Van Looy or Merckx, Rik I raced all winter on the velodromes, and came out in spring to use his track speed to snatch a major result or two which would mean more work in the winter. As well as a remarkable triple of world titles, Rik I came close to winning the Giro d'Italia in 1951 – not bad for a non-climber – and got the better of Fausto Coppi in two remarkable classics, the 1952 Paris–Roubaix and the 1949 Flèche Wallonne.

One of cycling's true mercenaries, he would travel to Switzerland and return with his arms covered in watches to sell, and was said to use one pair of socks for an entire season. Bizarrely, for one so frugal, he was addicted to gambling, on which he frittered away his winnings.

NATIONALITY	Belgian
BORN	9 September 1924, Arendonk, Antwerp
NICKNAMES	the Boss; Rik I
PROFESSIONAL	1943–66
MAJOR WINS	
1943	Belgian national title.
1944	Tour of Flanders.
1945	Belgian national title.
1946	Tour of Flanders.
1948	Paris–Roubaix.
1949	World Road Championship; Flèche Wallonne.
1950	Paris–Brussels.
1952	Paris–Roubaix.
1954	Milan–San Remo; Belgian national title.
1956	World Road Championship.
1957	World Road Championship.
1958	Flèche Wallonne.

mate Abraham Olano, who rode for a rival trade team, to victory on a dank, drizzling day at Duitama in Colombia in 1995. Indurain, who had won the time trial title a few days earlier, crossed the line with his arms in the air a few seconds behind Olano. Sean Kelly made the same gesture a few metres behind Stephen Roche after the Dubliner clinched his incredible treble of Giro–Tour–world championship on the circuit in Villach, Austria, in 1987.

Sometimes, however, the greats simply disgrace themselves. The greatest cycling rivals, Bartali and Coppi, reached their nadir at Valkenberg in 1948 by refusing to race because it was simply too important that the other man lose. Victory was merely incidental. As the winning break of Bric Schotte, Lucien Teisseire, and Apo Lazarides rode away, Coppi and Bartali simply watched each other at the back of the bunch, impervious to the entreaties of the Italian fans and threats from the Italian Cycling Federation.

"They were like two villains who had done a robbery and were afraid that the other one would escape with the loot," wrote André Coste in *France-Soir*. Coppi explained: "Bartali had won the Tour de France which meant that I could afford less than ever to be beaten by him in the world championship. He just wanted to retain his popularity. All we could do was damage each other. When we learned the gap was 10 minutes, Bartali got worried: 'We should save our honour. Let's go, Fausto!' I said, 'I'm going to rest.'" The pair did a U-turn at the foot of the Cauberg, and were suspended for three months by the Italian Cycling Federation.

The curious tactics mean that the world championships become something of a lottery, where the normal ground rules of professional racing do not apply. Surprise winners are no longer a surprise in the Worlds. The 1985 championship, at Giavera del Montello, in Italy's cycling heartland of the Veneto, was one such, with Holland's Joop Zoetemelk sneaking away in the finale to win at the age of 38.

Sometimes the surprise is in a champion who manages to change register for a day, as happened to Johan Museeuw at Lugano in 1996. Museeuw was no climber, but for that single day the Flandrian made the climbs of the Cormano and Crespera his own. He infiltrated the winning break early on, and survived as the Italian *squadra* fell to bits behind, with its leaders squabbling and riding for themselves. "Who would have expected Museeuw to win?" asked the bitter Italian leader, Michele Bartoli. Who indeed? The course was too hilly for him, and the weekend before, after a disastrous Paris–Tours, he had announced that he was retiring.

Tom Simpson's cunning win in the Basque Country in 1965 – Britain's only victory in the professional road race – fell into the same category. Simpson was not high among the list of favourites, and when he escaped in the finale with Rudi Altig of Germany it was assumed that the German, a more rapid sprinter, would take gold. But Simpson "played dead" according to Altig, pretending that his legs were tiring and his strength fading, and he then surprised the German as he changed gear for the sprint.

Just up the Alpine road from Sallanches in 1989, Greg LeMond and Laurent Fignon re-fought their epic Tour de France on the rainsoaked Côte de la Montagnole, trading attack for attack before LeMond took the final sprint. The American had been saying for the entire day that he wanted to abandon, but the rainbow jersey – at the expense of a distraught Sean Kelly – clinched his comeback from near death in a shooting accident.

RIGHT A youthful Eddy Merckx, centre, enters the big time at Heerlen, Holland, in 1967. "The cannibal" has just won the first of his three professional titles. Jan Janssen, left, won silver on home soil; Ramon Saez, right, nicknamed "Tarzan", took a rare Spanish medal with his bronze.

A HISTORY OF CONTROVERSY

Sometimes a totally obscure figure wins. The late Rudy Dhaenens, winner in Japan in 1990, was a strong domestique who never did justice to the rainbow jersey. Most obscure of all, however, was Harm Ottenbros of Holland, world champion in 1969 on the Zolder motor-racing circuit in Belgium. Eddy Merckx was the favourite, but he was so heavily marked that he eventually just climbed off. Ottenbros escaped with Merckx's team-mate Julien Stevens, who was generally expected to take the sprint in front of the 150,000-strong Belgian crowd, who began celebrating well before the pair came into the finishing straight. But Stevens was tired, having tried to help Merckx earlier in the race, and Ottenbros won the sprint by 15 cm (6 in). Stevens burst into tears, and Ottenbros, from the nation the Belgians love to hate, had to be escorted to the podium by police.

Two venues have a particular history of controversial world championships: the little Dutch town of Valkenburg, and the Belgian town of Renaix, or Ronsse.

As well as Bartali and Coppi's mutual destruction in 1948, Valkenburg was also where Bartali's team-mates bizarrely deserted him 10 years before. 1979, however, saw controversy of a different kind.

That year's scandal involved team-mates helping their leader too zealously. In the early laps of the 275-km (172-mile) race, the Dutch television cameras filming the event repeatedly broadcast images of the Dutch team leaders, Jan Raas and Gerrie Knetemann, saving their strength by either being pushed up the Cauberg by their orange-jerseyed team-mates or holding on to their jerseys. Hinault saw it too, and stopped in the French team's cabin in the pit area to shout: "Raas and Knetemann are barely even pedalling on the climb."

JAN ULLRICH

Cycling commentators and former stars were almost unanimous that Jan Ullrich would win another five Tours de France after his dominant 1997 win, when he blew the field apart on the steep slope leading to the Arcalis ski station in Andorra and became the first German to triumph in "la Grande Boucle". Ullrich clearly has raw talent to burn. He finished the 1996 Tour, his first, in better shape than his team leader Bjarne Riis, and was capable of dominating races such as the 1999 Vuelta and Sydney Olympic road race in 2000.

However, he has continually fallen foul of his own lack of discipline. He has tended to gain weight in winter, making him vulnerable to illness and injury in spring, and as a result his Tour record is more reminiscent of Raymond Poulidor than Eddy Merckx. Additionally, in 2002 he blotted his copybook with a drunk driving charge and a positive test for amphetamines.

NATIONALITY	German
BORN	2 December 1973, Rostock
NICKNAME	the Kaiser
PROFESSIONAL	1995 to date
MAJOR WINS	
1993	(amateur): World Road Race Championship.
1996	Regio Tour.
1997	Tour de France; German national title.
1998	Rund um Berlin.
1999	Vuelta a España; World Time Trial Championship.
2000	Olympic road race title; Coppa Agostoni.
2001	German national title; Giro dell'Emilia; World Time Trial Championship.

Raas would go on to win an epic sprint from the German Dietrich Thurau, but the pushing and pulling was what grabbed the headlines. A race commissaire on a motorbike took a megaphone into the heart of the bunch to warn the Dutch leader, but no action was taken. The practice, which was widespread at the time among team leaders – a meeting among the Italians later that winter agreed that they would end it – was actually exposed because of a running dispute between the Dutch cyclists and the television station. The cyclists had refused to be interviewed at the Tour de France due to the reporting of a positive drug test for one of their number, Joop Zoetemelk, so the television reporters duly took their revenge.

Pushing of a different kind is what Renaix/Ronsse became famous for in 1963. The Belgian team at the championships had been stumbling from one crisis to another since 1957, due to continual conflicts between Rik I – Van Steenbergen – and the young pretender Rik II – Van Looy. By 1963 Rik II had become "the Emperor", twice a world champion, and King of the Classics. On home soil for what he hoped would be his third title, he had promised the team bonuses, but the day before they asked for more money: Van Looy walked out of the meeting, slamming the door behind him.

Van Looy was perfectly placed to win the title, reeling in Tom Simpson with 350 metres to go, just as he began his sprint for the line. Gilbert Desmet, who was supposed to lead him out, was nowhere to be seen. Another team-mate, Benoni Beheyt, was at the front, but Beheyt had earlier refused to lead out Van Looy, on the pretext that he was suffering from cramp.

In the final metres, Van Looy veered from one side of the road to the other, so that he and Beheyt came side by side to the line. As they did so, Beheyt put his hand on his leader's back and either fended him off, or pulled him backwards, depending on who you believe. Whether or not it was treachery barely mattered: it was treated as the ultimate betrayal by Van Looy, who used his influence to ensure that Beheyt made no money from his new status, and ended his career in obscurity.

RIGHT Claude Criquielion is outraged as he limps up the finishing straight in the main street of the town of Renaix, dragging his broken bike after coming a cropper in a close sprinting encounter with Steve Bauer of Canada. His lawsuit for assault against the Canadian would fail.

A quarter of a century later came the second "Renaix affair", again involving a Belgian favourite, this time Claude Criquielion, world champion four years earlier. As he and the Canadian Steve Bauer sprinted for the line with about 100 metres to go, "Criq" tried to come through the tiny gap between the Canadian and the crowd barriers. Bauer moved across slightly to block him. "Criq" persisted, and Bauer seemed to elbow him. The Belgian grazed a policeman, and hit a stanchion, falling to the ground. Bauer was put off, and the Italian Maurizio Fondriest raced to a surprise gold medal.

When "Criq" walked across the line, his mangled bike in his hand, he was in 11th place. "He deliberately made me fall," he alleged. Bauer was disqualified from the silver medal. "He was the one that ran into me first and lost his balance," insisted Bauer. Whatever, neither was world champion. Bauer had to be given protection by the Belgian police, while Criquielion took out a lawsuit for assault which was unsuccessful and smacked mainly of sour grapes.

Lugano, on the other hand, is famous for scandal of a different kind. The prosperous little Swiss border town north of Milan was where Fausto Coppi finally took the world title in 1953, over the same climbs where Johan Museeuw would triumph at the expense of the *squadra* 43 years later. It was a typical victory by the campionissimo: a lone escape with the rest of the field way behind, but it generated a photo that made the headlines. When Coppi stood on the podium to receive the rainbow jersey, the figure of an attractive dark-haired woman in a white coat could be made out behind him. "Coppi's Lady in White" was the headline in one of the Italian newspapers. For the first time, the liaison between the campionissimo and his mistress, "la Dama Bianca", both already married, was out in public.

It was a deeply symbolic moment. For many of Coppi's supporters, he would never race with the same intensity again, thanks to the malign influence of "the White Lady", they said. In Italy, the scandal would be immense, far more important than either of the Renaix affairs, because it had a dimension way beyond sport, symbolizing a nation on the cusp of a deeply Catholic past and a secular future.

RIGHT Fausto Coppi celebrates after winning his world title at Lugano in 1953, and peeping over his shoulder is "the White Lady", his mistress Giulia Occhini. Pictures of the pair a few minutes later on the podium would make their liaison public for the first time.

NATIONALITY	American
DATE OF BIRTH	18 September 1971, Plano, Texas
NICKNAME	Big Tex
PROFESSIONAL	8 August 1992 to date
PROFESSIONAL TEAMS	
1992–6	Motorola (USA)
1997	Cofidis (France)
1998–Present	US Postal Service
MAJOR WINS	
1993	World Road Championship; Laigueglia Trophy; US national championship (Tour of Philadelphia); K-Mart Classic.
1994	Thrift Drug Classic.
1995	San Sebastian Classic; DuPont Tour; West Virginia Mountain Classic.
1996	Flèche Wallonne; DuPont Tour.
1998	Tour of Lower Saxony; Tour of Luxembourg; Cascade Classic; 56K Criterium.
1999	Tour de France.
2000	Tour de France; Grand Prix des Nations; GP Eddy Merckx.
2001	Tour de France; Tour of Switzerland.
2002	Tour de France; Midi Libre; Dauphiné Libéré.
OTHER RESULTS	1998: Vuelta d'España, fourth; World Time Trial Championship, fourth. 2000: bronze medal, Olympic time trial.
	Tour de France: 15 stages; 45 days in yellow jersey.
	68 professional wins.

LANCE ARMSTRONG

On 25 July 1999, the Stars and Stripes flew over the Champs-Elysées to greet a unique winner of the Tour de France, a man who had completed a personal odyssey unmatched in sporting history, let alone that of cycling.

Lance Armstrong had completely outclassed the other 179 starters from day one, but this was eclipsed by his victory over life-threatening testicular cancer. As Armstrong's best-selling autobiography, *It's Not About the Bike*, was memorably to sum up: "The Tour was the least of the story."

A child who never knew his father and grew up close to his hardworking mother Linda, Armstrong was a precocious cycling talent. When he sprinted into Verdun in 1993, he was the youngest man to win a stage in the Tour de France since World War II, and two months later in Oslo he became one of a select handful of cyclists to become world champions while still under 22.

A CRUSHING BLOW

By 1996 he had become established as a top name in world cycling, winning two one-day Classics and a second stage in the Tour, and with a brash, confident personality to match. A long and lucrative career beckoned – until 3 October that year, when he was diagnosed with advanced cancer in his testicles, stomach, lungs, and brain. The tumours had been growing even as Armstrong dominated races such as the Flèche Wallonne and the DuPont Tour that year.

To his face, doctors told Armstrong he had a 40 per cent chance of recovery: in fact, they did not expect him to survive. Surgery and chemotherapy reduced the champion to a coughing, vomiting shadow of himself, with two crescent-shaped scars on his bald scalp where the brain lesions had been cut out.

"If I wasn't in pain I was vomiting, and if I wasn't vomiting I was thinking about what I had. Chemo was a burning in my veins, a matter of being slowly eaten from the inside out by a destroying river of pollutants," he wrote. And when he was at his lowest ebb, representatives of his new sponsor, the French finance firm Cofidis, turned up at his bedside to tell him that his salary was to be cut by three-quarters.

FIGHTING BACK TO FITNESS

Armstrong's rehabilitation was lengthy, and began from a point where, when he was out on his bike, women on shopping bikes could pedal sedately past the former world champion as he gasped for breath. But Armstrong had to come back to cycling. "When they told me about the cancer, I can't remember which hit me first: I might die, or I might lose my cycling career. I'm a cyclist, I was born to race a bike."

Even when declared cancer-free, and with the toxins of chemotherapy gone from his body, the mental scars remained alongside the patchwork of white burns from his treatment. Twice Armstrong temporarily gave up riding his bike, convinced that the cancer was returning. And by the end of 1997, no European team believed that he could return to the top. None would pay him a salary worthy of his former status.

But by the end of 1998, Armstrong had finished fourth in the Vuelta a España and the world championships, and in December that year he received an e-mail from his new team manager, the Belgian Johan Bruyneel, saying that he would look good in the yellow jersey of the Tour de France the next year.

VICTORY

His victory in the 1999 race was one of the most convincing of the decade, born of domination in the stages against the watch – all of which he won – and of one memorable escape to the Alpine ski station of Sestrière. Afterwards, he returned to the US to be greeted by Bill Clinton, and president-to-be George W. Bush.

A second victory in 2000, at the expense of the 1997 winner Jan Ullrich and the 1998 victor Marco Pantani, confirmed that Armstrong was cycling's new number one. His earnings were estimated at $7.5m, and he was worth $100,000 per speaking appearance. *It's Not About the Bike* topped the US best-seller lists. In 2001 he joined LeMond and Bobet with a hat trick, and in 2002 he added a fourth.

Stardom notwithstanding, Armstrong still saw himself as a man who had beaten cancer. "If you asked me to choose between winning the Tour de France and having cancer I would choose cancer," he writes, "… because of what it has done for me as a human being, a man, a husband, a son and a father."

LEFT: Lance Armstrong proudly carries the US flag on the Champs-Elysées after winning the 1999 Tour de France.

AUTUMN CLASSICS

As the nights close in, the curtain is drawn on the professional cycling year by two Classics, the run south-west through France from Paris to Tours, and the loop around northern Italy that is the Giro di Lombardia. Completely different in nature – Paris–Tours is pancake flat; Lombardia hilly, if not verging on the mountainous – they nonetheless have this in common: they offer struggling champions one last chance to resurrect their careers, and they have an end-of-term feel to them, as the cyclists bid each other farewell and prepare for their winter holidays.

Lombardy, autumn 2001: mists, mellow fruitfulness, and a group of 200 cyclists trundling along together during the early phase of the "Race of the Falling Leaves", final Classic of the season.

PARIS – TOURS

THE FINAL PHASE OF THE CYCLING YEAR OPENS WITH THE LENGTHY TREK SOUTH-WEST FROM PARIS TO THE CATHEDRAL CITY OF TOURS IN THE ONLY CLASSIC OF THE YEAR WHERE A BUNCH SPRINT IS THE RULE.

Autumn comes early to the plains south of Paris. By the first weekend of October, the fields ploughed for winter wheat are often flecked with frost and shrouded in mist, with shooting parties plodding through the mud as the peloton passes during the final French Classic of the year. The autumn winds push the cyclists south-westward, or blast the bunch to bits from the side, but most often just slow them down as they trudge towards the Loire Valley.

Team line-ups are sometimes just the minimum five or six riders: most are longing for the winter rest. The men of the Tour de France and Giro d'Italia are already on holiday, and it is only those who want to hone their skills for the world championships – held the following Sunday – or make up for a lacklustre year who make the effort to race between Paris and Tours.

Not that Paris–Tours is to be underestimated. It has been going since 1896, when the magazine *Paris-Vélo* announced the first race, intended – like Paris–Roubaix earlier the same year – to coincide with the opening of the local velodrome. It was an amateur event, open to bicycles, tricycles, tandems, triplets, and quadruples; every starter would receive a medal if they made it to Tours by 6 p.m.

The prizes for the 151 starters were eclectic: the winner received a classical statue of the young Jupiter, 1.4 metres (5 feet) high in bronze. The starters were also provided with coupons offering three months' free subscription to *Paris-Vélo*, which they could offer to the locals in exchange for assistance with repairs and so on if they hit difficulty en route.

The race's start, close to Paris' Porte Maillot, was disrupted by a carriage containing four ladies who were determined to pass through the line of cyclists waiting for the order to leave. The coach driver tried to force a passage with his whip, but was pulled out of his seat by one of the cyclists and forcibly made to go a different way.

The finish, in Tours' Avenue de Grammont, was attended by 12,000 people who blocked the road, so that the order of the surviving 42 cyclists had to be decided on the outskirts of town. "A crazy, unheard of, unhoped for success" said the headline in *Paris-Vélo*, but this did not guarantee its status. It was 1901 before the magazine organized the race again, then another five years before it was run again, this time by *l'Auto* – the newspaper responsible for running the first Tour de France. Since 1906 the race has remained in the stable of major French events run by *l'Auto*, its successor *l'Equipe*, and now the Tour's parent company Amaury Sport Organization.

THE SPRINTERS' CLASSIC

Paris–Tours no longer begins in Paris. The start is now to the south, in the little town of Saint Remy de Chevreuse. There are no hills, apart from a couple of little rises outside Tours, so the Avenue de Grammont remains the most distinctive feature of this Classic: a wide 3-km (1¾-mile) straight lined with trees, which is perfectly suited to a bunch sprint. And that is how France's last Classic of the year markets itself: the sprinters' race, a rapid run from Paris followed by a hectic cut and thrust up the Avenue.

Its relaunch as the sprinters' Classic followed a period of confusion between 1974 and 1987, when the race was run in the opposite direction, from the Loire Valley to Paris, as Blois–Chaville – the finish being in a small suburb of Paris – and the Grand Prix d'Automne. The change to the original route in 1988 has given it a proper identity, and the idea that the sprinters should have a Classic of their own has some merit, as there are Classics for climbers, cobble specialists, and "punchy" riders who like short steep climbs.

Appropriately, a chilly, still autumn day in 1994 saw a young German with a very outdated "mullet" haircut

RIGHT With the sprinting peloton only a few seconds behind, Richard Virenque makes his point to the world on the Avenue de Grammont in Tours as he scores the win in 2001 that will enable his career to continue after a lengthy drugs ban.

Saint-Arnoult-en-Yvelines

START

The Start
This was moved out of Paris early on, first to Versailles and finally to Saint Arnoult, about 50 km (30 miles) south-west of the French capital.

THE ROUTE

The "Sprinters' Classic" has known many variations, being run sometimes from Tours or the nearby chateau city of Blois to Paris or its suburbs, and sometimes being known as the Grand Prix d'Automne. Since 1988, however, it has kept to the set, traditional course to preserve its distinctive status as the only Classic where the sprinters can expect to shine. This is easy on paper, given the pancake flat route, but much depends on the morale of the domestiques, and the weather. South-westerly winds blow in the faces of the riders, making it relatively easy to keep breakaways within reach; a tail wind or crosswind makes it more likely that the field will split before the finish, usually on the exposed roads after Amboise or on the couple of tiny climbs before the race crosses the river Loire for the finish in Tours.

Chartres

Voves

Brou

Bonneval

KEY

Route

Calais **BELGIUM**
Lille
Paris
Tours
FRANCE

Le Gault-du-Perche

Saint Ago

Savigny-sur-Braye

Montoire-sur-la-Loire

Tours
Boasts the longest finish straight in any one-day cycling Classic: the tree-lined Avenue de Grammont is a mile and a half long – perfect for sprinters.

Chateau Renault

Amboise
In the heart of the chateaux of the Loire, the course crosses the river here.

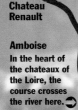

FINISH

Esvres-sur-Indre

Côte de Petit-Pas de l'Ane
"Donkey's footstep" hill is the only climb in the finale, a short burst up a lane above the banks of the Loire. It's the last chance for the non-sprinters to attack but is rarely tough enough to split the field.

ABOVE There was nothing mellow or fruitful about the 1921 Paris–Tours, run through a blizzard and won by the great Francis Pelissier, second of the three great French cycling brothers.

sprint up the Avenue in the pink colours of the Deutsche Telekom team. Few knew it then, but this was highly significant: the day that Erik Zabel scored the first major win of his career. He has since gone on to win the points jersey of the Tour de France a record six times, and has taken three victories in Milan–San Remo.

The Avenue de Grammont has not always seen bunch sprint finishes – far from it. In recent years, in fact, the tendency has been for a breakaway of one or two cyclists, with the bunch hot on their heels. And, particularly at this time of year, they are often men with a point to prove. The 2000 winner, Andrea Tafi of Italy, desperately wanted to show the world championship team selector, Antonio Fusi, that he had made a big mistake in leaving him out of the squadra, and duly won after a heroic late attack.

Most emphatic of all, however, was the 2001 victory by Richard Virenque, only the second French winner since 1956. Virenque had just returned from an eight-month ban for using drugs. In the spring, not a single team had wanted to hire him, due partly to his reputation, and partly because it was unclear whether he would race again at the highest level, so when he eventually landed a contract at the Domo-Farm Frites team, it was for the minimum wage, $1,100 (£800) a month.

Virenque started the 2001 Paris–Tours with no guarantee of employment for 2002, and launched an attack shortly after the start, together with the 1998 winner Jacky Durand, who has made suicide moves his speciality. It looked like a lunatic move that would simply earn the pair some valuable television time before the bunch closed in on them well before the finish. Neither the field nor the two riders believed the attack could succeed.

Instead, the bunch gave the pair too much rope and waited until too late to begin the chase. Durand fell back just outside Tours, but Virenque somehow managed to hang on, with the bunch in hot pursuit over the final kilometres. They were right on his heels as he crossed the line with his fist in the air and a great yell of anger. It was an epic win which did much for his credibility and pushed this autumn Classic back onto the front pages.

RIGHT Gino Bartali as the Italians love to remember him: crossing a mountain pass in the Giro d'Italia with the fans applauding his every pedal stroke.

GINO BARTALI

"Il Pio Gino" symbolized the links between cycling and Catholic culture, with his habit of attending mass every day during the Tour de France – no matter what the disruption to his daily routine – his nomination by the Vatican as a role model, his links with Catholic youth groups, and finally the little chapel he set up in a room of his home in Tuscany.

If Bartali is now defined largely by his rivalry with Fausto Coppi, he was also one of cycling's greatest climbers, winning the mountains jersey in the Giro and Tour on eight occasions. A champion of great longevity, he is the only cyclist to have won two Tours de France 10 years apart, and he remains one of the oldest Tour victors.

Incredibly, he won his first Italian national title in 1935, his last in 1952.

SAVIOUR OF THE STATE

His influence extended far beyond cycling. Ordered by Mussolini to go and win the 1938 Tour for the sake of Italian national pride, 10 years later he would save the state from collapse, following the attempted assassination of the Communist minister Palmiro Togliatti.

With the country in chaos, Bartali was personally telephoned at the start of the Alpine stages by the Italian Prime Minister, who asked if he could manage something to distract the restive masses. He went on to win the race,

thanks to a lone escape over the Izoard pass, Italy calmed down, and Togliatti's first words on coming out of his coma were "How is Bartali getting on?"

Bartali's name is also credited with saving 21 prisoners in the concentration camp at Dachau in 1943: "Do you know Bartali?" a guard asked a Florentine prisoner, Antonio Davitti. Davitti showed a photograph of the cyclist, and was asked to prepare a list of 20 men to be sent to the prison factory, not the gas chamber.

For half a century, Bartali remained an iconic figure in Italian cycling: shortly before his death he was asked what he would say to his great rival in paradise, and joked, "I'd prefer purgatory, there will be more hills there."

NATIONALITY	Italian
DATES	18 July 1914–5 May 2000
NICKNAMES	il Pio (the Pious One); the Iron Man
PROFESSIONAL	1935–54
MAJOR WINS	
1935	Italian national title; Tour of Basque Country.
1936	Giro d'Italia and King of the Mountains; Giro di Lombardia.
1937	Giro d'Italia & King of the Mountains; Italian national title; Giro del Piemonte.
1938	Tour de France and King of the Mountains.
1939	Milan–San Remo; Giro di Lombardia.
1940	Italian national title; Milan–San Remo; Giro di Lombardia.
1946	Giro d'Italia and King of the Mountains. Championship of Zurich; Tour of Switzerland.
1947	Milan–San Remo; Tour of Switzerland.
1948	Tour de France and King of the Mountains. Championship of Zurich.
1949	Tour de Romandie
1950	Milan–San Remo.
1951	Giro del Piemonte.
1952	Italian national title.
OTHER RESULTS	1939: Giro d'Italia, second. 1947: Giro d'Italia, second; 1949: Tour de France, second; Giro d'Italia, second. 1950: Giro d'Italia, second.
	Tour de France: 12 stage wins; 20 days in yellow jersey. Giro d'Italia: 17 stage wins; 50 days in pink jersey.

GIRO DI LOMBARDIA

FIRMLY ROOTED IN THE HILLS AROUND THE TWIN LAKES OF COMO AND LECCO, THE "RACE OF THE FALLING LEAVES" CLOSES THE CYCLING YEAR, JUST AS MILAN–SAN REMO STANDS FOR ITS OPENING.

One building symbolizes the end of the cycling season: a little chapel at a crossroads on a wooded hillside above Lake Como. The Madonna del Ghisallo, to whom the chapel is dedicated, was designated the protectress of cyclists by Pope Pius XII in 1949. Since then this has been the cyclists' chapel, and the close of another cycling year is heralded by the ringing of the bells to welcome the season's final Classic, the Giro di Lombardia, as it passes over the climb.

The chapel is crammed with cycling memorabilia. Bikes belonging to Coppi, Bartali, and Merckx; pink jerseys from the Giro, signed by the champions; yellow jerseys from the great days of the campionissimi. The cyclists' prayer before the altar asks the Madonna for health, safety when training, and fraternity among the two-wheeled brethren. Poignantly, a whole wall is covered with tiny photographs of cyclists who have died on the roads of Italy.

The climb up from the lake is smoothly tarmacked now, but it is steeped in cycling history. A 500-lire prize for the first cyclist to cross the summit was what tempted Alfredo Binda to make the leap from amateur racing in Nice to professionalism in 1924: he won the "prime" and never looked back. The following year he returned, in bitter cold and pouring rain, and won alone, eating 28 raw eggs en route that were handed up by friends he had placed in strategic positions along the course.

The Ghisallo is the last link with the race's distant past, and in recent years has seen farce – Tony Rominger fell off on the descent en route to victory in 1992 while attempting to urinate on the move – and symbolism, such as Sean Kelly's attack on the "Super-Ghisallo", a narrow lane rearing up from the descent after the chapel, which gave him his second Lombardy win in the autumn of his career in 1991.

The Giro di Lombardia is not Italy's oldest race: that honour falls to Milan–Turin, first run in 1876, dropped for 20 years, but still going now and run four days before Lombardy. Together with the Giro del Piemonte, the three races now form an elegant triptych to close the cycling year. Lombardy has a greater significance, though: it was Italy's first major international race, predating both Milan–San Remo and the Giro d'Italia.

In the early 1900s there was a common awareness in Italy that a major event was needed to develop the nation's cycling. Milan–Turin existed, but there were doubts about the quality of its organization. Other events had come and gone: Rome–Naples–Rome; Milan–Mantua; a Giro del Veneto. A Giro di Lombardy was proposed in 1903, but the difficulty lay with the region's roads. They were little more than mule tracks.

The course was devised in the winter of 1904–5, and was anxiously inspected by the cyclists: there were places where they had to push their machines for hundreds of metres at a time. In other places the tracks were barely 45 cm (18 in) wide. Between Milan and Lodi, the route used a tram track.

Passo Intelvi
The high point of the route most commentators regard as the definitive one, from Milan to Como via the mountains around the two lakes. This spectacular pass with its pink cobble stones, rising to 760 m (2,500 feet) above sea level, was often the key point.

Varese
START

Como
The finish from 1961 to 1984, often on the banked concrete velodrome by the lake, with the decisive action usually coming on the little hill of San Fermo della Battaglia, just outside town. The start point until 1990.

Zurich
SWITZERLAND
Geneva
Milan
ITALY
Bologna
Nice

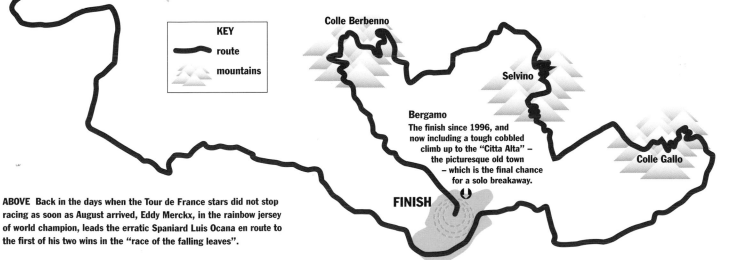

Madonna del Ghisallo
This climb from the shores of Lake Lecco is a hallowed place in Italian cycling, with a chapel at the summit dedicated to cyclists that contains souvenirs donated by the greats of the sport. It's also the only climb left in the race from the traditional route in the mountains around the two lakes.

Como

Lake Lecco

Lecco

THE ROUTE
Traditionally the route for the "Race of the Falling Leaves" included either Milan or Como, where the race started and finished from 1961 to 1990. For the next five years start and finish were in the town of Monza, of motor-racing fame, before the move to a start in Varese and a finish in Bergamo, as shown here in the 2002 map.

KEY

—— route

mountains

Colle Berbenno

Selvino

Bergamo
The finish since 1996, and now including a tough cobbled climb up to the "Citta Alta" – the picturesque old town – which is the final chance for a solo breakaway.

Colle Gallo

FINISH

ABOVE Back in the days when the Tour de France stars did not stop racing as soon as August arrived, Eddy Merckx, in the rainbow jersey of world champion, leads the erratic Spaniard Luis Ocana en route to the first of his two wins in the "race of the falling leaves".

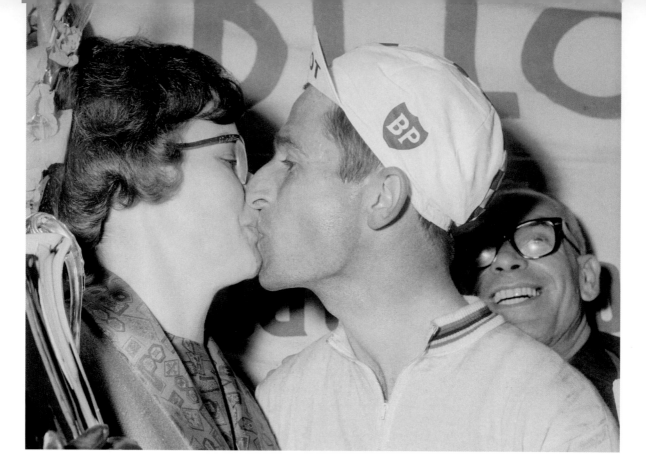

The route has gone through many incarnations since then. The finish on the velodrome in Como was a fixture for many years. Milan has hosted the finish, and so has the grim little town of Monza, to the north. Currently the route is fixed between Varese to the west and Bergamo to the east, with the hills around Bergamo offering a test that can split the field, but not to excess. The great passes around Lake Como, such as the Valico di Esino Lario, which were used until the mid-1990s, are now considered too tough.

THE RACE OF THE FALLING LEAVES

Lone victories and bad weather are common phenomena in the event the Italians call "the Race of the Falling Leaves". Winter is just around the corner, and sometimes snow can be seen flecking the Alpine peaks to the north. Lombardy is notorious for its fog, but cold rain often hits the race. Binda's first victory, in 1925, was, he recalled, "on a day so cold and wet that bending your arm to get something out of a jersey pocket was a victory in itself".

On one extremely wet day, during the 1992 race, the leaves themselves played a defining role. The local rider and newly crowned world champion Gianni Bugno was the favourite, and the route had been rearranged to finish in his home town of Monza, just north of Milan. But Bugno was a nervous character, and could not cope

with the descents, which had been turned into skating rinks by the fallen leaves and the heavy rain, and retired.

The consummate champion of Lombardy remains Fausto Coppi, whose four successive victories between 1946 and 1949, lone wins with the opposition trailing far behind, epitomized the campionissimo's greatest years. On the other hand, his defeat on the Vigorelli velodrome in Milan by the sprinter Andre Darrigade in 1956 was the last time he made a meaningful contribution to a major race.

Coppi was 37, and was riding partly to publicize his own brand of bikes. He desperately needed a major win to re-establish his reputation in Italy after his divorce. He attacked on the Ghisallo, was only caught on the outskirts of Milan by a large chasing group, and led the sprint on the Vigorelli from 500 metres. Just two metres from the line, Darrigade surged past. The campionissimo collapsed in tears: from then on his career was in slow decline as he struggled to keep up with the younger men while refusing to retire.

Sean Kelly is also indelibly associated with the race. The 1983 finish, a tight sprint in Como between Kelly, Greg LeMond, Adri van der Poel, Hennie Kuiper, and Francesco Moser, was where the Irishman's reign as

"King of the Classics" began: he would be unstoppable for the next four years. 1991 was also Kelly's year. He broke away on a new climb, the viciously steep "Super-Ghisallo", and outsprinted the Frenchman Martial Gayant to produce his unique victory salute – arms thrown back behind his head – in Monza's Viale dell'Industria, which was as unromantic as it sounds.

That year Kelly had overcome a broken collarbone which put him out of the Classics, a mass illness in his PDM team which had ended his Tour de France, and the death of his elder brother. The final straw could have been a crash while training: a car knocked him off and injured his knee. In the early miles of Lombardy he came close to climbing off his bike, but kept going merely to see what happened. On such tiny things do great wins turn.

Bernard Hinault had an epic lone win in 1984, marking the resurgence of "the Badger" after his knee operation of 1983. The following year he would go on to equal Merckx and Anquetil by winning his fifth Tour de France. Tony Rominger's lengthy lone break into Milan in 1989 was when his career, which would include a hat trick in the Vuelta a España, truly took off. In 1993, a smiling Swiss named Pascal Richard relaunched his career in the race, and would go on three years later to win the first Olympic road title open to professionals. Much is now expected of the 2001 winner: the blonde haired Italian Danilo di Luca, whose film-star looks have earned him the nickname "Di Caprio".

The finest achievement in Lombardy is victory while wearing the world champion's rainbow jersey, now awarded just the week before. The rainbow stripes make the wearer highly visible and easily marked by the opposition, who know the world champion's is a good wheel to follow. This makes the "double" a rare feat, most recently managed by the Swiss Oscar Camenzind in 1998, following in the wheelmarks of Binda in 1931, Tom Simpson in 1965, and Eddy Merckx in 1971.

EFFORT AND EXULTATION

The little chapel surrounded by the avid fans, the tifosi, on a Saturday in October underlines the fact that in racing up the climb from the lake, these men are continuing a cycling tradition that goes back almost a century. Overlooking the lake and the distant Alps is a bust of Coppi, whose exploits on these roads can never be equalled, and who remains Italian cycling's most evocative and tragic figure.

The bust's inscription sums up why the tifosi are here to yell at their heroes as they pass, why they flock to the Turchino pass to welcome the cycling season when it starts in March with Milan–San Remo, and why they and their fellows around Europe line roadsides every weekend of the intervening months. "God created the bicycle for men to use as an instrument of effort and exaltation on the hard road of life." Memorabilia inside for the past, hard racing outside for the present, and as eloquent a statement of cycling's purpose as you can get. For another year, the effort and exaltation are over. But next year, the tifosi will be back.

TOM SIMPSON

Much loved across Europe for his daring and charisma, Simpson has a place in sporting history as the only Briton to win the World Road Championship, and the only rider to die on the roads of the Tour de France with drugs in his veins. Born to a mining family in Co Durham, Simpson adapted seamlessly to racing in Europe, and produced a string of major wins, which no Briton has yet come close to matching. His finest win was probably the 1965 Giro di Lombardia, which he won alone in the manner of his early hero Fausto Coppi while wearing the rainbow jersey of world champion.

Simpson was a man of searing wit and wild dreams, whose ambitions included owning a vintage train and a plane. He was also courageous and often drove his body beyond its limits. Finally, he went too far while trying to stay with the leaders on the Mont Ventoux in the 1967 Tour de France. The cocktail of alcohol and amphetamines in his system killed him.

NATIONALITY	British
DATES	30 November 1937–13 July 1967
NICKNAMES	Four-stone Coppi; Major Simpson
PROFESSIONAL	August 1959–July 1967
MAJOR WINS	
1961	Tour of Flanders.
1963	Bordeaux–Paris.
1964	Milan–San Remo.
1965	World Road Championship; Giro di Lombardia; London–Holyhead.
1967	Paris–Nice.

NATIONALITY	Italian
DATES	15 Sept 1919–2 Jan 1960
NICKNAME	il campionissimo
PROFESSIONAL	1940–59
PROFESSIONAL TEAMS	1940: Legnano. 1940–42 and 1945–55: Bianchi. 1956–7: Carpano-Coppi. 1958–9: Bianchi.
MAJOR WINS	
1940	Giro d'Italia.
1941	Giro di Toscana; Giro del Veneto; Giro dell'Emilia; Tre Valle Varesine.
1942	Italian national championship.
1946	Milan–San Remo; Giro di Lombardia; Giro di Romagna; GP des Nations.
1947	Italian national championship; Giro di Lombardia; Giro d'Italia; Giro di Romagna; Giro del Veneto; Giro dell'Emilia; GP des Nations.
1948	Milan–San Remo; Giro di Lombardia; Tre Valle Varesine; Giro dell'Emilia.
1949	Italian national championship; Tour de France and King of the Mountains; Giro d'Italia and King of the Mountains; Milan–San Remo; Giro di Lombardia; Giro di Romagna; Giro del Veneto.
1950	Paris–Roubaix; Fleche Wallonne.
1952	Tour de France and King of the Mountains; Giro d'Italia and King of the Mountains.
1953	World Road Championship.
1954	Giro di Lombardia; Giro di Campania.
1955	Italian national championship; Giro dell'Appennino; Tre Valle Varesine.
OTHER RESULTS:	1946: Giro d'Italia, second; 1955: Giro d'Italia, second. World hour record 1942 – 45.871 km.
	Tour de France: nine stage wins; 19 days in yellow jersey. Giro d'Italia: 22 stage wins.
	158 wins as a professional.

FAUSTO COPPI

Italian cycling is still overshadowed by the tortured figure of "il campionissimo", whose epic solo victories, painful injuries, controversial private life and tragic early death have spawned a minor industry of books, magazines and films.

Fausto Coppi was born of peasant farming stock in Liguria, delivered sausages on his bike as a boy, and turned professional at 20, winning his first Giro in 1940. The war intervened – although before joining up he managed to break the world hour record as bombs fell on Milan – and he was captured and imprisoned by the English in North Africa.

THE LEGENDARY DOUBLES

His greatest years were 1949, when he became the first rider to win the Giro d'Italia and Tour de France in the same year, and 1952, when he repeated the feat. His first "double" included a legendary escape across the Alps to destroy Bartali in the Giro, and an epic comeback in the Tour after a crash in Brittany left him 36 minutes behind the leader Jacques Marinelli.

In utter depression, he threatened to quit the race, and was only made to stay by the pleading of the Italian team manager Alfredo Binda. In Paris, Marinelli would be 25 minutes behind. Bartali was almost 11 minutes back: out of consideration for his great rival, Coppi did not seek to stretch his lead further.

Coppi rides alone to the stage win in Briancon during the 1951 Tour de France, which he started against his will shortly after the tragic death of his brother Serse. A memorial on the bleak scree of the Col d'Izoard, where this picture is taken, commemorates the "campionissimo".

Three years later, his second "double" was clinched with a 52-mile escape across the Alps to win at the Sestriere ski resort, and also included the first stage win at the ski resort of l'Alpe d'Huez. At the finish in Paris, the runner-up, Stan Ockers, was 28 minutes behind, which remains the biggest winning margin in the Tour since World War II. So outrageous was his dominance that the organisers had to double the prize for second place to restore some interest in the race.

INSPIRATIONAL STYLE

Coppi's perfect style on the bike inspired lyrical prose, such as this from Tour winner turned journalist André Leducq in 1949: "He seems to caress the handlebars, while his torso seems fixed by screws in the saddle. His long legs stretch to the pedals like the limbs of a gazelle. At the end of each pedal stroke his ankles flex with a grace which it would be wonderful to analyse in slow motion on a cinema screen. All the moving parts turn as if in oil. His long face is like a knifeblade as he climbs with no apparent effort, like a great artist painting a water colour."

SCANDAL

After becoming Italy's biggest sporting star following his battles with Gino Bartali, Coppi scandalized the country by his love affair with a doctor's wife, Giulia Occhini, immortalized as "the white lady". Both were already married, convulsing Catholic Italy: they were excommunicated, thrown briefly into prison for adultery, and "la dama bianca" was forced to leave the country in order to have Coppi's children.

On 2 January 1960, Coppi died from malaria, which he had caught on a hunting trip in Africa, and which was not diagnosed until too late. His home at Castellania in Liguria, where thousands gathered for the funeral, is now a museum dedicated to his memory.

HIS RUN OF BAD LUCK

29 June 1942: training crash in Turin – broken collarbone.
2 June 1950: crash during Vicenza–Primolano stage of Giro – broken pubis.
11 March 1951: crash at finish of Milan–Turin – broken collarbone.
29 June, 1951: death of brother Serse from head injuries after crash in Giro del Piemonte.
7 August 1952: crash on track in Perpignan – broken shoulder blade.
7 July 1954: hit by wheel falling off a lorry while training near Pavia – twisted knee, broken skull.
1956: crash during Mantova–Rimini stage of the Giro d'Italia – sprained Achilles, dislocated vertebra.
1 March 1957: crash in criterium at Sassari – broken leg (femur).

ALL THE WINNERS

This section lists the winners of the races described in the book (years when the races were not run have been omitted), with an additional section on the Olympic Games road race, as this event is now open to professionals, plus a brief guide to the various season-long competitions that have been intended to decide the best cyclist in a given year.

TOUR DE FRANCE

YEAR	WINNER	TIME (hour-min-sec)	DISTANCE (km)
1900			
1903	Maurice Garin (Fra)	94.33.00	2,428
1904	Henri Cornet (Fra)	96.05.00	2,388
1905	Louis Trousselier (Fra)	112.18.09	2,975
1906	Rene Pottier (Fra)	185.47.26	4,637
1907	Lucien Petit-Breton (Fra)	156.22.30	4,488
1908	Lucien Petit-Breton (Fra)	156.09.31	4,488
1909	Francois Faber (Lux)	156.55.10	4,497
1910			
1910	Octave Lapize (Fra)	163.52.38	4,700
1911	Gustave Garrigou (Fra)	195.35.25	5,544
1912	Odile Defraye (Bel)	184.50.00	5,229
1913	Philippe Thys (Bel)	197.54.00	5,387
1914	Philippe Thys (Bel)	200.28.49	5,414
1919	Firmin Lambot (Bel)	231.07.15	5,560
1920			
1920	Philippe Thys (Bel)	228.36.00	5,503
1921	Leon Scieur (Bel)	221.50.00	5,484
1922	Firmin Lambot (Bel)	222.08.06	5,378
1923	Henri Pelissier (Fra)	222.15.30	5,386
1924	Ottavio Bottechia (Ita)	226.18.21	5,427
1925	Ottavio Bottechia (Ita)	219.10.13	5,430
1926	Lucien Buysse (Bel)	238.44.25	5,475
1927	Nicolas Frantz (Lux)	198.16.42	5,348
1928	Nicolas Frantz (Lux)	192.48.58	5,377
1929	Maurice Dewaele (Bel)	186.39.16	5,286
1930			
1930	Andre Leducq (Fra)	172.12.10	4,818
1931	Antonin Magne (Fra)	177.10.03	5,095
1932	Andre Leducq (Fra)	154.11.49	4,502
1933	Georges Speicher (Fra)	147.51.37	4,395
1934	Antonin Magne (Fra)	147.03.58	4,363
1935	Romain Maes (Bel)	141.32.00	4,302
1936	Sylvere Maes (Bel)	142.47.32	4,442
1937	Roger Lapebie (Fra)	138.58.31	4,415
1938	Gino Bartali (Ita)	148.29.12	4,694
1939	Sylvere Maes (Bel)	132.03.17	4,224
1940			
1947	Jean Robic (Fra)	148.11.25	4,648
1948	Gino Bartali (Ita)	147.10.36	4,813
1949	Fausto Coppi (Ita)	149.40.49	4,813
1950			
1950	Ferdi Kubler (Swi)	145.36.56	4,776
1951	Hugo Koblet (Swi)	142.20.14	4,474
1952	Fausto Coppi (Ita)	151.57.20	4,707
1953	Louison Bobet (Fra)	129.23.25	4,479
1954	Louison Bobet (Fra)	140.06.50	4,855
1955	Louison Bobet (Fra)	130.29.26	4,495

YEAR	WINNER	TIME (hour-min-sec)	DISTANCE (km)
1956	Roger Walkowiak (Fra)	124.01.16	4,528
1957	Jacques Anquetil (Fra)	135.44.42	4,665
1958	Charly Gaul (Lux)	116.59.05	4,319
1959	Federico Bahamontes (Spa)	113.50.54	4,363
1960			
1960	Gastone Nencini (Ita)	112.08.42	4,172
1961	Jacques Anquetil (Fra)	122.01.33	4,394
1962	Jacques Anquetil (Fra)	114.31.54	4,274
1963	Jacques Anquetil (Fra)	113.30.05	4,141
1964	Jacques Anquetil (Fra)	127.09.44	4,505
1965	Felice Gimondi (Ita)	116.42.06	4,176
1966	Lucien Aimar (Fra)	117.34.21	4,329
1967	Roger Pingeon (Fra)	136.53.50	4,780
1968	Jan Janssen (Ned)	133.49.42	4,675
1969	Eddy Merckx (Bel)	116.16.02	4,102
1970			
1970	Eddy Merckx (Bel)	119.31.49	4,367
1971	Eddy Merckx (Bel)	96.45.14	3,689
1972	Eddy Merckx (Bel)	108.17.18	3,847
1973	Luis Ocana (Spa)	122.25.34	4,140
1974	Eddy Merckx (Bel)	116.16.58	4,098
1975	Bernard Thévenet (Fra)	114.35.31	3,999
1976	Lucien van Impe (Bel)	116.22.23	4,016
1977	Bernard Thévenet (Fra)	115.38.30	4,000
1978	Bernard Hinault (Fra)	108.18.00	4,103
1979	Bernard Hinault (Fra)	103.06.50	4,108
1980			
1980	Joop Zoetemelk (Ned)	109.19.14	3,996
1981	Bernard Hinault (Fra)	96.19.38	3,740
1982	Bernard Hinault (Fra)	92.08.46	3,573
1983	Laurent Fignon (Fra)	105.07.52	3,750
1984	Laurent Fignon (Fra)	112.03.40	3,900
1985	Bernard Hinault (Fra)	113.24.23	4,006
1986	Greg LeMond (USA)	110.35.19	3,833

TOUR FACTS AND FIGURES

- Winning margins: the smallest margin of victory remains Greg LeMond's eight-second victory over Laurent Fignon in 1989. The biggest margin was that of Maurice Garin in the first Tour – 2 hours, 49 minutes, 45 sec – but since World War II, the most decisive victory was that of Fausto Coppi in 1952, with 28 min, 17 sec in hand on Stan Ockers of Belgium.

- The quickest ever Tour stage dates back to Chris Boardman's victory in the 1994 prologue time trial: 55.152 kph (34.47 mph) for the 4.5 miles. The quickest road race stage ever was won by Mario Cipollini, between Laval and Blois in 1999, at 50.355 kph, (31.47 mph) for the 122 miles.

- The record for the greatest number of stage wins in a single Tour is eight, held by Charles Pelissier (1930), Eddy Merckx (1970 and 1974), and Freddy Maertens (1976).

YEAR	WINNER	TIME (hour-min-sec)	DISTANCE (km)
1987	Stephen Roche (Ire)	115.27.42	4,235
1988	Pedro Delgado (Spa)	84.27.53	3,300
1989	Greg LeMond (USA)	87.38.35	3,250
1990			
1990	Greg LeMond (USA)	90.43.20	3,449
1991	Miguel Indurain (Spa)	101.01.20	3,915
1992	Miguel Indurain (Spa)	100.49.30	3,983
1993	Miguel Indurain (Spa)	95.57.09	3,720
1994	Miguel Indurain (Spa)	103.38.38	3,972

YEAR	WINNER	TIME (hour-min-sec)	DISTANCE (km)
1995	Miguel Indurain (Spa)	92.44.59	3,535
1996	Bjarne Riis (Den)	95.57.16	3,753
1997	Jan Ullrich (Ger)	100.30.35	3,942
1998	Marco Pantani (Ita)	92.50.17	3,850
1999	Lance Armstrong (USA)	91.32.16	3,687
2000			
2000	Lance Armstrong (USA)	92.33.08	3,662
2001	Lance Armstrong (USA)	86.17.28	3,453
2002	Lance Armstrong (USA)	82.05.12	3,278

MILAN–SAN REMO

YEAR	WINNER	DISTANCE (km)	AV. SPEED (kph)
1900s			
1907	Lucien Petit Breton (Fra)	281	26.206
1908	Cyrille van Hauwert (Bel)	281	25.108
1909	Luigi Ganna (It)	281	30.420
1910	Eugène Christophe (Fra)	281	23.330
1911	Gustave Garrigou (Fra)	281	29.570
1912	Henri Pelissier (Fra)	281	29.722
1913	Odile Defraye (Bel)	281	31.143
1914	Ugo Agostoni (It)	281	27.200
1915	Ezio Corlaita (It)	281	27.263
1917	Gaetano Belloni (It)	281	22.500
1918	Costante Girardengo (It)	281	24.279
1919	Angelo Gremo (It)	281	24.800
1920			
1920	Gaetano Belloni (It)	281	30.317
1921	Costante Girardengo (It)	281	30.105
1922	Giovanni Brunero (It)	281	27.293
1923	Costante Girardengo (It)	281	27.996
1924	Pietro Linari (It)	281	26.400
1925	Costante Girardengo (It)	281	27.722
1926	Costante Girardengo (It)	281	29.284
1927	Pietro Chiesi (It)	281	29.485
1928	Costante Girardengo (It)	281	24.680
1929	Alfredo Binda (It)	281	31.628
1930			
1930	Michele Mara (It)	269	29.485
1931	Alfredo Binda (It)	281	29.843
1932	Alfredo Bovet (It)	281	34.432
1933	Learco Guerra (It)	281	36.138
1934	Jos Demuysère (Bel)	281	35.978
1935	Giuseppe Olmo (It)	281	36.089
1936	Angelo Varetto (It)	281	36.479
1937	Cesare del Cancia (It)	281	37.408
1938	Giuseppe Olmo (It)	281	38.517
1939	Gino Bartali (It)	281	37.386
1940			
1940	Gino Bartali (It)	286	36.670
1941	Pierino Favalli (It)	281	36.155
1942	Adolfo Leoni (It)	281	34.469
1943	Cino Cinelli (It)	281	34.753
1946	Fausto Coppi (It)	292	35.940
1947	Gino Bartali (It)	285	33.300
1948	Fausto Coppi (It)	281	37.284
1949	Fausto Coppi (It)	290	39.397
1950			
1950	Gino Bartali (It)	282	38.853

THE ITALIAN DOUBLE

Reflecting a period of dominance over a whole season, the "Italian double" of Milan–San Remo and Giro di Lombardia was most frequent in the early years of cycling, with Costante Girardengo (1921), Michele Mara (1930), Alfredo Binda (1931), and Gino Bartali all managing the feat. Post-war, Fausto Coppi managed this double an incredible three times in 1946, 1948, and 1949. Inevitably, the only cyclist to manage it since then is Eddy Merckx, in 1971 and 1972.

YEAR	WINNER	DISTANCE (km)	AV. SPEED (kph)
1951	Loulson Bobet (Fra)	282	37.578
1952	Loretto Petrucci (It)	282	38.270
1953	Loretto Petrucci (It)	282	40.340
1954	Rik van Steenbergen (Bel)	282	39.344
1955	German Derycke (Bel)	282	39.927
1956	Alfred de Bruyne (Bel)	281	40.415
1957	Miguel Poblet (Spain)	282	40.667
1958	Rik van Looy (Bel)	282	42.176
1959	Miguel Poblet (Spain)	281	41.575
1960			
1960	René Privat (Fra)	288	42.640
1961	Raymond Poulidor (Fra)	288	34.474
1962	Emile Daems (Bel)	288	42.342
1963	Joseph Groussard (Fra)	288	41.178
1964	Tom Simpson (GB)	288	43.420
1965	Arie den Hertog (Hol)	287	41.641
1966	Eddy Merckx (Bel)	288	43.182
1967	Eddy Merckx (Bel)	288	44.805
1968	Rudi Altiig (Ger)	288	41.945
1969	Eddy Merckx (Bel)	288	43.425
1970			
1970	Michele Dancelli (It)	288	43.976
1971	Eddy Merckx (Bel)	288	39.152
1972	Eddy Merckx (Bel)	288	43.909
1973	Roger de Vlaeminck (Bel)	288	41.782
1974	Felice Gimondi (It)	288	42.533
1975	Eddy Merckx (Bel)	288	37.530
1976	Eddy Merckx (Bel)	288	42.015
1977	Jan Raas (Hol)	288	42.986
1978	Roger de Vlaeminck (Bel)	288	42.386
1979	Roger de Vlaeminck (Bel)	288	40.588
1980			
1980	Pierino Gavazzi (It)	288	42.972
1981	Alfons de Wolf (Bel)	288	43.081
1982	Marc Gomez (Fra)	294	41.584

YEAR	WINNER	DISTANCE (km)	AV. SPEED (kph)
1983	Giuseppe Saronni (It)	294	41.216
1984	Francesco Moser (It)	294	39.871
1985	Hennie Kuiper (Hol)	294	38.636
1986	Sean Kelly (Ire)	294	42.126
1987	Erich Maechler (Swi)	294	41.913
1988	Laurent Fignon (Fra)	294	41.376
1989	Laurent Fignon (Fra)	297	41.181

1990

YEAR	WINNER	DISTANCE (km)	AV. SPEED (kph)
1990	Gianni Bugno (It)	294	45.806
1991	Claudio Chiappucci (It)	294	42.342
1992	Sean Kelly (Ire)	294	39.052

YEAR	WINNER	DISTANCE (km)	AV. SPEED (kph)
1993	Maurizio Fondriest (It)	297	39.989
1994	Giorgio Furlan (It)	294	41.445
1995	Laurent Jalabert (Fra)	294	43.519
1996	Gabriele Colombo (It)	294	41.995
1997	Eric Zabel (Ger)	294	42.223
1998	Eric Zabel (Ger)	294	41.001
1999	Andrei Tchmil (Bel)	294	42.752

2000

YEAR	WINNER	DISTANCE (km)	AV. SPEED (kph)
2000	Eric Zabel (Ger)	294	40.882
2001	Eric Zabel (Ger)	287	38.852
2002	Mario Cipollini (It)	287	43.105

NORTHERN CLASSICS

TOUR OF FLANDERS

YEAR	WINNER	DISTANCE (km)	AV. SPEED (kph)
1910			
1913	Paul Deman (Bel)	324	26.880
1914	Marcel Buysse (Bel)	280	27.097
1919	H. van Lerberghe (Bel)	203	26.421
1920			
1920	Jules van Hevel (Bel)	248	26.105
1921	Rene Vermandel (Bel)	250	25.168
1922	Leon de Vos (Bel)	253	27.956
1923	Henri Suter (Swi)	243	27.956
1924	Gerard Debaets (Bel)	284	27.528
1925	Julien Delbecque (Bel)	228	25.680
1926	Denis Verschueren (Bel)	217	30.104
1927	Gerard Debaets (Bel)	205	27.528
1928	Jan Mertens (Bel)	225	32.530
1929	Josef Dervaes (Bel)	216	30.713
1930			
1930	Frans Bonduel (Bel)	227	32.199
1931	Romain Gijssels (Bel)	227	33.058
1932	Romain Gijssels (Bel)	227	32.506
1933	Alfonse Schepers (Bel)	227	33.139
1934	Gaston Rebry (Bel)	239	33.172
1935	Louis Duerloo (Bel)	260	34.899
1936	Louis Hardiquest (Bel)	250	33.333
1937	Michel D'hooghe (Bel)	267	35.679
1938	Edgar de Caluwe (Bel)	260	33.766
1939	Karel Kaers (Bel)	230	35.204
1940			
1940	Achiel Buysse (Bel)	211	34.972
1941	Achiel Buysse (Bel)	198	35.148
1942	Bric Schotte (Bel)	226	34.242
1943	Achiel Buysse (Bel)	205	33.424
1944	Rik van Steenbergen (Bel)	224	35.091
1945	Sylvain Grysolle (Bel)	222	34.961
1946	Rik van Steenbergen (Bel)	275	37.062
1947	Emiel Faignaert (Bel)	275	38.823
1948	Bric Schotte (Bel)	257	38.263
1949	Fiorenzo Magni (Ita)	268	36.462
1950			
1950	Fiorenzo Magni (Ita)	273	33.090
1951	Fiorenzo Magni (Ita)	274	35.503
1952	Roger Decock (Bel)	258	34.630
1953	Wim van Est (Hol)	253	34.578
1954	Raymond Impanis (Bel)	255	33.774

YEAR	WINNER	DISTANCE (km)	AV. SPEED (kph)
1955	Louison Bobet (Fra)	263	35.302
1956	Jean Forestier (Fra)	238	38.690
1957	Fred de Bruyne (Bel)	240	40.223
1958	Germain Derijcke (Bel)	239	37.602
1959	Rik van Looy (Bel)	242	38.823
1960			
1960	Arthur de Cabooter (Bel)	227	38.693
1961	Tom Simpson (GB)	255	40.052
1962	Rik van Looy (Bel)	256	38.823
1963	Noel Foré (Bel)	249	40.683
1964	Rudi Altig (Ger)	236	40.990
1965	Jo de Roo (Hol)	235	40.577
1966	Ward Sels (Bel)	243	41.303
1967	Dino Zandegu (Ita)	245	39.050
1968	Walter Godefroot (Bel)	249	42.443
1969	Eddy Merckx (Bel)	259	40.984
1970			
1970	Eric Leman (Bel)	255	41.406
1971	Evert Dolman (Hol)	268	43.225
1972	Eric Leman (Bel)	250	41.152
1973	Eric Leman (Bel)	260	41.379
1974	Cees Bal (Hol)	256	41.513
1975	Eddy Merckx (Bel)	225	40.690
1976	Walter Planckaert (Bel)	261	42.324
1977	Roger de Vlaeminck (Bel)	264	39.207
1978	Walter Godefroot (Bel)	260	41.935
1979	Jan Raas (Hol)	267	40.971
1980			
1980	Michel Pollentier (Bel)	265	39.810
1981	Hennie Kuiper (Hol)	266	40.650
1982	Rene Martens (Bel)	267	40.320
1983	Jan Raas (Hol)	272	41.087
1984	Johan Lammerts (Hol)	268	38.941
1985	Eric Vanderaerden (Bel)	271	39.650
1986	Adri van der Poel (Hol)	275	38.297
1987	Claude Criquielion (Bel)	274	37.350
1988	Eddy Planckaert(Bel)	279	37.810
1989	Edwig van Hooydonck (Bel)	264	37.624
1990			
1990	Moreno Argentin (Ita)	265	39.026
1991	Edwig van Hooydonck (Bel)	261	36.683
1992	Jacky Durand (Fra)	260	38.810
1993	Johan Museeuw (Bel)	263	40.305
1994	Gianni Bugno (Ita)	268	39.671

YEAR	WINNER	DISTANCE (km)	AV. SPEED (kph)
1995	Johan Museeuw (Bel)	261	39.505
1996	Michele Bartoli (Ita)	269	41.705
1997	Rolf Sorensen (Den)	256	42.023
1998	Johan Museeuw (Bel)	277	39.580
1999	Peter van Petegem (Bel)	270	43.200

2000

YEAR	WINNER	DISTANCE (km)	AV. SPEED (kph)
2000	Andrei Tchmil (Bel)	269	39.531
2001	Gianluca Bortolami (Ita)	269	43.580
2002	Andrea Tafi (Ita)	264	38.354

HET VOLK

1940

YEAR	WINNER	DISTANCE (km)	AV. SPEED (kph)
1945	Jean Bogaerts (Bel)	187	33.006
1946	Andre Pieters (Bel)	225	35.809
1947	Albert Sercu (Bel)	240	32.832
1948	Sylvain Grisolle (Bel)	240	35.997
1949	Andre Declerck (Bel)	239	33.271

1950

YEAR	WINNER	DISTANCE (km)	AV. SPEED (kph)
1950	Andre Declerck (Bel)	235	37.852
1951	Jean Bogaerts (Bel)	204	36.519
1952	Ernest Sterckx (Bel)	221	36.660
1953	Ernest Sterckx (Bel)	220	35.967
1954	Karel de Baere (Bel)	228	36.286
1955	Lode Anthonis (Bel)	233	33.049
1956	Ernest Sterckx (Bel)	227	34.417
1957	Norbert Kerckhove (Bel)	207	38.490
1958	Jef Planckaert (Bel)	203	37.270
1959	Seamus Elliott (Irl)	209	40.965

1960

YEAR	WINNER	DISTANCE (km)	AV. SPEED (kph)
1961	Arthur de Cabooter (Bel)	177	43.164
1962	Robert de Middeleir (Bel)	218	38.866
1963	Rene van Meenen (Bel)	181	39.926
1964	Frans Melckenbeeck (Bel)	194	42.637
1965	Noel de Pauw (Bel)	223	41.424
1966	Jo de Roo (Hol)	213	41.225
1967	Willy Vekemans (Bel)	203	40.735
1968	Herman van Springel (Bel)	193	40.278
1969	Roger de Vlaeminck (Bel)	193	40.774

1970

YEAR	WINNER	DISTANCE (km)	AV. SPEED (kph)
1970	Frans Verbeeck (Bel)	185	40.068
1971	Eddy Merckx (Bel)	198	41.684
1972	Frans Verbeeck (Bel)	198	40.824
1973	Eddy Merckx (Bel)	198	42.888
1974	Jos Bruyère (Bel)	193	42.109
1975	Jos Bruyère (Bel)	198	43.352
1976	Willem Peeters (Bel)	202	42.377
1977	Freddy Maertens (Bel)	201	42.918
1978	Freddy Maertens (Bel)	218	42.310
1979	Roger de Vlaeminck (Bel)	215	40.396

1980

YEAR	WINNER	DISTANCE (km)	AV. SPEED (kph)
1980	Jos Bruyère (Bel)	216	39.754
1981	Jan Raas (Hol)	224	38.731
1982	Alfons de Wolf (Bel)	217	39.817
1983	Alfons de Wolf (Bel)	220	39.639
1984	Eddy Planckaert (Bel)	226	41.662
1985	Eddy Planckaert (Bel)	223	36.859
1987	Teun van Vliet (Hol)	237	38.852
1988	Ronny van Holen (Bel)	246	42.171
1989	Etienne de Wilde (Bel)	244	36.059

1990

YEAR	WINNER	DISTANCE (km)	AV. SPEED (kph)
1990	Johan Capiot (Bel)	198	36.553

YEAR	WINNER	DISTANCE (km)	AV. SPEED (kph)
1991	Andreas Kappes (Ger)	201	42.095
1992	Johan Capiot (Bel)	208	41.462
1993	Wilfried Nelissen (Bel)	202	38.971
1994	Wilfried Nelissen (Bel)	200	41.670
1995	Franco Ballerini (It)	205	39.850
1996	Tom Steels (Bel)	205	40.196
1997	Peter van Petegem (Bel)	200	38.960
1998	Peter van Petegem (Bel)	202	39.351
1999	Frank Vandenbroucke (Bel)	202	38.846

2000

YEAR	WINNER	DISTANCE (km)	AV. SPEED (kph)
2000	Johan Museeuw (Bel)	204	40.664
2001	Michele Bartoli (Ita)	200	41.096
2002	Peter van Petegem (Bel)	200	41.436

GHENT–WEVELGEM

1930

YEAR	WINNER	DISTANCE (km)	AV. SPEED (kph)
1934*	Gustave van Belle (Bel)	–	–
1935	Albert Debreitere (Bel)	–	–
1936	Robert van Eenaeme (Bel)	–	–
1937	Robert van Eenaeme (Bel)	–	–
1938	Hubert Godart (Bel)	–	–
1939	André Declerck (Bel)	–	–

1940

YEAR	WINNER	DISTANCE (km)	AV. SPEED (kph)
1945	Robert van Eenaeme (Bel)	200	35.820
1946	Ernest Sterckx (Bel)	200	35.088
1947	Maurice Desempelaere (Bel)	230	34.074
1948	Valeré Ollivier (Bel)	276	36.720
1949	Marcel Kint (Bel)	250	33.708

1950

YEAR	WINNER	DISTANCE (km)	AV. SPEED (kph)
1950	Bric Schotto (Bol)	255	37.872
1951	André Rosseel (Bel)	250	36.363
1952	Raymond Impanis (Bel)	240	37.210
1953	Raymond Impanis (Bel)	240	30.784
1954	Rolf Graf (Swi)	235	35.968
1955	Bric Schotte (Bel)	232	37.120
1956	Rik van Looy (Bel)	228	35.905
1957	Rik van Looy (Bel)	207	40.142
1958	Noel Foré (Bel)	231	41.597
1959	Leon van Daele (Bel)	221	42.776

1960

YEAR	WINNER	DISTANCE (km)	AV. SPEED (kph)
1960	Frans Aerenhouts (Bel)	253	38.430
1961	Frans Aerenhouts (Bel)	231	41.202
1962	Rik van Looy (Bel)	237	39.964
1963	Benoni Beheyt (Bel)	231	39.449
1964	Jacques Anquetil (Fra)	233	41.572
1965	Noel de Pauw (Bel)	235	41.964
1966	Herman van Springel (Bel)	251	38.324
1967	Eddy Merckx (Bel)	242	39.349
1968	Walter Godefroot (Bel)	246	42.171
1969	Willy Vekemans (Bel)	250	43.346

1970

YEAR	WINNER	DISTANCE (km)	AV. SPEED (kph)
1970	Eddy Merckx (Bel)	233	40.195
1971	Georges Pintens (Bel)	237	44.576
1972	Roger Swerts (Bel)	245	42.000
1973	Eddy Merckx (Bel)	250	39.682
1974	Barry Hoban (GB)	244	44.383
1975	Freddy Maertens (Bel)	250	40.106
1976	Freddy Maertens (Bel)	262	41.892

* The first Ghent–Wevelgem was a junior race, while until 1945 the race was run for independents, a half-way category between professional and amateur.

YEAR	WINNER	DISTANCE (km)	AV. SPEED (kph)
1977	Bernard Hinault (Fra)	277	41.191
1978	Ferdi van den Haute (Bel)	244	38.281
1979	Francesco Moser (Ita)	252	43.448

1980

YEAR	WINNER	DISTANCE (km)	AV. SPEED (kph)
1980	Henk Lubberding (Hol)	264	42.127
1981	Jan Raas (Hol)	254	43.988
1982	Frank Hoste (Bel)	245	39.200
1983	Leo van Vliet (Hol)	255	39.331
1984	Guido Bontempi (Ita)	255	41.463
1985	Eric Vanderaerden (Bel)	262	41.957
1986	Guido Bontempi (Ita)	250	44.776
1987	Teun van Vliet (Hol)	243	42.384
1988	Sean Kelly (Ire)	275	38.364
1989	Gerrit Solleveld (Hol)	265	39.750

1990

YEAR	WINNER	DISTANCE (km)	AV. SPEED (kph)
1990	Herman Frison (Bel)	210	35.139
1991	Djamolidin Abduzhaparov (Usb)	210	39.036
1992	Mario Cipollini (Ita)	210	43.599
1993	Mario Cipollini (Ita)	210	38.989

YEAR	WINNER	DISTANCE (km)	AV. SPEED (kph)
1994	Wilfried Peeters (Bel)	210	40.909
1995	Lars Michaelsen (Den)	207	41.959
1996	Tom Steels (Bel)	208	42.593
1997	Philippe Gaumont (Fra)	208	43.368
1998	Frank Vandenbroucke (Bel)	190	40.784
1999	Tom Steels (Bel)	210	40.000

2000

YEAR	WINNER	DISTANCE (km)	AV. SPEED (kph)
2000	Geert van Bondt (Bel)	214	42.650
2000	George Hincapie (USA)	215	42.881
2002	Mario Cipollini (Ita)	215	44.781

THE IMPOSSIBLE TRIPLE

- No cyclist has ever won Het Volk, Ghent–Wevelgem, and the Tour of Flanders in the same year. Jan Raas of Holland came close to the feat in 1981, when he won Ghent–Wevelgem and Het Volk, and finished third in "De Ronde", while Eddy Merckx managed the same placings in 1973. The only other cyclists to manage the Het Volk-Wevelgem double are Noel de Pauw (1965) and most recently Tom Steels in 1996.

PARIS–ROUBAIX

YEAR	WINNER	DISTANCE (km)	AV. SPEED (kph)

1890

YEAR	WINNER	DISTANCE (km)	AV. SPEED (kph)
1896*	Josef Fischer (Ger)	280	30.162
1897	Maurice Garin (Fra)	280	28.124
1898	Maurice Garin (Fra)	268	32.599
1899	Albert Champion (Fra)	268	31.976

1900

YEAR	WINNER	DISTANCE (km)	AV. SPEED (kph)
1900	Emile Bouhours (Fra)	268	37.352
1901	Lucien Lesna (Fra)	280	25.861
1902	Lucien Lesna (Fra)	268	28.088
1903	Hippolyte Aucouturier (Fra)	268	29.104
1904	Hippolyte Aucouturier (Fra)	268	32.518
1905	Louis Trousselier (Fra)	268	33.206
1906	Henri Cornet (Fra)	270	27.034
1907	Georges Passerieu (Fra)	270	30.971
1908	Cyrille van Hauwaert (Bel)	271	25.63
1909	Octave Lapize (Fra)	276	30.469

1910

YEAR	WINNER	DISTANCE (km)	AV. SPEED (kph)
1910	Octave Lapize (Fra)	266	29.274
1911	Octave Lapize (Fra)	266	31.345
1912	Charles Crupelandt (Fra)	266	31.294
1913	François Faber (Lux)	265	35.333
1914	Charles Crupelandt (Fra)	274	30.332
1919	Henri Pelissier (Fra)	280	22.857

1920

YEAR	WINNER	DISTANCE (km)	AV. SPEED (kph)
1920	Paul Deman (Bel)	263	24.377
1921	Henri Pelissier (Fra)	263	29.068
1922	Albert Dejonghe (Bel)	262	34.69
1923	Henri Suter (Swi)	270	30.098
1924	Jules van Hevel (Bel)	270	25.962
1925	Felix Sellier (Bel)	260	28.031
1926	Julien Delbecque (Bel)	270	31.962
1927	Georges Ronsse (Bel)	260	30.449

* The race was run with pacers on bikes in 1896 and 1897, with pacing by cars from 1898 to 1900, then with pace bikes from 1901 to 1909. In 1908 and 1909 pace bikes were permitted as far as Beauvais.

YEAR	WINNER	DISTANCE (km)	AV. SPEED (kph)
1928	André Leducq (Fra)	260	33.597
1929	Charles Meunier (Bel)	260	29.168

1930

YEAR	WINNER	DISTANCE (km)	AV. SPEED (kph)
1930	Julien Vervaecke (Bel)	255	31.146
1931	Gaston Rebry (Bel)	255	36.342
1932	Romain Gijssels (Bel)	255	37.32
1933	Sylvère Maes (Bel)	255	36.523
1934	Gaston Rebry (Bel)	255	32.415
1935	Gaston Rebry (Bel)	255	37.363
1936	Georges Speicher (Fra)	262	36.137
1937	Jules Rossi (Ita)	255	34.935
1938	Lucien Storme (Bel)	255	30.936
1939	Emile Masson (Bel)	262	35.934

1940

YEAR	WINNER	DISTANCE (km)	AV. SPEED (kph)
1943	Marcel Kint (Bel)	250	41.822
1944	Maurice de Simpelaere (Bel)	246	39.897
1945	Paul Maye (Fra)	246	31.212
1946	Georges Claes (Bel)	246	34.055
1947	Georges Claes (Bel)	246	39.831
1948	Rik van Steenbergen (Bel)	246	43.612
1949	Ex aequo André Mahé (Fra) and Serse Coppi (It)	244	39.396

1950

YEAR	WINNER	DISTANCE (km)	AV. SPEED (kph)
1950	Fausto Coppi (Ita)	247	39.123
1951	Antonio Bevilacqua (Ita)	247	40.355
1952	Rik van Steenbergen (Bel)	245	41.938
1953	Germain Derycke (Bel)	245	43.522
1954	Raymond Impanis (Bel)	246	35.59
1955	Jean Forestier (Fra)	249	40.741
1956	Louison Bobet (Fra)	252	41.831
1957	Fred de Bruyne (Bel)	252	34.738
1958	Léon van Daele (Bel)	269	33.3
1959	Noël Foré (Bel)	262	42.76

1960

YEAR	WINNER	DISTANCE (km)	AV. SPEED (kph)
1960	Pino Cerami (Bel)	262	43.538
1961	Rik van Looy (Bel)	263	41.7
1962	Rik van Looy (Bel)	258	38.321

YEAR	WINNER	DISTANCE (km)	AV. SPEED (kph)
1963	Emile Daems (Bel)	266	37.681
1964	Peter Post (Ned)	265	45.129
1965	Rik van Looy (Bel)	267	41.847
1966	Felice Gimondi (Ita)	262	37.546
1967	Jan Janssen (Hol)	263	36.824
1968	Eddy Merckx (Bel)	262	36.606
1969	Walter Godefroot (Bel)	264	38.939

1970

YEAR	WINNER	DISTANCE (km)	AV. SPEED (kph)
1970	Eddy Merckx (Bel)	266	41.644
1971	Roger Rosiers (Bel)	266	42.108
1972	Roger de Vlaeminck (Bel)	272	36.709
1973	Eddy Merckx (Bel)	272	36.37
1974	Roger de Vlaeminck (Bel)	274	37.567
1975	Roger de Vlaeminck (Bel)	277	40.406
1976	Marc de Meyer (Bel)	279	40.811
1977	Roger de Vlaeminck (Bel)	250	40.464
1978	Francesco Moser (Ita)	263	36.494
1979	Francesco Moser (Ita)	259	41.01

1980

YEAR	WINNER	DISTANCE (km)	AV. SPEED (kph)
1980	Francesco Moser (Ita)	264	43.106
1981	Bernard Hinault (Fra)	263	40.868
1982	Jan Raas (Hol)	270	36.733
1983	Hennie Kuiper (Hol)	274	40.308
1984	Sean Kelly (Irl)	265	36.074
1985	Marc Madiot (Fra)	265	36.109
1986	Sean Kelly (Irl)	268	39.374
1987	Eric Vanderaerden (Bel)	264	36.982
1988	Dirk de Mol (Bel)	266	40.324
1989	Jean-Marie Wampers (Bel)	265	39.164

1990

YEAR	WINNER	DISTANCE (km)	AV. SPEED (kph)
1990	Eddy Planckaert (Bel)	265	34.855
1991	Marc Madiot (Fra)	266	37.332

CONTROVERSIAL VICTORIES

- On no fewer than four occasions, outright victory in Paris–Roubaix has been denied to the rider who crossed the line in first place. As well as the Roger Lapébie episode in 1934 and the André Mahé–Serse Coppi debacle in 1949, the 1930, and 1936 races deserve a mention.

  In 1930, Jean Maréchal finished first, but was accused of causing Julien Vervaecke to crash, and victory was given to Vervaecke. The consensus now is that pressure was applied by Vervaecke's team, Alcyon, the most powerful sponsor of the time.

  Six years later, Romain Maes of Belgium clearly finished first, and photographs of the finish show this. However, the judges ruled otherwise, and gave victory to Georges Speicher of France. The fact that Belgians had won the previous seven was presumably mere coincidence.

- Only seven riders have managed the double of winning Paris–Roubaix and its cobbled spring sister the Tour of Flanders in the same year, beginning with Henri Suter in 1923.

YEAR	WINNER	DISTANCE (km)	AV. SPEED (kph)
1992	Gilbert Duclos-Lassalle (Fra)	267	41.48
1993	Gilbert Duclos-Lassalle (Fra)	267	41.652
1994	Andreï Tchmil (Rus)	270	36.16
1995	Franco Ballerini (Ita)	266	41.303
1996	Johan Museeuw (Bel)	262	43.31
1997	Frédéric Guesdon (Fra)	267	40.28
1998	Franco Ballerini (Ita)	267	38.505
1999	Andrea Tafi (Ita)	273	40.519

2000

YEAR	WINNER	DISTANCE (km)	AV. SPEED (kph)
2000	Johan Museeuw (Bel)	272	40.098
2001	Servais Knaven (Hol)	254.5	39.191
2002	Johan Museeuw (Bel)	261	39.350

ARDENNES CLASSICS

FLECHE WALLONNE

YEAR	WINNER	DISTANCE (km)	AV. SPEED (kph)

1930

YEAR	WINNER	DISTANCE (km)	AV. SPEED (kph)
1936[1]	Philippe de Meersman (Bel)	236	33.376
1937[1]	Adolphe Braeckeveldt (Bel)	291	31.285
1938[1]	Emile Masson Jr (Bel)	300	35.785
1939[2]	Edmund Delathouwer (Bel)	285	35.668

1940

YEAR	WINNER	DISTANCE (km)	AV. SPEED (kph)
1941[2]	Sylvain Grysolle (Bel)	205	38.198
1942[3]	Karel Thijs (Bel)	208	35.657
1943[3]	Marcel Kint (Bel)	208	36.705
1944[3]	Marcel Kint (Bel)	208	33.638
1945[4]	Marcel Kint (Bel)	213	34.344
1946[2]	Désiré Keteleer (Bel)	253	36.246
1947[2]	Ernest Sterckx (Bel)	276	31.663
1948[5]	Fermo Camellini (Ita)	234	34.400
1949[5]	Rik van Steenbergen (Bel)	231	36.410

1950

YEAR	WINNER	DISTANCE (km)	AV. SPEED (kph)
1950[5]	Fausto Coppi (Ita)	235	36.654
1951[5]	Ferdi Kübler (Swi)	220	34.556
1952[5]	Ferdi Kübler (Swi)	220	36.668
1953[5]	Stan Ockers (Bel)	220	34.337
1954[5]	Germain Derycke (Bel)	220	33.350
1955[5]	Stan Ockers (Bel)	220	35.453

YEAR	WINNER	DISTANCE (km)	AV. SPEED (kph)
1956[5]	Richard van Genechten (Bel)	221	36.520
1957[5]	Raymond Impanis (Bel)	226	37.477
1958[5]	Rik van Steenbergen (Bel)	235	36.061
1959[5]	Joseph Hoevenaars (Bel)	218	36.524

1960

YEAR	WINNER	DISTANCE (km)	AV. SPEED (kph)
1960[6]	Pino Cérami (Bel)	208	36.535
1961[6]	Willi Vannitsen (Bel)	193	39.569
1962[6]	Henri de Wolf (Bel)	201	35.321
1963[6]	Raymond Poulidor (Fra)	213	34.667
1964[6]	Gilbert Desmet (Fra)	215	34.246
1965[7]	Roberto Poggiali (Ita)	214	33.630
1966[7]	Michele Dancelli (Ita)	233	38.614
1967[7]	Eddy Merckx (Bel)	223	37.373
1968[7]	Rik van Looy (Bel)	222	36.575
1969[7]	Joseph Huysmans (Bel)	222	38.034

1970

YEAR	WINNER	DISTANCE (km)	AV. SPEED (kph)
1970[7]	Eddy Merckx (Bel)	225	38.682
1971[7]	Roger de Vlaeminck (Bel)	225	38.028
1972[8]	Eddy Merckx (Bel)	249	38.880
1973[8]	André Dierickx (Bel)	249	36.479
1974[9]	Frans Verbeeck (Bel)	225	38.028
1975[9]	André Dierickx (Bel)	225	38.711
1976[9]	Joop Zoetemelk (Hol)	227	39.569

YEAR	WINNER	DISTANCE (km)	AV. SPEED (kph)
1977[9]	Francesco Moser (Ita)	223	37.630
1978[9]	Michel Laurent (Fra)	223	37.545
1979[10]	Bernard Hinault (Fra)	248	39.586

1980

YEAR	WINNER	DISTANCE (km)	AV. SPEED (kph)
1980[11]	Giuseppe Saronni (Ita)	248	38.313
1981[12]	Daniel Willems (Bel)	240	41.260
1982[13]	Mario Beccia (Ita)	251	37.450
1983[14]	Bernard Hinault (Fra)	248	36.650
1984[14]	Kim Andersen (Den)	247	39.538
1985[14]	Claude Criquielion (Bel)	219	38.071
1986[15]	Laurent Fignon (Fra)	248	38.685
1987[15]	Jean Claude Leclerq (Swii)	245	38.747
1988[15]	Rolf Gölz (Ger)	243	37.194
1989[15]	Claude Criquielion (Bel)	253	38.960

1990

YEAR	WINNER	DISTANCE (km)	AV. SPEED (kph)
1990[15]	Moreno Argentin (Ita)	208	38.878
1991[15]	Moreno Argentin (Ita)	203	39.571
1992[15]	Giorgio Furlan (Ita)	204	37.162
1993[15]	Maurizio Fondriest (Ita)	206	38.870
1994[15]	Moreno Argentin (Ita)	205	41.550
1995[15]	Laurent Jalabert (Fra)	203	41.960
1996[15]	Lance Armstrong (US)	201	42.960
1997[15]	Laurent Jalabert (Fra)	200	39.190
1998[15]	Bo Hamburger (Den)	201	39.300
1999[16]	Michele Bartoli (Ita)	200	40.988

2000

YEAR	WINNER	DISTANCE (km)	AV. SPEED (kph)
2000[16]	Francesco Casagrande (Ita)	200	40.937
2001[16]	Rik Verbrugghe (Bel)	198	40.958
2002[16]	Mario Aerts (Bel)	198	41.640

ALTERNATIVE ROUTES

Tournai–Liège[1] Mons–Liège[2] Mons–Marcinelle[3] Mons–Chaleroi[4]

Charleroi–Liège[5] Liège–Charleroi[6] Liège–Marcinelle[7]

Verviers–Marcinelle[8] Verviers–Verviers[9] Esneux–Marcinelle[10]

Mons–Spa[11] Spa–Mons[12] Charleroi–Spa[13] Huy–Huy[14]

Spa–Huy[15] Charleroi–Huy[16]

LIEGE–BASTOGNE–LIEGE

DATE	WINNER	DISTANCE (km)	AV. SPEED (kph)

1890

DATE	WINNER	DISTANCE (km)	AV. SPEED (kph)
1892	Léon Houa (Bel)	250	22.935
1893	Léon Houa (Bel)	250	24.509
1894[1]	Léon Houa (Bel)	223	25.150

1900s

DATE	WINNER	DISTANCE (km)	AV. SPEED (kph)
1908	A. Trousselier (Fra)	235	28.649
1909	Victor Fastre (Bel)	235	28.142
1911	Joseph van Daele (Bel)	234	28.631
1912	Omer Verschoore (Bel)	257	29.941
1913	M. Moritz (Bel)	233	30.490
1919	Léon Devos (Bel)	237	24.101

1920

DATE	WINNER	DISTANCE (km)	AV. SPEED (kph)
1920	Léon Scieur (Bel)	245	28.710
1921	Louis Mottiat (Bel)	209	28.306
1922	Louis Mottiat (Bel)	218	29.229
1923	René Vermandel (Bel)	218	29.376
1924	René Vermandel (Bel)	245	28.053
1925	Georges Ronsse (Bel)	231	28.755
1926	D. Smets (Bel)	231	27.176
1927	M. Raes (Bel)	231	31.862
1928	Ernest Mottard (Bel)	231	29.935
1929	Alfons Schepers (Bel)	231	24.864

ALTERNATIVE ROUTE Spa–Bastogne–Spa[1]

YEAR	WINNER	DISTANCE (km)	AV. SPEED (kph)

1930

YEAR	WINNER	DISTANCE (km)	AV. SPEED (kph)
1930	Herman Buse (Ger)	231	27.445
1931	Alfons Schepers (Bel)	213	28.435
1932	Marcel Hoyoux (Bel)	214	32.752
1933	Francois Gardier (Bel)	213	34.975
1934	Theo Heckenrath (Bel)	213	34.171
1935	Alfons Schepers (Bel)	240	36.219
1936	Albert Beckaert (Bel)	211	36.067
1937	Eloi Meulenbergh (Bel)	211	36.188
1938	Alfons Deloor (Bel)	211	37.051
1939	Albert Ritserveldt (Bel)	211	37.345

1940

YEAR	WINNER	DISTANCE (km)	AV. SPEED (kph)
1943	Richard Depoorter (Bel)	211	37.679
1945	Jean Engels (Bel)	204	32.929
1946	Prosper Depredomme (Bel)	205	33.974
1947	Richard Depoorter (Bel)	218	36.286
1948	Maurice Mollin (Bel)	205	34.943
1949	Camille Danguillaume (Fra)	256	36.775

1950

YEAR	WINNER	DISTANCE (km)	AV. SPEED (kph)
1950	Prosper Depredomme (Bel)	263	35.427
1951	Ferdi Kubler (Swi)	211	37.124
1952	Ferdi Kubler (Swi)	229	35.400
1953	Alois de Hertog (Bel)	236	34.215
1954	Marcel Ernzer (Lux)	236	34.016
1955	Stan Ockers (Bel)	238	34.747
1956	Alfred de Bruyne (Bel)	247	37.973
1957	Frans Schoubben (Bel)	255	34.386
1958	Alfred de Bruyne (Bel)	246	34.480
1959	Alfred de Bruyne (Bel)	240	35.511

1960

YEAR	WINNER	DISTANCE (km)	AV. SPEED (kph)
1960	Abe Geldermans (Hol)	248	36.401
1961	Rik van Looy (Bel)	251	37.224
1962	Jos Planckaert (Bel)	254	36.581
1963	Frans Melckenbeeck (Bel)	237	37.179
1964	Willy Bocklandt (Bel)	245	34.615
1965	Carmine Preziosi (Ita)	253	36.051
1966	Jacques Anquetil (Fra)	253	36.164
1967	Walter Godefroot (Bel)	256	35.971
1968	Valeer van Sweevelt (Bel)	268	36.380
1969	Eddy Merckx (Bel)	253	37.024

1970

YEAR	WINNER	DISTANCE (km)	AV. SPEED (kph)
1970	Roger de Vlaeminck (Bel)	235	35.971
1971	Eddy Merckx (Bel)	251	36.115
1972	Eddy Merckx (Bel)	239	36.488
1973	Eddy Merckx (Bel)	236	37.869
1974	Georges Pintens (Bel)	246	38.537
1975	Eddy Merckx (Bel)	247	38.247
1976	Jos Bruyere (Bel)	247	37.396
1977	Bernard Hinault (Fra)	243	37.654
1978	Joseph Bruyere (Bel)	242	36.464
1979	Dietrich Thurau (Ger)	242	36.713

1980

YEAR	WINNER	DISTANCE (km)	AV. SPEED (kph)
1980	Bernard Hinault (Fra)	244	34.716
1981	Josef Fuchs (Swi)	244	35.362
1982	Silvano Contini (Ita)	244	34.033
1983	Steven Rooks (Hol)	246	35.516
1984	Sean Kelly (Ire)	247	36.366
1985	Moreno Argentin (Ita)	245	37.021
1986	Moreno Argentin (Ita)	253	37.673
1987	Moreno Argentin (Ita)	258	38.700
1988	Adrie van der Poel (Hol)	260	38.801
1989	Sean Kelly (Ire)	268	36.243

YEAR	WINNER	DISTANCE (km)	AV. SPEED (kph)
1990			
1990	Eric van Lancker (Bel)	256	35.560
1991	Moreno Argentin (Ita)	267	36.627
1992	Dirk de Wolf (Bel)	262	35.882
1993	Rolf Sörensen (Den)	261	36.072
1994	Evgeni Berzin (Rus)	268	36.838
1995	Mauro Gianetti (Swi)	261	39.305
1996	Pascal Richard (Swi)	263	37.700
1997	Michele Bartoli (Ita)	262	36.650
1998	Michele Bartoli (Ita)	262	40.077
1999	Frank Vandenbroucke (Bel)	262	41.079
2000			
2000	Paolo Bettini (Ita)	264	40.769
2001	Oscar Camenzind (Swi)	258	38.507
2002	Paolo Bettini (Ita)	258	38.800

AMSTEL GOLD

YEAR	WINNER	DISTANCE (km)	AV. SPEED (kph)
1960			
1966	Jean Stablinski (Fra)	302	38.649
1967	Arie den Hartog (Hol)	213	43.711
1968	Harry Steevens (Hol)	245	41.704
1969	Gudio Reybrouck (Bel)	259	40.782
1970			
1970	Georges Pintens (Bel)	240	37.745
1971	Frans Verbeeck (Bel)	233	37.622
1972	Walter Planckaert (Bel)	237	37.653
1973	Eddy Merckx (Bel)	238	35.650
1974	Gerrie Knetemann (Hol)	238	38.963
1975	Eddy Merckx (Bel)	230	37.231
1976	Freddy Maertens (Bel)	230	39.078
1977	Jan Raas (Hol)	230	39.894
1978	Jan Raas (Hol)	237	37.803
1979	Jan Raas (Hol)	238	39.507
1980			
1980	Jan Raas (Hol)	237	41.417
1981	Bernard Hinault (Fra)	237	39.741
1982	Jan Raas (Hol)	242	38.354
1983	Phil Anderson (Aus)	247	41.434
1984	Jacques Hanegraaf (Hol)	242	40.584

THE ARDENNES DOUBLE

The Ardennes double – victory in Liège–Bastogne–Liège and the Flèche Wallone in the same year – has been managed on only five occasions: Ferdi Kubler in 1951 and 1952; Stan Ockers in 1955; Eddy Merckx in 1972; and Moreno Argentin in 1991.

From 1950 to 1964 the two races carried a combined classification – the "Ardennes Weekend", with rankings as follows: 1950 Raymond Impanis (Bel); 1951 Ferdi Kübler (Swi); 1952 Ferdi Kübler (Swi); 1953 Jan Storms (Bel); 1954 Marcel Ernzer (Lux); 1955 Stan Ockers (Bel); 1956 Richard van Genechten (Bel); 1957 Frans Schouben (Bel); 1958 Fred de Bruyne (Bel); 1959 Frans Schouben (Bel); 1960 Ab Geldermans (Bel); 1961 Rik van Looy (Bel); 1962 Jo Planckaert (Bel); 1963 Raymond Poulidor (Fra); 1964 Willi Bocklandt (Bel).

The Liège–Bastogne–Liège and Amstel Gold double is even more rare. Eddy Merckx, naturally, managed it twice, in 1973 and 1975, while the Swiss Mauro Gianetti pulled off two surprise wins in 1995 to take both. As a footnote, in 1973, Merckx also took second in the Flèche Wallonne, which is as close as anyone has come to winning all three Classics. No cyclist has achieved the Amstel-Flèche double in the same year.

YEAR	WINNER	DISTANCE (km)	AV. SPEED (kph)
1985	Gerrie Knetemann (Hol)	242	37.446
1986	Steven Rooks (Hol)	242	39.665
1987	Joop Zoetemelk (Hol)	242	38.943
1988	Jelle Nijdam (Hol)	242	37.386
1989	Erik van Lancker (Bel)	242	40.187
1990			
1990	Adri van der Poel (Hol)	249	41.507
1991	Frans Maassen (Hol)	244	40.135
1992	Olaf Ludwig (Ger)	248	38.219
1993	Rolf Järmann (Swi)	249	37.343
1994	Johan Museeuw (Bel)	249	37.260
1995	Mauro Gianetti (Swi)	250	39.261
1996	Stefano Zanini (Ita)	250	42.600
1997	Bjarne Riis (Den)	253	41.689
1998	Rolf Järmann (Swi)	258	38.280
1999	Michael Boogerd (Hol)	253	38.547
2000			
2000	Erik Zabel (Ger)	258	41.11
2001	Erik Dekker (Hol)	255	38.62
2002	Michele Bartoli (Ita)	254	37.370

GIRO D'ITALIA

YEAR	WINNER	TIME (hour-min-sec)	DISTANCE (km)
1900s			
1909	Luigi Ganna (Ita)	25pts*	2,448
1910	Carlo Galetti (Ita)	28pts	2,987
1911	Carlo Galetti (Ita)	50pts	3,530
1912	Atala	33pts	2,439
1913	Carlo Oriani (Ita)	37pts	2,932
1914	Alfonso Calzolari (Ita)	135.17.56	3,162
1919	Costante Girardengo (Ita)	112.51.29	2,984
1920			
1920	Gaetano Belloni (Ita)	102.47.33	2,632
1921	Giovanni Brunero (Ita)	120.24.39	3,107
1922	Giovanni Brunero (Ita)	119.43.00	3,095
1923	Costante Girardengo (Ita)	122.58.17	3,202

* 1909–13, the race was decided on points. In 1912, it was a team event.

YEAR	WINNER	TIME (hour-min-sec)	DISTANCE (km)
1924	Giuseppe Enrici (Ita)	143.43.37	3,613
1925	Alfredo Binda (Ita)	137.31.13	3.520
1926	Giovanni Brunero (Ita)	137.55.29	3,429
1927	Alfredo Binda (Ita)	144.15.35	3,758
1928	Alfredo Binda (Ita)	114.15.19	3,044
1929	Alfredo Binda (Ita)	107.18.24	2,920
1930			
1930	Luigi Marchisio (Ita)	115.11.55	3,097
1931	Francesco Camusso (Ita)	102.40.46	3,012
1932	Antonio Pesenti (Ita)	105.42.41	3,235
1933	Alfredo Binda (Ita)	111.01.52	3,343
1934	Learco Guerra (Ita)	121.17.17	3,706
1935	Vasco Bergamaschi (Ita)	113.22.46	3,577
1936	Gino Bartali (Ita)	120.12.30	3,766
1937	Gino Bartali (Ita)	122.25.40	3,840

YEAR	WINNER	TIME (hour-min-sec)	DISTANCE (km)
1938	Giovanni Valetti (Ita)	112.49.28	3,645
1939	Giovanni Valetti (Ita)	88.02.00	3,011
1940			
1940	Fausto Coppi (Ita)	107.31.10	3,574
1946	Gino Bartali (Ita)	95.32.20	3,039
1947	Fausto Coppi (Ita)	115.555.07	3,843
1948	Fiorenzo Magni (Ita)	124.51.52	4,164
1949	Fausto Coppi (Ita)	125.25.50†	4,088
1950			
1950	Hugo Koblet (Swi)	117.28.03	3,981
1951	Fiorenzo Magni (Ita)	121.11.37	4,153
1952	Fausto Coppi (Ita)	114.36.43	3,964
1953	Fausto Coppi (Ita)	118.37.26	4,035
1954	Carlo Clerici (Swi)	129.13.07	4,337
1955	Fiorenzo Magni (Ita)	108.56.12	3,871
1956	Charly Gaul (Lux)	101.39.46	3,523
1957	Gastone Nencini (Ita)	104.45.06	3,926
1958	Ercole Baldini (Ita)	92.09.30	3,341
1959	Charly Gaul (Lux)	101.50.26	3,657
1960			
1960	Jacques Anquetil (Fra)	94.03.54	3,841
1961	Arnaldo Pambianco (Ita)	111.25.38	4,004
1962	Franco Balmamion (Ita)	123.06.03	4,180
1963	Franco Balmamion (Ita)	116.50.16	4,063
1964	Jacques Anquetil (Fra)	115.10.27	4,119
1965	Vittorio Adorni (Ita)	121.08.18	4,151
1966	Gianni Motta (Ita)	111.10.48	3,916
1967	Felice Gimondi (Ita)	101.15.34	3,572
1968	Eddy Merckx (Bel)	108.42.27	3,917
1969	Felice Gimondi (Ita)	106.47.03	3,731
1970			
1970	Eddy Merckx (Bel)	90.08.47	3,292
1971	Gosta Pettersson (Swe)	97.24.03	3,567
1972	Eddy Merckx (Bel)	103.04.04	3,725
1973	Eddy Merckx (Bel)	106.54.41	3,796
1974	Eddy Merckx (Bel)	113.08.13	4,001
1975	Fausto Bertoglio (Ita)	111.31.24	3,963
1976	Felice Gimondi (Ita)	119.58.15	4,161
1977	Michel Pollentier (Bel)	107.27.16	3,968
1978	Johan de Muynck (Bel)	101.31.22	3,610
1979	Giuseppe Saronni (Ita)	89.29.18	3,301

GIRO RECORDS

- The youngest Giro winner is Fausto Coppi, victor in 1940 aged 20; the oldest Fiorenzo Magni, who took the 1955 race aged 35. The most successful stage winner is Alfredo Binda, with 41 stage wins; his record of 12 in one Giro, out of a possible 15 in the 1927 race will not be equalled, but he is being run close by Mario Cipollini, who reached 40 during the 2002 race.

- The fastest ever Giro stage was won by Rik Verbrugghe of Belgium, who took the 2001 prologue time trial at Pescara at an average of 58.874 kph (36.796 mph), the fastest ever stage in any of the three major Tours. The fastest road stage in any big Tour is Igor Gonzalez de Galdeano's stage win at Zaragoza in the 2001 Vuelta: 55.176 kph (34.485 mph).

YEAR	WINNER	TIME (hour-min-sec)	DISTANCE (km)
1980			
1980	Bernard Hinault (Fra)	112.08.20	4,025
1981	Giovanni Battaglin (Ita)	104.51.36	3,895
1982	Bernard Hinault (Fra)	110.07.55	4,010
1983	Giuseppe Saronni (Ita)	100.45.30	3,922
1984	Francesco Moser (Ita)	98.32.20	3,808
1985	Bernard Hinault (Fra)	105.46.51	3,998
1986	Roberto Visentini (Ita)	102.33.55	3,858
1987	Stephen Roche (Irl)	105.39.42	3,915
1988	Andrew Hampsten (USA)	97.18.56	3,579
1989	Laurent Fignon (Fra)	93.30.16	3,418
1990			
1990	Gianni Bugno (Ita)	91.51.08	3,450
1991	Franco Chioccioli (Ita)	99.35.43	3,715
1992	Miguel Indurain (Spa)	103.36.08	3,843
1993	Miguel Indurain (Spa)	98.09.44	3,702
1994	Evgeni Berzin (Rus)	100.41.21	3,721
1995	Tony Rominger (Swi)	97.39.50	3,736
1996	Pavel Tonkov (Rus)	105.20.23	3,990
1997	Ivan Gotti (Ita)	102.53.58	3,889
1998	Marco Pantani (Ita)	94.48.32	3,811
1999	Ivan Gotti (Ita)	99.55.56	3,757
2000			
2000	Stefano Garzelli (Ita)	98.30.14	3,698
2001	Gilberto Simoni (Ita)	89.02.58	3,144
2002	Paolo Savoldelli (Ita)	89.22.42	3,334

† Includes 10 minutes deducted in time bonuses.

VUELTA D'ESPANA

YEAR	WINNER	TIME (hour-min-sec)	DISTANCE (km)
1930/40			
1935	Gustaf Deloor (Bel)	120.01.02	3,431
1936	Gustaf Deloor (Bel)	150.07.54	4,349
1941	Julian Berrendero (Spa)	168.45.26	4,442
1942	Julian Berrendero (Spa)	134.05.09	3,634
1945	Delio Rodriguez (Spa)	135.43.55	3,723
1946	Dalmacio Langarica (Spa)	137.10.38	3,847
1947	Eduard van Dijck (Bel)	132.27.00	3,818
1948	Bernardo Ruiz (Spa)	155.06.30	4,090
1950			
1950	Emilio Rodriguez (Spa)	134.49.19	3,924
1955	Jean Dotto (Fra)	81.04.02	2,735
1956	Angelo Conterno (Ita)	105.37.52	3,204

YEAR	WINNER	TIME (hour-min-sec)	DISTANCE (km)
1957	Jesus Lorono (Spa)	84.44.06	2,943
1958	Jean Stablinski (Fra)	94.54.21	3,276
1959	Antonio Suarez (Spa)	84.36.20	3,060
1960			
1960	Franz de Mulder (Bel)	103.05.57	3,368
1961	Angelino Soler (Spa)	77.36.17	2,818
1962	Rudi Altig (Ger)	78.35.27	2,843
1963	Jacques Anquetil (Fra)	64.46.20	2,419
1964	Raymond Poulidor (Fra)	78.23.35	2,865
1965	Rolf Wolfshohl (Ger)	92.36.03	3,409
1966	Francisco Gabica (Spa)	78.53.55	2,950
1967	Jan Janssen (Hol)	76.38.04	2,941
1968	Felice Gimondi (Ita)	78.29.00	2,981

YEAR	WINNER	TIME (hour-min-sec)	DISTANCE(km)
1969	Roger Pingeon (Fra)	73.18.45	2,921
1970			
1970	Luis Ocana (Spa)	89.57.12	3,560
1971	Ferdinand Bracke (Bel)	73.50.05	2,793
1972	Jose-Manuel Fuente (Spa)	82.34.14	3,078
1973	Eddy Merckx (Bel)	84.40.50	3,056
1974	Jose-Manuel Fuente (Spa)	86.48.18	2,987
1975	Agustin Tamames (Spa)	88.00.56	3,075
1976	Jose Pesarrodona (Spa)	93.19.10	3,343
1977	Freddy Maertens (Bel)	78.54.36	2,785
1978	Bernard Hinault (Fra)	85.24.14	2,990
1979	Joop Zoetemelk (Hol)	94.57.05	3,373
1980			
1980	Faustino Ruperez (Spa)	88.23.21	3,216
1981	Giovanni Battaglin (Ita)	98.04.49	3,446
1982	Marino Lejaretta (Spa)*	95.47.23	3,456
1983	Bernard Hinault (Fra)	94.28.26	3,398
1984	Eric Caritoux (Fra)	90.08.03	3,593
1985	Pedro Delgado (Spa)	95.58.00	3,474
1986	Alvaro Pino (Spa)	98.16.04	3,666
1987	Luis Herrera (Col)	105.34.26	3,921
1988	Sean Kelly (Ire)	89.19.23	3,428
1989	Pedro Delgado (Spa)	93.01.17	3,683
1990			
1990	Marco Giovannetti (Ita)	94.36.50	3,711
1991	Melchior Mauri (Spa)	82.48.07	3,212

RARE DOUBLES AND TRIPLES

The double of Giro and Tour is the greatest stage racing feat, but the double of Giro and Vuelta is even rarer: only Eddy Merckx in 1973 and Giovanni Battaglin of Spain in 1981 have managed it. Hinault (1978) and Anquetil (1963) are the only cyclists to win Vuelta and Tour in the same season.

Winning all three majors over the course of a career is rare too: Merckx, Hinault, Anquetil, and Gimondi are the only cyclists to achieve it. Riding all three in the same season is rare but Marino Lejarreta of Spain set a unique record between 24 April and 22 July 1989: 20th in the Vuelta, 10th in the Giro, and 5th in the Tour. He rode all three in the next two seasons as well, with four more top 10 placings.

YEAR	WINNER	TIME (hour-min-sec)	DISTANCE(km)
1992	Tony Rominger (Swi)	96.24.50	3,395
1993	Tony Rominger (Swi)	96.07.03	3,605
1994	Tony Rominger (Swi)	92.07.48	3,531
1995	Laurent Jalabert (Fra)	95.30.33	3,637
1996	Alex Zülle (Swi)	97.31.46	3,947
1997	Alex Zülle (Swi)	91.15.55	3,759
1998	Abraham Olano (Spa)	93.44.08	3,781
1999	Jan Ullrich (Ger)	89.52.03	3,548
2000			
2000	Roberto Heras (Spa)	70.26.14	2,894
2001	Angel Casero (Spa)	70-49-05	2,986
2002	Aitor Gonzalez (Spa)	75-13-52	3,128

WORLD ROAD CHAMPIONSHIPS

YEAR	PLACE	WINNER
1920		
1927	Nurburgring (Ger)	Alfredo Binda (It)
1928	Budapest (Hung)	Georges Ronsse (Bel)
1929	Zurich (Sw)	Georges Ronsse (Bel)
1930		
1930	Liège (Bel)	Alfredo Binda (It)
1931	Copenhagen (Den)	Learco Guerra (It)
1932	Rome (It)	Alfredo Binda (It)
1933	Monthléry (Fr)	Georges Speicher (Fr)
1934	Leipzig (Ger)	Karel Kaers (Bel)
1935	Floreffe (Bel)	Jean Aerts (Bel)
1936	Berne (Sw)	Antonin Magne (Fr)
1937	Copenhagen (Den)	Eloi Meulenberg (Bel)
1938	Valkenburg (Hol)	Marcel Kint (Bel)
1940		
1946	Zurich (Sw)	Hans Knecht (Switz)
1947	Reims (Fr)	Theo Middelkamp (Hol)
1948	Valkenburg (Hol)	Bric Schotte (Bel)
1949	Copenhagen (Den)	Rik van Steenbergen (Bel)
1950		
1950	Moorslede (Bel)	Briek Schotte (Bel)
1951	Varese (It)	Ferdi Kubler (Sw)
1952	Luxembourg	Heinz Muller (Ger)
1953	Lugano (It)	Fausto Coppi (It)
1954	Solingen (Ger)	Louison Bobet (Fr)
1955	Frascati (It)	Stan Ockers (Bel)
1956	Ballerup (Den)	Rik van Steenbergen (Bel)
1957	Waregem (Bel)	Rik van Steenbergen (Bel)
1958	Reims (Fr)	Ercole Baldini (It)

YEAR	PLACE	WINNER
1959	Zandtvoort (Hol)	Andre Darrigade (Fr)
1960		
1960	Sachsenring (Ger)	Rik van Looy (Bel)
1961	Berne (Sw)	Rik van Looy (Bel)
1962	Salo (It)	Jean Stablinski (Fr)
1963	Ronse (Bel)	Benoni Beheyt (Bel)
1964	Sallanches (Fr)	Jan Janssen (Hol)
1965	Lasarte (Sp)	Tom Simpson (GB)
1966	Nurburgring (Ger)	Rudi Altig (Ger)
1967	Heerlen (Hol)	Eddy Merckx (Bel)
1968	Imola (It)	Vittorio Adorni (It)
1969	Zolder (Bel)	Harm Ottenbros (Hol)
1970		
1970	Leicester (GB)	Jean-Pierre Monséré (Bel)
1971	Mendrisio (Sw)	Eddy Merckx (Bel)
1972	Gap (Fr)	Marino Basso (It)
1973	Montjuich (Sp)	Felice Gimondi (It)
1974	Montreal (Can)	Eddy Merckx (Bel)
1975	Yvoir (Bel)	Hennie Kuiper (Hol)
1976	Ostuni (It)	Freddy Maertens (Bel)
1977	San Cristobal (Ven)	Francesco Moser (It)
1978	Nurburgring (Ger)	Gerrie Knetemann (Hol)
1979	Valkenburg (Hol)	Jan Raas (Hol)
1980		
1980	Sallanches (Fr)	Bernard Hinault (Fr)
1981	Prague (Czech)	Freddy Maertens (Bel)
1982	Goodwood (GB)	Giuseppe Saronni (It)
1983	Altenrhein (Sw)	Greg LeMond (USA)
1984	Barcelona (Sp)	Claude Criquielion (Bel)

YEAR	PLACE	WINNER
1985	Giavera (It)	Joop Zoetemelk (Hol)
1986	Colorado Springs (USA)	Moreno Argentin (It)
1987	Villach (Aust)	Stephen Roche (Ire)
1988	Ronse (Bel)	Maurizio Fondriest (It)
1989	Chambéry (Fr)	Greg LeMond (USA)

1990

YEAR	PLACE	WINNER
1990	Utsunomiya (Japan)	Rudy Dhaenens (Bel)
1991	Stuttgart (Ger)	Gianni Bugno (It)
1992	Benidorm (Sp)	Gianni Bugno (It)
1993	Oslo (Nor)	Lance Armstrong (USA)
1994	Agrigento (It)	Luc Leblanc (Fr)
1995	Duitama (Col)	Abraham Olano (Sp)
1996	Lugano (Sw)	Johan Museeuw (Bel)
1997	San Sebastian (Sp)	Laurent Brochard (Fr)
1998	Valkenburg (Hol)	Oscar Camenzind (Sw)
1999	Verona (It)	Oscar Freire (Sp)

2000

YEAR	PLACE	WINNER
2000	Plouay (Fr)	Romans Vainsteins (Latvia)
2001	Lisbon (Port)	Oscar Freire (Sp)
2002	Zolder (Bel)	Mario Cipollini (It)

THE CURSE OF THE RAINBOW JERSEY

Cycling lore has it that the winner of the world championships will struggle to win races wearing the rainbow jersey, and that he will be more likely to suffer bad luck than those around him. Here are six of the unluckiest world champions: decide for yourselves.

Jean-Pierre Monséré (Belgium): killed in a racing accident the year after winning the title in 1970.

Rudy Dhaenens (Belgium): never won a major race after taking the 1990 title; killed in a car accident in 1999.

Laurent Brochard (France): involved in a major drug scandal in the Tour de France the year after taking the 1997 title.

Luc Leblanc (France): an old knee injury flared up after he won the 1994 title, and his financially shaky sponsor pulled the plug on his team midway through the season.

Stephen Roche (Ireland): missed most of the season after taking the 1987 title, and never rose again to the level he reached in winning the Giro, Tour, and world championship that year.

Freddy Maertens (Belgium): won the 1981 title in Prague, and was never seen at the front of a bike race ever again. Lost all his money to the taxman. Now living in obscurity.

AUTUMN CLASSICS

PARIS–TOURS

YEAR	WINNER	DISTANCE (km)	AV. SPEED (kph)
1896	E. Prevost (Fra)	250	31.200

1900s

YEAR	WINNER	DISTANCE (km)	AV. SPEED (kph)
1901	Jean Fischer (Fra)	253	26.982
1906	Lucien Petit-Breton (Fra)	234	29.557
1907	Georges Passerieu (Fra)	245	32.186
1908	Omer Beaugendre (Fra)	248	30.690
1909	Francois Faber (Lux)*	248	30.680
1910	Francois Faber (Lux)	248	32.105
1911	Octave Lapize (Fra)	248	27.054
1912	Louis Heusghem (Bel)	246	26.348
1913	Charles Crupelandt (Fra)	246	33.931
1914	Oscar Egg (Swi)	316	32.147
1917	Philippe Thys (Bel)	246	34.009
1918	Charles Mantelet (Fra)	248	30.182
1919	Hector Thiberghien (Bel)	342	27.178

1920

YEAR	WINNER	DISTANCE (km)	AV. SPEED (kph)
1920	Eugène Christophe (Fra)	342	25.570
1921	Francis Pélissier (Fra)	342	22.893
1922	Henri Pélissier (Fra)	342	29.653
1923	Paul Deman (Bel)	342	25.014
1924	Louis Mottiat (Bel)	342	28.423
1925	Den. Verschueren (Bel)	342	27.469
1926	Henri Suter (Swi)	324	28.230
1927	Henri Suter (Swi)	253	35.324
1928	Den. Verschueren (Bel)	253	34.746
1929	Nicolas Frantz (Bel)	253	27.355

1930

YEAR	WINNER	DISTANCE (km)	AV. SPEED (kph)
1930	Jean Maréchal (Fra)	253	34.112
1931	André Leducq (Fra)	240	31.276
1932	Julien Moineau (Fra)	253	37.251
1933	Jules Merviel (Fra)	243	37.528
1934	Gustave Danneels (Bel)	243	38.358
1935	René Le Grevès (Fra)	251	37.900
1936	Gustave Danneels (Bel)	251	41.455

YEAR	WINNER	DISTANCE (km)	AV. SPEED (kph)
1937	Gustave Danneels (Bel)	251	41.092
1938	Jules Rossi (Ita)	251	42.097
1939	Frans Bonduel (Bel)	251	39.655

1940

YEAR	WINNER	DISTANCE (km)	AV. SPEED (kph)
1941	Paul Maye (Fra)	249	36.096
1942	Paul Maye (Fra)	248	36.024
1943	Gaby Gaudin (Fra)	241	37.422
1944	Lucien Teisseire (Fra)	253	41.452
1945	Paul Maye (Fra)	253	37.161
1946	Bric Schotte (Bel)	251	37.714
1947	Bric Schotte (Bel)	251	35.678
1948	Louis Caput (Fra)	251	43.096
1949	Albert Ramon (Bel)	251	41.377

1950

YEAR	WINNER	DISTANCE (km)	AV. SPEED (kph)
1950	André Mahé (Fra)	251	39.536
1951	Jacques Dupont (Fra)	251	41.691
1952	Raymond Guégan (Fra)	253	40.861
1953	Jozef Schils (Bel)	253	43.529
1954	Gilbert Scodeller (Fra)	253	40.881
1955	Jacques Dupont (Fra)	253	43.766
1956	Albert Bouvet (Fra)	251	40.844
1957	Alfred de Bruyne (Bel)	251	42.842
1958	Gilbert de Smet (Bel)	251	37.148
1959	Rik van Looy (Bel)	267	37.791

1960

YEAR	WINNER	DISTANCE (km)	AV. SPEED (kph)
1960	Jo de Haan (Hol)	267	40.001
1961	Jos Wouters (Bel)	267	38.407
1962	Jo de Roo (Hol)	267	44.903
1963	Jo de Roo (Hol)	255	39.162
1964	Guido Reybroeck (Bel)	248	36.466
1965†	Gerben Karstens (Hol)	247	45.029
1966	Guido Reybroeck (Bel)	249	43.355
1967	Rik van Looy (Bel)	249	41.720
1968	Guido Reybroeck (Bel)	249	44.584
1969	Herman Vanspringel (Bel)	286	43.038

YEAR	WINNER	DISTANCE (km)	AV. SPEED (kph)
1970			
1970	Jurgen Tschan (Ger)	286	41.011
1971	Rik van Linden (Bel)	285	40.766
1972	Noel Vantyghem (Bel)	292	40.679
1973	Rik van Linden (Bel)	264	42.076
1974[1]	Francesco Moser (Ita)	254	43.268
1975[1]	Freddy Maertens (Bel)	247	41.241
1976[1]	Ronald de Witte (Bel)	253	43.519
1977[1]	Joop Zoetemelk (Hol)	259	44.531
1978[2]	Jan Raas (Hol)	271	38.896
1979[3]	Joop Zoetemelk (Hol)	228	41.838
1980			
1980[3]	Daniel Willems (Bel)	228	40.449
1981[3]	Jan Raas (Hol)	228	40.113
1982[3]	Luc Vandenbroucke (Bel)	228	40.777
1983[3]	Ludo Peeters (Bel)	237	43.431
1984[3]	Sean Kelly (Irl)	249	41.411
1985[4]	Ludo Peeters (Bel)	249	38.607
1986[1]	Phil Anderson (Aus)	253	40.765
1987[1]	Adri van Der Poel (Hol)	255	38.734
1988	Peter Pieters (Hol)	290	34.202
1989	Jelle Nijdam (Hol)	283	39.402
1990			
1990	Rolf Sorensen (Dan)	283	39.601
1991	Johan Capiot (Bel)	286	38.406
1992	Hendrik Redant (Bel)	286	46.745
1993	Johan Museeuw (Bel)	251	38.142
1994	Erik Zabel (Ger)	250	39.934
1995	Nicola Minali (Ita)	250	43.363
1996	Nicola Minali (Ita)	249	44.860
1997	Andrei Tchmil (Ukr)	254	48.400
1998	Jacky Durand (Fra)	254	44.231
1999	Marc Wauters (Bel)	254	41.281
2000			
2000	Andrea Tafi (Ita)	254	38.300
2001	Richard Virenque (Fra)	254.5	36.484
2002	Jakob Storm Piil (Den)	257	45.46

* First three riders disqualified for taking the wrong course.

† Run without derailleur gears

ALTERNATIVE ROUTES:

Tours–Paris[1]   Blois–Montlhery[2]

Blois–Chaville[3] (Grand Prix d'Automne)

Creteil–Chaville[4] (Grand Prix d'Automne)

GIRO DI LOMBARDIA

YEAR	WINNER	DISTANCE (km)	AV. SPEED (kph)
1900s			
1905	Giovanni Gerbi (Ita)	230	24.950
1906	Giuseppe Brambilla (Ita)	197	26.452
1907	Gustave Garrigou (Fra)	210	27.668
1908	Francois Faber (Lux)	210	28.750
1909	Giovanni Cuniolo (Ita)	193	20.850
1910	Giovanni Micheletto (Ita)	232	27.030
1911	Henri Pélissier (Fra)	232	30.660
1912	Carlo Oriani (Ita)	235	31.298
1913	Henri Pélissier (Fra)	235	30.400
1914	Lauro Bordin (Ita)	235	32.290
1915	Gaetano Belloni (Ita)	190	28.330
1916	Leopodo Torricelli (Ita)	232	25.330
1917	Philippe Thijs (Bel)	204	29.280

THE AUTUMN DOUBLE

The double of both autumn Classics in the same year is a remarkably rare feat, presumably because of the difffferent skills required to win each one – Paris–Tours usually fell traditionally to a sprinter, while the Giro di Lombardia was for the climbers.

The first man to achieve the double was Philippe Thys in 1917, which offers further grounds for believing that the Belgian would have won far more if World War I had not cut his career short. As it was, he was still the first man to take three Tours de France.

Thys was followed, 42 years later, by Rik van Looy, confirming the status of the "Emperor" as perhaps the greatest Classics rider of all time, given that he is also the only cyclist ever to have managed the "cobbled Grand Slam" of Tour of Flanders, Paris–Roubaix, and Ghent–Wevelgem, in 1962.

The surprise, however, is the Dutchman Jo de Roo, an all-round Classics specialist, whose only claim to fame is that he managed the autumn double in 1962 and 1963. His first win, at an average speed of 44.903 kph (28.081 mph) was the fastest ever speed in a Classic at the time, the unofficial *ruban jaune* or "yellow riband". That was not surprising: its flat route means that Paris–Tours has always been one of the fastest of Classics, and Andrei Tchmil's 1997 average of 47.539 kph (29.711 mph) is the current "yellow riband".

More coveted than the "autumn double" is the double of world championship and Giro di Lombardia, achieved by only six men: Alfredo Binda in 1927, Tom Simpson in 1965, Eddy Merckx in 1971, Felice Gimondi in 1973 – after Merckx's disqualification – Giuseppe Saronni in 1982, and Oscar Camenzind in 1998. The double of Paris–Tours and world championship has yet to be achieved.

YEAR	WINNER	DISTANCE (km)	AV. SPEED (kph)
1918	Gaetano Belloni (Ita)	190	26.500
1919	Costante Girardengo (Ita)	256	26.391
1920			
1920	Henri Pélissier (Fra)	241	28.819
1921	Costante Girardengo (Ita)	261	27.449
1922	Costante Girardengo (Ita)	246	27.349
1923	Giovanni Brunero (Ita)	250	26.497
1924	Giovanni Brunero (Ita)	250	28.935
1925	Alfredo Binda (Ita)	251	28.804
1926	Alfredo Binda (Ita)	251	26.120
1927	Alfredo Binda (Ita)	252	28.182
1928	Gaetano Belloni (Ita)	248	27.606
1929	Piero Fossati (Ita)	238	28.958
1930			
1930	Michele Mara (Ita)	237	30.913
1931	Alfredo Binda (Ita)	234	27.385
1932	Antonio Negrini (Ita)	265	30.576
1933	Domenico Piemontesi (Ita)	230	32.502
1934	Learco Guerra (Ita)	245	32.368
1935	Enrico Mollo (Ita)	238	32.268
1936	Gino Bartali (Ita)	241	35.616
1937	Aldo Bini (Ita)	252	33.297
1938	Cino Cinelli (Ita)	232	34.974
1939	Gino Bartali (Ita)	231	33.715
1940			
1940	Gino Bartali (Ita)	225	34.405
1941	Mario Ricci (Ita)	217	33.670
1942	Aldo Bini (Ita)	184	36.073
1945	Mario Ricci (Ita)	222	36.177
1946	Fausto Coppi (Ita)	231	36.046
1947	Fausto Coppi (Ita)	222	32.876
1948	Fausto Coppi (Ita)	222	37.849
1949	Fausto Coppi (Ita)	222	38.002

YEAR	WINNER	DISTANCE (km)	AV. SPEED (kph)
1950			
1950	Renzo Soldani (Ita)	222	38.093
1951	Louison Bobet (Fra)	226	38.626
1952	Giuseppe Minardi (Ita)	226	37.293
1953	Bruno Landi (Ita)	222	36.812
1954	Fausto Coppi (Ita)	222	37.415
1955	Cleto Maule (Ita)	222	38.670
1956	André Darrigade (Fra)	238	38.468
1957	Diego Ronchini (Ita)	240	38.945
1958	Nino Defilippis (Ita)	243	39.705
1959	Rik van Looy (Bel)	240	40.899
1960			
1960	Emile Daems (Bel)	226	40.627
1961	Vito Taccone (Ita)	253	35.604
1962	Jo de Roo (Hol)	253	35.633
1963	Jo de Roo (Hol)	263	37.085
1964	Gianni Motta (Ita)	266	38.550
1965	Tom Simpson (GB)	266	39.613
1966	Felice Gimondi (Ita)	266	38.272
1967	Franco Bitossi (Ita)	266	38.473
1968	Herman van Springel (Bel)	266	38.092
1969	Jean-Pierre Monseré (Bel)	266	40.009
1970			
1970	Franco Bitossi (Ita)	266	38.241
1971	Eddy Merckx (Bel)	266	39.365
1972	Eddy Merckx (Bel)	266	39.127
1973	Felice Gimondi (Ita)	266	37.315
1974	Roger de Vlaeminck (Bel)	266	37.290
1975	Francesco Moser (Ita)	266	35.945
1976	Roger de Vlaeminck (Bel)	253	39.326

YEAR	WINNER	DISTANCE (km)	AV. SPEED (kph)
1977	Gian-Battista Baronchelli (Ita)	257	36.453
1978	Francesco Moser (Ita)	266	39.213
1979	Bernard Hinault (Fra)	251	40.008
1990			
1980	Alfons de Wolf (Bel)	255	35.747
1981	Hennie Kuiper (Hol)	259	39.642
1982	Giuseppe Saronni (Ita)	248	40.754
1983	Sean Kelly (Ire)	253	39.164
1984	Bernard Hinault (Fra)	251	40.831
1985	Sean Kelly (Ire)	255	41.208
1986	Gian-Battista Baronchelli (Ita)	262	37.329
1987	Moreno Argentin (Ita)	265	38.576
1988	Charly Mottet (Fra)	260	38.134
1989	Tony Rominger (Swi)	260	38.368
1990			
1990	Gilles Delion (Fra)	246	39.704
1991	Sean Kelly (Ire)	242	39.176
1992	Tony Rominger (Swi)	241	39.311
1993	Pascal Richard (Swi)	242	39.821
1994	Vladislav Bobrik (Rus)	244	34.378
1995	Gianni Faresin (Ita)	252	42.116
1996	Andrea Tafi (Ita)	250	42.642
1997	Laurent Jalabert (Fra)	250	43.013
1998	Oscar Camenzind (Swi)	253	42.282
1999	Mirko Celestino (Ita)	262	41.170
2000			
2000	Raimondas Rumsas (Ltu)	258	40.892
2001	Danilo di Luca (Ita)	256	38.847
2002	Michele Bartoli (Ita)	251	40.91

OLYMPIC GAMES

YEAR	CITY	WINNER	DIST (km)/TIME (h-m-s)
ROAD RACE			
1896	Athens	Aristidis Konstantanides (Gr)	87 / 3.22.31
1900	Paris	Not held	
1906	Athens	Fernand Vast (France)	84 / 2.41.28
TIME TRIAL			
1908	London	not held	
1912	Stockholm	Rudolph Lewis (S Afr)	300 / 10.42.39
1920	Antwerp	Harry Stenquist (Swe)	175 / 4.40.01
1924	Paris	Armand Blanchonnet (Fra)	188 / 6.20.48
1928	Amsterdam	Henry Hansen (Den)	169 / 4.47.18
1932	Los Angeles	Attilio Pavesi (It)	100 / 2.28.05
ROAD RACE			
1936	Berlin	Robert Carpentier (Fra)	100 / 2.33.05
1948	London	José Bayaert (Fra)	199 / 5.18.12
1952	Helsinki	André Noyelle (Bel)	190 / 5.06.03
1956	Melbourne	Ercole Baldini (It)	187 / 5.21.17
1960	Rome	Viktor Kapitonov (USSR)	175 / 4.20.30
1964	Tokyo	Mario Zanin (It)	194 / 4.39.51
1968	Mexico	Pier Franco Vianelli (It)	196 / 4.41.25
1972	Munich	Hennie Kuiper (Hol)	182 / 4.14.37
1976	Montreal	Bernt Johansson (Swe)	175 / 4.46.52
1980	Moscow	Sergei Soukhoroutchenkov (USSR)	189 / 4.48.28
1984	Los Angeles	Alexei Grewal (USA)	190 / 4.59.57
1988	Seoul	Olaf Ludwig (E Ger)	196 / 4.32.22
1992	Barcelona	Fabio Casartelli (It)	194 / 4.35.21

YEAR	CITY	WINNER	DIST (km)/TIME (h-m-s)
ROAD RACE AND TIME TRIAL			
1996	Atlanta		
	road race	Pascal Richard (Swi)	221.8 / 4.53.56
	time trial	Miguel Indurain (Sp)	52 / 1.04.05
2000	Sydney		
	road race	Jan Ullrich (Ger)	239 / 5.29.08
	time trial	Viatcheslav Ekimov (Rus)	46 / 0.57.40

AMATEURS, PROFESSIONALS, AND THE ELITE

The Olympic Games road titles opened to professionals only from 1996; at the same time the amateur and professional ranks were officially abolished, and for administrative purposes the top echelons of the two categories were combined as "elite".

Before the shake-up, few amateurs went on to race with success as professionals after winning the Olympic title. One of the main exceptions was Ercole Baldini of Italy, winner of the Olympic road race in Melbourne in 1956, and the professional road race in Reims, France, two years later. Baldini also took the Giro d'Italia, the world hour record, and numerous Italian one-day events.

He was emulated by Hennie Kuiper of Holland in the 1970s: Kuiper was Olympic champion in Munich in 1972, and world champion in 1975 at Yvoir, Belgium, and went on to win Paris–Roubaix, the Tour of Flanders, and the Giro di Lombardia, also finishing second twice in the Tour de France.

WORLD RANKINGS

CHALLENGE DESGRANGE–COLOMBO

1948	Bric Schotte (Bel)
1949	Fausto Coppi (Ita)
1950	Ferdi Kubler (Swi)
1951	Louson Bobet (Fra)
1952	Ferdi Kubler (Swi)
1953	Loretto Petrucci (Ita)
1954	Ferdi Kubler (Swi)
1955	Stan Ockers (Bel)
1956	Fred de Bruyne (Bel)
1957	Fred de Bruyne (Bel)
1958	Fred de Bruyne (Bel)

SUPER PRESTIGE

1959	Jean Forestier (Fra)
1960	Henri Anglade (Fra)
1961	Jean Graczyk (Fra)
1962	Jo de Roo (Hol)
1963	Jacques Anquetil (Fra)
1964	Raymond Poulidor (Fra)
1965	Jacques Anquetil (Fra)
1966	Jacques Anquetil (Fra)
1967	Jan Janssen (Hol)
1968	Herman van Springel (Bel)
1969	Eddy Merckx (Bel)
1970	Eddy Merckx (Bel)
1971	Eddy Merckx (Bel)
1972	Eddy Merckx (Bel)
1973	Eddy Merckx (Bel)
1974	Eddy Merckx (Bel)
1975	Eddy Merckx (Bel)

1976	Freddy Maertens (Bel)
1977	Freddy Maertens (Bel)
1978	Francesco Moser (Ita)
1979	Bernard Hinault (Fra)
1980	Bernard Hinault (Fra)
1981	Bernard Hinault (Fra)
1982	Bernard Hinault (Fra)
1983	Greg LeMond (USA)
1984	Sean Kelly (Ire)
1985	Sean Kelly (Ire)
1986	Sean Kelly (Ire)
1987	Sean Kelly (Ire)

UCI WORLD CUP

1989	Sean Kelly (Irl)
1990	Gianni Bugno (Ita)
1991	Maurizio Fondriest (Ita)
1992	Olaf Ludwig (Ger)
1993	Maurizio Fondriest (Ita)
1994	Gianluca Bortolami (Ita)
1995	Johan Museeuw (Bel)
1996	Johan Museeuw (Bel)
1997	Michele Bartoli (Ita)
1998	Michele Bartoli (Ita)
1999	Andrei Tchmil (Bel)
2000	Eric Zabel (Ger)
2001	Erik Dekker (Hol)
2002	Erik Zabel (Ger)

UCI WORLD RANKINGS (No 1 at year end)

1986	Sean Kelly (Ire)
1987	Sean Kelly (Ire)
1988	Sean Kelly (Ire)
1989	Laurent Fignon (Fra)
1990	Gianni Bugno (Ita)
1991	Gianni Bugno (Ita)
1992	Miguel Indurain (Spa)
1993	Miguel Indurain (Spa)
1994	Tony Rominger (Swi)
1995	Laurent Jalabert (Fra)
1996	Laurent Jalabert (Fra)
1997	Laurent Jalabert (Fra)
1998	Michele Bartoli (Ita)
1999	Laurent Jalabert (Fra)
2000	Francesco Casagrande (Ita)
2001	Eric Zabel (Ger)
2002	Eric Zabel (Ger)

VELO MAGAZINE'S VELODOR MONDIAL

1992	Miguel Indurain (Spa)
1993	Miguel Indurain (Spa)
1994	Tony Rominger (Swi)
1995	Laurent Jalabert (Fra)
1996	Johan Museeuw (Bel)
1997	Jan Ullrich (Ger)
1998	Marco Pantani (Ita)
1999	Lance Armstrong (USA)
2000	Lance Armstrong (USA)
2001	Lance Armstrong (USA)
2002	Mario Cipollini (It)

WORLD RANKINGS

One of the great conundrums of professional cycling is designating the best cyclist of a given year. The debate was launched shortly after World War II when the world's leading race organizers got together to found an annual prize based on performances in their events during that season: the Challenge Desgrange–Colombo, named after the founders of the Tour de France and Giro d'Italia. The Challenge was decided on points awarded for both stage and one-day events, and eventually mutated into the Super Prestige, sponsored for many years by Pernod.

The Super Prestige died at the end of the 1980s, and it has been succeeded by two slightly differing competitions. The Union Cycliste Internationale's annual World Cup – taking its name from an annual team competition founded in 1961 – rewards the year's best one-day rider, as it is decided on points awarded for a series of 10 or 12 one-day events that always includes the sport's five "monuments" – Milan–San Remo, the Tour of Flanders, Paris–Roubaix, Liège–Bastogne–Liège, and the Giro di Lombardia – as well as the Amstel Gold, Paris–Tours, and Spain's San Sebastian Classic, plus specially devised events at various times in England, Canada, and Germany.

A more accurate reflection of which cyclist has dominated a given season is provided by the UCI's world points rankings, founded in 1986 according to a system devised by the current Tour de France organiser Jean-Marie Leblanc, and based that of on the ATP tennis world rankings. Points are scored for all events on the world calendar, which are ranked according to toughness and prestige, and as a given day's points are added, last year's are deducted.

Neither system provides perfect clarity. In 1989, for example, Greg LeMond was indisputably the performer of the season, winning the double of Tour de France and world championship. But the World Cup went to Sean Kelly, bronze medallist in the world championship, while the world rankings were topped by Laurent Fignon, runner-up in the Tour, but a consistent winner from March to October.

At present, neither system reflects Lance Armstrong's current status as the world's No. 1 cyclist by a vast margin in terms of earnings and public profile. In the days of Merckx and Sean Kelly, a simple look at the number of races won was a good indicator – now, however, the year's biggest winners may well be going for quantity rather than quality. A better indication, perhaps, is the French magazine Vélo's Velodor (Golden Bike) Mondial award, elected by an international panel of journalists.

INDEX

PICTURE CREDITS